WORKING LONGER

WORKING LONGER
The Solution to the Retirement Income Challenge

Alicia H. Munnell

Steven A. Sass

BROOKINGS INSTITUTION PRESS
Washington, D.C.

331.3
MUN

Copyright © 2008
THE BROOKINGS INSTITUTION
1775 Massachusetts Avenue, N.W., Washington, D.C. 20036
www.brookings.edu

Library of Congress Cataloging-in-Publication data
Munnell, Alicia Haydock.
  Working longer : the solution to the retirement income challenge / Alicia H. Munnell and Steven A. Sass.
       p.   cm.
  Summary: "Investigates the prospects for moving the average retirement age to 66 from 63. Examines companies' incentives to employ older workers and what government can do to promote continued participation in the workforce. Considers the challenge of ensuring a secure retirement for low-wage workers and those unable to continue to work"—Provided by publisher.
  Includes bibliographical references and index.
  ISBN 978-0-8157-5898-3 (cloth : alk. paper)
  1. Older people—Employment—United States. 2. Age and employment—United States. 3. Retirement age—United States. 4. Retirement income—United States. I. Sass, Steven A., 1949– II. Title.
  HD6280.M86 2008
  331.3'980973—dc22   2008007242

9 8 7 6 5 4 3 2 1

Typeset in Adobe Garamond

Composition by Peter Lindeman
Arlington, Virginia

Printed by R. R. Donnelley
Harrisonburg, Virginia

Contents

Acknowledgments

The authors thank the Prudential Foundation for its generous support of this project. In addition, we thank the Atlantic Philanthropies, whose support stimulated our initial interest in this topic. We suspect that the case for working longer—due to the contraction of the retirement income system and increasing life expectancy—has become even stronger since this book was conceived. We hope that the arguments presented in this volume lead to changes by individuals, employers, and the government that will allow people to extend their careers and enjoy secure retirements.

The authors would also like to thank Jerilyn Libby and Dan Muldoon for their excellent research assistance. Katharine Abraham and Robert Hutchens read the manuscript in its entirety and provided helpful comments, as did three anonymous reviewers. David Cutler and Dora Costa also provided helpful comments on a paper that has become the health chapter.

1

Introduction

Every morning more than 100 million Americans wake up and head out to work. They grab a bite, get the news, then turn their attention to the issues they'll face that day. At times, however, it becomes necessary to look beyond this workaday routine and deal with issues that could disrupt one's life if not addressed. This is one of those times, and the issue is retirement.

A wake-up call regarding one's retirement should come as no surprise. The press is filled with calls to fix Social Security, shore up employer pensions, and make 401(k) plans work better. Indeed, Social Security benefits—relative to earnings—are declining. Employer pensions have become increasingly scarce. And 401(k) balances are generally inadequate. At the same time, longevity is steadily rising. The retirement challenge is typically framed as a financial problem, requiring more saving and better asset management or cuts in promised benefits. The challenge, however, is in many ways better framed as an employment problem.

According to the standard life-cycle model, rational actors respond to a rise in longevity and decline in Social Security and employer pensions in three ways. They spread the burden across the life cycle by consuming less and setting aside more of their income while working; they remain in the labor force longer; and they live on less in retirement. But the baby boom generation has not set aside more of its income while working. Nor do subsequent cohorts seem to be saving much more. This lack of saving puts more weight on the other two responses: working longer and consuming less in retirement. A failure to work longer shifts the entire burden to lower retirement consumption, implying a steep reduction in living standards upon exiting the labor force. Alternatively, the most effective lever for securing a comfortable retirement, especially for the baby boom generation now at the cusp with little opportunity to save, is to remain in the work force longer.

At first blush, it may seem strange to say: "You need to reduce your retirement to ensure your retirement." But it's not nearly as bad as it sounds. Because life expectancy has increased dramatically over the past several decades while the average age of retirement has fallen, working longer does not mean having fewer years in retirement than workers earlier in the post-war era. The working-longer prescription is not about no retirement at all; it's about beginning your retirement somewhat later.

Spending a few additional years in the labor force can make a big difference. It directly increases current income; it avoids the actuarial reduction in Social Security benefits; it allows people to contribute more to their 401(k) plans; it allows those plans to accumulate more investment income; and it shortens the period of retirement. By and large, those who continue to work until their mid-60s or beyond should have a reasonably comfortable retirement.

Working longer, however, will not be simple. It requires thought and planning on the part of individuals. It also requires employers to retain, train, and even hire older workers. Government also has a role to play. And the sooner everybody realizes that staying in the labor force is the best way to ensure a secure retirement, the better.

The Retirement Income Challenge

The major reason that people have to work longer is that the retirement income system is contracting. This system—Social Security and publicly subsidized and regulated employer-sponsored plans—is the major source of support for people as they withdraw from the labor force and as earnings decline.[1] But Social Security and employer-sponsored retirement income plans will provide relatively less in the future than they do today. Employers have also backed away from offering retiree health insurance, leaving households exposed to rapidly rising health care costs. In addition, life expectancy is rising: for men, life expectancy at age 65 was less than fifteen years in 1980 but in 2020 is projected to be nearly eighteen years. Workers in the future

Figure 1-1. *Social Security Replacement Rates, Medium Earner, 2002 and 2030*

Percent

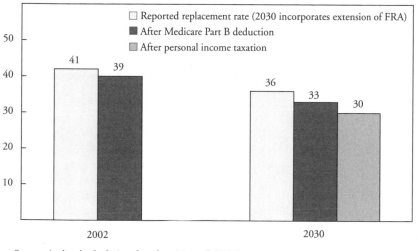

Source: Authors' calculations based on Munnell (2003).
FRA = full retirement age.

will thus need more resources, not fewer, if they continue to retire at the same ages as they do today.

The Outlook for Social Security

At any given retirement age, Social Security benefits will replace a smaller fraction of preretirement earnings than in the past. Today, the hypothetical average earner retiring at age 65 receives benefits equal to about 41 percent of previous earnings. After payment of the Medicare part B premium, which is automatically deducted from Social Security benefits, the replacement rate is 39 percent. But under current law Social Security replacement rates are scheduled to decline for three reasons. First, the full retirement age is currently in the process of moving from 65 to 67, which is equivalent to an across-the-board cut.[2] Second, Medicare part B premiums are slated to increase sharply due to rising health care costs.[3] Finally, Social Security benefits will be taxed more under the personal income tax, as the exemption amounts are not indexed to inflation. These three factors alone will reduce the net replacement rate for the average worker who claims at age 65 from 39 percent in 2002 to 30 percent in 2030 (figure 1-1). This percentage does not include premiums for the part D drug benefit, which will also claim an increasing share of the Social Security check. Nor does it include any addi-

Figure 1-2. *Wage and Salary Workers with Pension Coverage, by Type of Plan, 1983, 1992, and 2004*

Percent

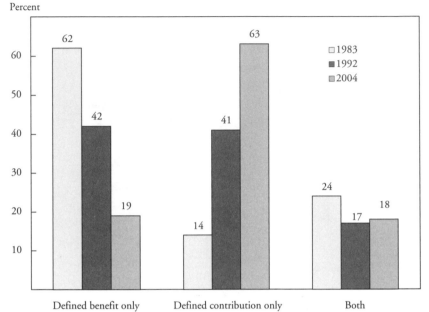

Source: Munnell and Sundén (2006) based on the U.S. Federal Reserve Board (1983, 1992, 2004).

tional benefit cuts enacted to shore up the solvency of the Social Security program.[4]

The Outlook for Private Sector, Employer-Sponsored Pensions

With a diminished role for Social Security, retirees will be increasingly dependent on employer-sponsored pensions. At any moment in time, however, less than half of the private sector workforce ages 25–64 participates in an employer-sponsored plan of any type. This fraction has remained virtually unchanged since the late 1970s and is unlikely to improve.[5] Since pension participation tends to increase with earnings, only middle- and upper-income individuals can count on receiving meaningful benefits from employer-sponsored pension plans.

While the level of pension coverage has remained flat, the nature of coverage has changed dramatically. Twenty-five years ago, most people with pension coverage had a traditional defined benefit plan that pays a lifetime annuity at retirement.[6] Today the world looks very different (figure 1-2). Most

Figure 1-3. *Actual and Simulated Accumulations, 401(k) and IRA Plans, by Age Group, 2004*

Age group

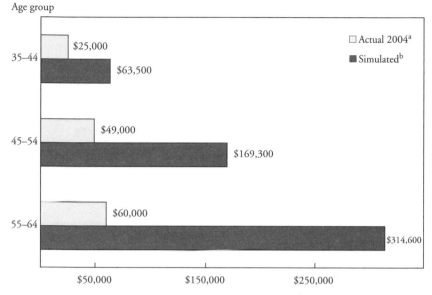

Source: Munnell and Sundén (2006).

a. Figures from U.S. Federal Reserve (2004).

b. Assumes that the worker's earnings rise with the growth of average wages in the economy and with the rise and fall of earnings across the typical worker's career. The worker begins contributing 6 percent of earnings to a 401(k) at age 30, gets an employer match of 3 percent, and 401(k) balances earn 4.6 percent above inflation. At age 64, the last year before retirement, the worker earns $58,000 and ends the year with a 401(k) balance of $380,000, 6.5 times final earnings.

people with a pension have a defined contribution plan, typically a 401(k) plan, which is like a savings account.[7] In theory workers could accumulate substantial wealth in a 401(k) and offset the decline in both Social Security and employer-provided pensions. Simulations suggest that the worker in the middle of the earnings distribution, who contributes regularly throughout his work life, should end up at retirement with about $300,000 in his 401(k) or individual retirement account (IRA). (Most IRA assets are rolled-over balances from 401(k) plans.) This amount, when combined with Social Security, could easily provide an adequate retirement income. But reality looks quite different. The Federal Reserve's 2004 Survey of Consumer Finances reports that the typical household head approaching retirement (ages 55–64) had combined 401(k) and IRA balances of only $60,000.[8] Nor do younger cohorts seem to be on track to accumulate sufficient wealth to support themselves in retirement (figure 1-3).[9]

Figure 1-4. *Private Saving Rate, Personal Saving Rate, and Rate of Personal Saving Less Pension Saving, Working-Age Population, 1980–2003*

Percent

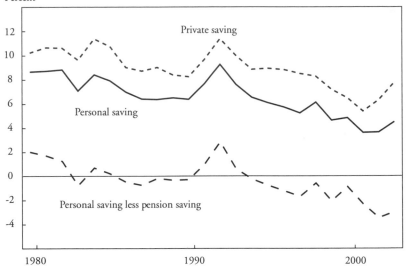

Source: Munnell, Golub-Sass, and Varani (2005).

The Outlook for Individual Saving

Given the decline in Social Security and employer-provided pensions and the rise in longevity, the standard life-cycle model would expect the working-age population to decrease the share of income it consumes and increase the share it saves. This saving does not have to be in a 401(k). Workers could set aside more of their income for retirement in bank deposits or investments in businesses, securities held outside a retirement account, home equity, or investment real estate. But a study estimating saving by the working-age population, based on the U.S. National Income and Product Accounts, shows that this has not occurred.[10] Both the personal saving rate of the working-age population, which includes 401(k) saving and employer contributions to defined benefit pension plans, and a broader private saving measure, which includes business saving (retained earnings) by businesses owned directly or through equities, have declined. The study also finds that virtually all personal saving occurred in pension plans and that saving outside such plans, in recent years, has actually been negative (figure 1-4).

This disconcerting finding is corroborated by a study based on the Survey of Consumer Finances. It finds that median household wealth, excluding

Figure 1-5. *Ratio of Wealth to Income in the Survey of Consumer Finances, by Age Group, Selected Years 1983–2004*

Ratio

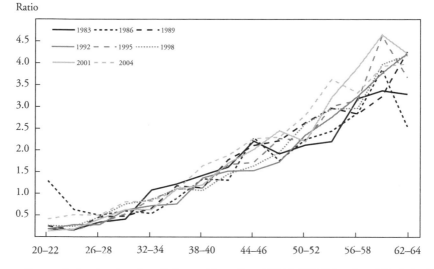

Source: Authors' update from Delorme, Munnell, and Webb (2006) based on U.S. Federal Reserve Board (1983–2004).

Social Security and employer-defined benefit pensions, has remained remarkably constant relative to household income (figure 1-5). Households have not increased their accumulation of wealth to offset the demise of employer-defined benefit plans or the scheduled reduction in Social Security replacement rates.[11]

Retiree Health Insurance

The preceding discussion focuses on the decline in cash benefits. Employers have also cut back on postretirement health care benefits. Between 1989 and 2006 the percentage of large firms offering such benefits dropped from 66 percent to 35 percent.[12] The decline in participating firms actually understates the extent of the cutback, because the generosity of the benefits has also been reduced. In response to the rising costs of health care, employers have increased retiree premium contributions, copayments, deductibles, and out-of-pocket limits. Moreover, many of those providing postretirement health benefits today have terminated such benefits for new retirees. Thus workers will need more income than they did in the past to cover health care costs that were previously borne by the employer.

In summary, the outlook for retirement income for future retirees is dismal.[13] People are not going to be able to continue to retire at age 63—the average retirement age for men today—and maintain their preretirement living standards over an increasingly long period of retirement. Moreover, dramatically rising health care costs are going to erode already diminished pension income.[14] Working longer is the obvious solution for the baby boom generation, which has little time to accumulate more retirement savings. Even if saving rates in subsequent generations increase, working longer will continue to be an effective lever for securing a comfortable retirement.

Will We Have to Work Forever?

Future retirees need not panic. Although the replacement rate reductions are significant, a few years of work can make retirees in 2030 as well off as those in the current generation. In other words, working longer does not mean working forever.

Each additional year in the workforce increases income directly through earnings from work and investments. It also actuarially increases Social Security benefits by 7–8 percent a year and produces a similar increase, on a risk-adjusted basis, on income from balances in 401(k) plans. The implications on the need for retirement savings are striking.[15] The Congressional Budget Office estimates that in 2004 a married couple earning in the middle of the income distribution could reduce the assets needed to achieve their target replacement rate from $550,000 if they retire at age 62 to $325,000 if they retire at age 66 and to $130,000 if they retire at age 70.[16]

So, how much longer do most people need to work? The easiest calculation is the required response to the increase in the full retirement age. By definition, a worker in 2030 will have to work until age 67 to receive the same replacement rate as a worker retiring at 65 today.[17] Similarly, those who would have chosen actuarially reduced benefits at age 63 in 2002 will have to delay claiming benefits to age 65 in 2030 to receive the same replacement rate.

With a simple model, it is possible to calculate the increase in required work life to offset the projected increase in the Medicare premium and taxation of Social Security benefits.[18] In 2030 the reduction from the Medicare part B premium can be reversed in about six months, and that from taxes can be reversed in about thirteen months. To compensate for all the foreseeable changes to the Social Security replacement rate, workers will need to extend their work lives by about four years.

Workers who reach retirement with significant assets in their 401(k) plans or other accounts will have to work less than four years to offset the projected reductions in Social Security replacement rates. The reason is that additional years of work, assuming financial assets are left untouched, increase the ultimate annual income that can be derived from 401(k) accumulations. Part of the increase comes from the additional investment income.[19] The other part of the story is that by working longer, expected years in retirement decrease, raising the income available for each retirement year.[20] To make income from 401(k)s comparable with Social Security benefits, which are indexed for inflation, 401(k) proceeds would be used to purchase an inflation-indexed annuity. Thus a medium earner who reaches age 63 with 401(k) assets that could buy a real annuity that would produce a replacement rate of 20 percent will only need to work for about twenty-eight months to offset reductions in Social Security. This increase is significantly less than that for workers without financial assets, because the additional income from the 401(k) assets makes up for some of the loss.

The important message is that continued employment means two to four more years of work to maintain today's level of income replacement. This prescription is equivalent to moving the current average retirement age—the age at which half the cohort is out of the labor market—from 63 to about 66. Interestingly, 66 was the average retirement age for men in 1960. This book explores the potential for making such a change.

Organization of the Book

This book is organized around the notion that working longer requires older workers to be healthy enough to work and willing to work. But the decision is not one sided. Employers also have to be willing to hire them. Since both sides of this equation appear uncertain, the question is what individuals, employers, and the government can do to make continued employment more likely.

To set the stage for labor supply decisions, chapter 2 explores whether future generations of workers will be healthy enough to work beyond the current retirement age of 63. Intuitively, people's health affects their ability and desire to work, an intuition that is confirmed by a substantial body of research. People's health can also affect their attractiveness to employers. This chapter explores the extent to which health today compares to health in 1960, when the retirement age for men was 66.

Certainly life expectancy for both men and women has increased since the 1960s. But the relationship between increases in longevity and improvements in health is complicated. If medical advancements keep frail people alive, the overall health of a population can look like it has deteriorated. Indeed in the 1970s, when health trends appeared to be worsening, experts accepted the outcome as the "failure of success." Therefore, it is important to look closely at health trends for both older people (those 65 and over) and for older workers (those 55–64). The trends for these age groups are likely related because presumably if those 65 and over are healthier, those 55–64 should also be healthier.

The evidence suggests that the health of older people, as opposed to older workers, showed little improvement in the 1970s, mixed results in the 1980s, and marked improvement since the 1990s. The improvement for older workers most likely began earlier, in the 1980s. Today, the health of older workers appears to be at least as good as it was forty years ago. And today's jobs are less physically demanding. Thus if half of the male population was healthy enough to work until age 66 in 1960, the same percentage should be able to do so today. Two notes of caution are needed. First, 15–20 percent of the older population will not be able to work that long. Second, some studies suggest that the improvements seen to date may not continue and might even reverse.

Given that improved health should enable most people to work longer, chapters 3 and 4 turn to the question of whether older men and older women are likely to want to work. It is necessary to deal with men and women separately, because women's work patterns reflect the increasing participation of cohorts over time as well as the factors that affect retirement behavior. Putting the two together muddies the waters.

Some indication that older men might be willing to work longer comes from the fact that the century-long downward trend in their labor force participation has clearly ceased and that participation has actually been rising for much of the population since the mid-1990s. The question is whether this recent upward trend in participation will broaden and continue.

Some key changes in the nation's retirement income system should encourage greater labor force participation by older workers going forward. Social Security replacement rates at any given age are falling. And retirement income from employer-sponsored plans at any given age is also likely to fall, given rising longevity and the meager balances in the now dominant 401(k)s. The "income effect" of such reductions should increase labor force participation. In addition, changes in Social Security and the decline in traditional defined benefit pensions have essentially eliminated subsidies for early retirement and penalties for later retirement. The "substitution effect" of these changes—raising the cost of retirement relative to work (to its actuarially appropriate level)—should increase participation.

Impediments still remain, however, to the continued employment of older workers. The most important is the availability of Social Security benefits at age 62. Even today, with the elimination of the earnings test after the full retirement age and an actuarially fair delayed retirement credit, the majority of workers continue to claim their benefits as soon as they become available. Another important factor is the increased mobility of older workers, which exposes them to the vagaries of the labor market. Extended and difficult job searches as well as the prospect of low wages may cause many older workers to simply give up. Moreover, older people have a strong preference for part-time work and flexible schedules, which to date employers have been reluctant to accommodate.

On balance, the evidence suggests that work rates for both those aged 55–64 and those 65 and over should continue to increase. By 2030 these rates may even exceed official government projections. But they are unlikely to reach 1960s levels, given the increase in wealth since then (some of which workers want to spend on more leisure at the end of their work life) and the availability of Social Security benefits at age 62. Further, the nature of employment for older workers may be less than optimal, at least in financial terms. It would probably be best if older workers remained in their career job. But the trend toward shorter tenures suggests that more and more older workers will end up in short-term, spot-market jobs. These jobs will pay less. The good news is that many workers who have moved into such positions report that their jobs are more enjoyable.

Chapter 4 investigates the likelihood of increased labor supply of older women. Women have a lot to gain by working longer. Today nearly 30 percent of elderly nonmarried women, who represent a majority of households at older ages, are classified as poor or near poor. Some of these women were nonmarried and poor as they entered retirement. But many were married and suffered a large drop in income when their spouse died. Thus women would be better off if they had their own Social Security earnings record and employer pension benefits. Moreover, given the importance of joint decision-making for couples, the continued employment of married women may be the best way to keep their husbands working, thereby ensuring the largest Social Security benefit for their husband and the largest widow's benefit for themselves.

In some ways, the work prospects for older women look fairly bright. Labor force participation of women in their prime years has risen significantly. Increasingly their work decisions and careers look more like those of men. And early baby boomer married women claim they are going to retire more than a year later than their immediate predecessors. Indeed, the changing incentives in the retirement income system should encourage more employment for both men and women. But good plans often go awry. Given their weaker attachment to the labor force, smaller financial incentives, and tendency to coordinate retirement with their—typically older—husbands, the challenge for women to join and stay in the labor force is greater than that facing men.

So assume that more older workers will want to work. Will employers want to hire them? This question is the subject of chapter 5. The advent of retirement and the long decline in the age of retirement were to a significant degree the result of employer decisions. Employers dismissed or eased out older employees whose strength and acuity had declined and created mandated retirement policies that forced workers out at a specified age. Large employers, and employers with a unionized workforce, offered pensions to facilitate orderly exits and then sweetened the benefits to induce even earlier separations. And employers rarely hired older workers except for a narrow subset of jobs. Presumably, employers found it unprofitable to retain older, higher paid, and relatively less educated workers when a large supply of younger, cheaper, and better educated workers was available.

Similarly, going forward, employers will employ older workers if it is profitable to do so—if the value of what they produce is greater than what they are paid. So chapter 5 compares trends in productivity with the cost to the employer as people age. The evidence suggests that productivity from ages 55 to 70 at best remains level but in all likelihood falls. Declining physical strength, stamina, and agility, factors that are much less significant than in the past, still impair the productivity of some older workers. Older workers generally retain job knowledge and the ability to do what they did in the past, but cognitive flexibility and the ability to learn decline. Most older workers have sufficient mental agility to learn and adapt if given the necessary training, but few get trained, and many fail to learn and adapt on their own.

While the productivity of older workers remains level or falls, the compensation employers pay older workers generally remains level or rises over time. Wages, the largest component of compensation, tend to be "sticky" downward. Employers generally avoid cutting an employee's wage, as this creates various personnel management problems. Thus the wages of long-service workers are typically high. Further, the cost of traditional defined benefit plans and health insurance unquestionably rises with age.

In recent surveys, employers claim they are reasonably comfortable with the productivity-compensation trade-off for the older workers they currently employ, but they are not keen on retaining those who want to stay on beyond the company's traditional retirement age.

Many observers say employer attitudes will change. Today's older workers are in many ways more capable than those of the past (for example, they have more education), and work is less physically taxing. The shift from defined benefit pensions to 401(k)s has eliminated a major financial impediment to the employment of older workers. Many observers also say that employers face the prospect of labor shortages and the loss of valuable institutional knowledge when the baby boom generation retires, which will make older workers much more attractive. But the shift away from career employment also suggests a decline in the value that employers place on institutional intelligence. And employers face a global supply of labor in today's economy that far offsets the slowing of labor force growth as the baby boom generation retires.

The conclusion that emerges from chapters 2 through 5 is that most people will be healthy enough to work longer, some older people will want to work longer, but employers may be lukewarm about employing older workers. Chapter 6 explores what can be done by individuals, companies, and the government to improve the outlook.

The most important change that can occur at the federal government level is to increase the earliest eligibility age (EEA) under Social Security. Raising the EEA is charged with controversy, since it does little to improve Social Security finances, has the potential to disadvantage short-lived people (a large percentage of whom are minorities), and requires some provision for those in their early 60s who are either physically incapable of working or who cannot find a job.[21] Yet without an increase in the EEA, most workers will continue to claim benefits at age 62 and to retire early.

A host of other changes could also be helpful. These include making Medicare, rather than the employer, the primary payer for the health costs of workers 65 and over; perhaps increasing the number of years in the Social Security benefit calculation from thirty-five years to forty, giving workers an incentive to work longer to avoid a cut in benefits; and eliminating payroll taxes for workers age 62 and over. At the state level, programs that help match older workers with new jobs could be extremely valuable.

For older individuals, the most important change is to recognize that working longer is the key to their financial security and to then devise a plan and stick to it. Currently, workers say the right thing but do not follow through. Year after year in EBRI's Retirement Confidence Survey, workers respond that they plan to work to age 65. But year after year, they retire at 62. Things happen as workers get older. Their health deteriorates. They get a new young boss whom they don't like and, seeing that Social Security benefits are available, retire earlier than planned. They endure a horrible business trip, decide they never want that kind of experience again, and quit. In other words, employees are buffeted by events that change their target date of retirement. If instead they were committed to a later retirement, employers might also be more likely to invest in them through training and promotion.

On the employer side, companies will have to adapt to an older workforce. Older workers have different sets of skills than younger workers; they are better with people and at operating well-developed systems, while younger workers are better at physically demanding tasks and in developing innovative technologies. So employers will need to adjust their operations as older workers make up a larger share of the labor pool. They will also need to adjust their compensation systems so that compensation costs, especially the cost of health insurance, do not price older workers out of a job. Employers also need to provide more opportunities for older workers to upgrade their skills.

Chapter 7 concludes that the continued employment of older workers looks like so many other economic challenges facing Americans. The people who will most need to work longer—namely, lower-paid workers who will depend primarily on a contracting Social Security system—will be the ones most likely to be in poor health or with limited job prospects. Higher paid workers, those most capable of saving on their own, will likely be the ones to stay in the labor force. Indeed, studies show that higher income, better educated workers are responsible for the reversal in labor force participation rates among older men. Thus working longer may be the prescription for the bulk of Americans. But thought needs to be given to ensure that those at the low end of the pay scale also have a secure retirement.

Finally, the shift to 401(k) plans and the increased mobility of older workers also means that retirement is going to become a much messier process than it was in the past. With mandatory retirement, both parties knew that, as of a certain age, the relationship would end. Employers also used traditional defined benefit plans to structure an orderly departure. No such structure exists in a 401(k) environment. Employers face the prospect of workers with declining productivity and inadequate 401(k) balances hanging on much longer than desirable. Employers will need new tools, including an orderly severance process, to manage an older workforce. Without such tools, employers will avoid older workers. Severance could be structured using carrots, such as a generous retirement package, or a stick, such as some form of mandatory retirement. Of course, the latter would be extremely controversial. But it is important to recognize that, in the absence of employer-defined benefit plans, the structure that eased employees into retirement no longer exists. Without such a structure, employers could become quite reluctant about employing older workers.

2

Will Older People Be Healthy Enough to Work Longer?

As recently as the mid-1960s, the median retirement age for men—the age at which half of all men are no longer in the labor force—was 66. Today, it is 63. But given the scheduled decline in Social Security replacement rates, increased longevity, and the relatively low balances in 401(k) accounts, Americans risk serious income shortfalls, especially at older ages, if they continue to retire at age 63. As discussed in the introduction, a rational response is to move the average retirement age back to 66 or even older. A key consideration is whether people will be healthy enough to work longer. This chapter compares the health status of older people today with those forty years ago and explores what happens to people's health as they age.

The chapter is structured as follows. The first section reviews the relationship between health and work. As a prelude to investigating changes in the health of older people, the second section reports on various measures of the increase in life expectancy. The third section describes the trends in disability for those 65 and over, since most of the research has focused on this age group. If those 65 and over are healthier, presumably those 55–64 should also be enjoying better health. The fourth section turns to the trends in disability among these older workers. Section five reports on studies that point to the possible worsening of health outcomes among the baby boom generation. The following section concludes the discussion.

The bottom line is that the health of older people (those ages 65 and older), as opposed to older workers (those ages 55 to 64), showed little improvement in the 1970s, mixed results in the 1980s, and marked improvement since the 1990s. For older workers, a marked improvement most likely began earlier, in the 1980s. Today, the health of older workers appears to be at least as good as it was forty years ago. Thus if half of the male population was then healthy enough to work until age 66, the same percentage should be able to do so today. Two notes of caution are needed. First, 15–20 percent of the population will not be physically able to work that long. Second, some studies suggest that the improvements seen to date may not continue.

Health and Work

Intuitively, people's health affects their ability and desire to work. Poor health can make work seem very difficult and unpleasant, leading people to withdraw from the labor force. Poor health can reduce people's productivity, leading to lower wages, and lower wages reduce the incentive to work. Poor health can make people less attractive to employers and therefore less likely to be hired. In 1969 intuition carried the day, as shown by the following observation by the day's leading experts: "That the labor force status of an individual will be affected by his health is an unassailable proposition [because] a priori reasoning and casual observation tell us it must be so, not because there is a mass of supporting evidence."[1]

Today, we have the evidence. In the last thirty-five years research into the impact of health on labor force activity has become a major industry, and virtually all studies show that poor health has a negative effect on the likelihood of being in the labor force, the expected retirement age, as well as hours worked and wages.[2]

The size of the effect of health on work, however, is sensitive to the measurement of health status. Most studies use a measure of self-assessed health (very good, good, fair, poor, or very poor) or whether respondents report health limitations that affect their ability to work. Researchers have also used objective measures such as whether the person has a problem with activities of daily living or the presence of a chronic or acute condition.

It turns out that self-reported health status is actually a pretty good indicator of a person's medically determined health status. These self-reports, however, are sensitive to other parts of the employment picture, which creates problems for researchers attempting to establish relationships between health and work. For example, people who like their work downplay their health problems and work longer, while those who dislike their work emphasize health issues and retire sooner. Similarly, people who have cut back on their work are more likely to report a health problem, either because they want to justify their decision or because they may be eligible for government benefits if they are unhealthy.[3] Despite these possible biases, using self-reported health information may be the best approach to determining how health affects work. While the justification phenomenon tends to bias the estimated effect of health on work upward, experts suggest that measurement error biases the results downward, and the two biases tend to cancel each other out. In contrast, objective measures of health are often not good indicators of whether people can work or not. For example, difficulty walking up stairs may have little effect on a person's ability to work as a computer programmer. Including objective measures in an equation may simply bias the effect of health on work toward zero.

A huge body of literature now confirms that health affects work.[4] Originally, researchers simply added some measure of poor health to an equation explaining labor force participation and found negative effects. Increasingly, the studies have become more sophisticated, to address the biases discussed above. Regardless of the approach and the measurement of health and work activity, the studies provide overwhelming evidence that poor health reduces the likelihood of work. Therefore it is important to determine whether older people will be healthy enough to work.[5]

Survival Expectancies

Death is the end point, so a natural starting place for exploring the ability of older people to work is life expectancy. An increase in life expectancy raises the possibility of increased health and a longer work life. One would not expect, however, a one-year increase in healthy life expectancy to translate into a one-year increase in work. Under reasonable assumptions, people would be likely to allocate part of that additional year to work and part to retirement. For example, people might want to keep their ratio of working years to retirement years unchanged and allocate an additional year proportionately. But improvement in life expectancy is the first step for arguing that people are able to work longer.

We have chosen life expectancy at age 55, as a proxy for the ability of older people to work. The pattern at age 65 looks very similar. Life expectancy at age 55 over the twentieth century was higher for women than for men. But the pattern of increase in life expectancy was very different for

Figure 2-1. *Life Expectancy at Age 55, Males and Females, 1905–2005*

Years

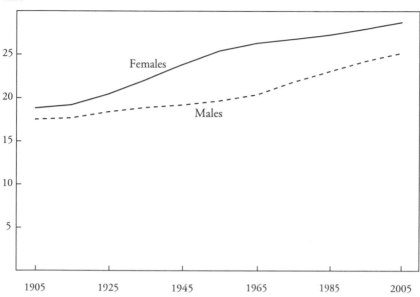

Source: U.S. Social Security Administration (2003).

men and women (figure 2-1). For men life expectancy at older ages rose slowly at the beginning of the century and then accelerated toward the end of the century. In fact, life expectancy for men at 55 was not very different in 1965 than in 1905: twenty versus eighteen years. After 1965, however, life expectancy at 55 took off, rising to twenty-five years in 2005.[6] The pattern for women is quite different. Women experienced a seven-year gain in life expectancy at age 55 between 1905 and 1965 but saw only a four-year increase between 1965 and 2005. But both men and women at age 55 can look forward to more years of life than they could have in 1965, when retirement ages were much higher than they are today.[7]

Some experts suggest that a useful way for determining how long people can work is to consider years from death.[8] That is, if in 1960 men had an average retirement age of 66, the average man who retired at that age could expect to live 12.7 years. The question is at what age in subsequent decades could the average man retire and expect to live the same 12.7 years. For men, the retirement age would have increased to 69 by 1980 and to 71 by 2000 (table 2-1). The increase is less for women, who at 66 had 16.8 years of life expectancy in 1960 and the same life expectancy at 68 in 1980 and at 69 in 2000. So 71-year-old men and 69-year-old women today have as much life

Table 2-1. *Ages of Men and Women with Same Number of Years Remaining, as a Sixty-Six-Year-Old in 1960, 1960–2000*[a]

Year	Men	Women
1960	66	66
1970	67	68
1980	69	68
1990	70	68
2000	71	69

Source: U.S. Social Security Administration (2003).
a. Number of years remaining in 1960: men, 12.7; women, 16.8.

expectancy as 66-year-old men and women in 1960. Thus if workers' goals were to keep their years in retirement constant, they could have increased their working life by three to five years. Although people would most likely want to allocate some of their additional life span to retirement as well as to work, rising longevity suggests that retirement ages could rise.

Another study took a different approach to measuring how much longer people might be able to work.[9] It looked at the percentage of men at each age who are near death, which they define as within two years of dying. The two-year period was selected because disability rates are very high within two years of death. Figure 2-2 presents results for men in 1960 and 2003. In 1960 the two-year mortality rate for men aged 66 (the average retirement age in that year) was 7.8 percent. In 2003 the two-year mortality rate did not reach that percentage until age 73. This suggests that men are not just living longer but also have gained even more in terms of disability-adjusted life expectancy.

Trends in Disabilities among Those 65 and Over

Proximity to death, however, might not be a consistent marker for identifying how long people can work. The relationship between improvement in mortality and health is complicated. In the old days when death was caused by acute diseases, say typhoid, eliminating typhoid would let more people live longer and also reduce the incidence of illness. But when health is dominated by chronic diseases, the relationship becomes unclear. People have offered a number of theories. One expert suggests that better management of the risks leading to chronic diseases would delay their onset so that the period of illness would become "compressed."[10] By delaying the onset, improvements in mortality would be accompanied by reduced prevalence of illness. Another expert predicts better management of chronic diseases so that

Figure 2-2. *Percentage of Men within Two Years of Death, 1960 and 2003*

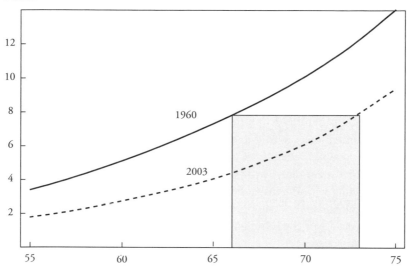

Percent

Source: Authors' calculations based on Cutler, Liebman, and Smyth (2006) and National Center for Health Statistics, Life Tables (1964, 2006).

people with the disease would live longer.[11] Since the duration of the disease would increase, improved mortality would be accompanied by increased prevalence of illness. A third theory, which has been dubbed the "failure of success," posits that success in treating once-fatal illnesses would increase the number of frail individuals and increase the incidence of disability.[12] Improved mortality would thus be accompanied by an increase in the number of frail and ill individuals. For example, a reduction in mortality due to success with stroke victims would reduce the health of the surviving population, since stroke survivors are often quite disabled. Mortality would decline, but the incidence of illness would increase.

It is possible to measure health along a scale of well-being. At the high end would be questions of how vigorously a person can exercise or engage in other strenuous activities. At the low end, questions revolve around people's ability to undertake daily tasks and to care for themselves. In assessing people's ability to work, the low end is the relevant criterion. And the ability to function at the low end turns on the notion of disability.

What Is a Disability?

Disablement is generally defined as a process. It begins with a pathology, a change in a person's body caused by disease, infection, or some other factor.[13] An example is hypertension, whereby high blood pressure stretches the walls of the arteries. A pathology can then lead to an impairment, which makes it difficult for a person to function. For example, hypertension can lead to angina (the chest pain or discomfort that occurs when your heart muscle does not get enough blood) or to heart attack or stroke. The impairment can then lead to an inability to perform work or household tasks. Finally, the functional limitations can lead to dependence.

For older people, dependence usually means that they have difficulty with the basic activities of daily living (ADLs), such as eating, bathing, and dressing; or difficulty with the instrumental activities of daily living (IADLs), such as doing light housework, shopping, and preparing meals. ADL disability is generally considered the most severe because it is generally associated with long-term care needs.

With a focus on work, the key question is the extent to which older people have disabilities that might limit their labor force activity. Our primary concern is with older workers, people aged 55–64. But we first look at trends in disability among the population 65 and over, because substantial research has been conducted for this age group, and presumably a healthier group of retirees would imply a healthier cohort of older workers. The following section reports the more limited survey results for older workers.

Trends in Disability

Trends during the 1970s led a number of researchers to conclude that increased longevity had led to increased frailty among the surviving population. For a period of time, researchers accepted the failure of success theory. But since the early 1990s it seems irrefutable that the health of the older population has been improving.[14]

In 2002 a technical working group examined trends in disability for older Americans across five major national surveys.[15] The group concluded that, when standardizing for the definition of disability, time period, and consistent inclusion or exclusion of the nursing home population, all five surveys showed steady downward trends for two common disability measures—difficulty with daily activities and help with daily activities—beginning in the early to mid-1990s. The evidence for change in the 1980s and for a third measure of disability (the use of help or equipment with daily activities) remained mixed.

Figure 2-3. *Older Americans with Disability, by Age Group, Selected Years 1984 to 2004–05*

Percent

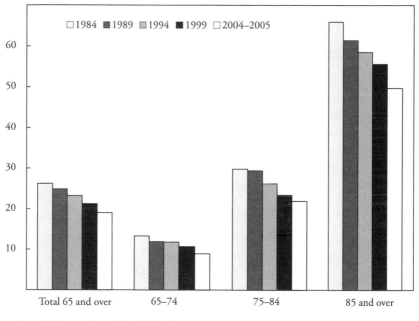

Source: Manton, Gu, and Lamb (2006).

The most consistently positive findings regarding the health of those 65 and over come from the National Long-Term Care Survey (NLTCS). The NLTCS, a longitudinal survey of the Medicare-enrolled population ages 65 and over, was conducted in 1982, 1984, 1989, 1994, 1999, and 2004. In each survey, approximately 20,000 people were screened for chronic limitations in activities of daily living and instrumental activities of daily living.[16] Researchers put a lot of weight on this survey because the questions have remained virtually unchanged since the beginning.

Figure 2-3 shows the percentage of the total 65-and-over population that was dependent, where *dependent* is defined as having an ADL or IADL difficulty or as residing in a nursing home. Between 1984 and 2004, the share of the elderly that lacked the ability to function independently with ease declined from 26.2 percent to 19.0 percent.[17] The figure also shows the prevalence of dependency by age. Although dependency rises sharply by age, the pattern of decreasing dependency was evident for all age groups.

Experts cite a number of reasons for this improvement in the health of those 65 and over. Since the change has occurred so recently and so rapidly, environmental factors—as opposed to genetic or evolutionary developments—must clearly play a major role.[18] The usual suspects include better medical care, reduced exposure to childhood diseases, improved lifestyles, fewer occupational hazards, and increased education and income. Understanding the source of the improvements for those 65 and over should shed light on whether and when older workers would also be expected to enjoy better health. For example, to the extent that most of the improvements for those 65 and over were the result of Medicare-driven improved medical care, those under 65 would be less likely to benefit. But to the extent that they were the result of other factors such as reduced exposure to early childhood disease and improved working conditions, the improvement should be evident in those under 65 but show up roughly a decade earlier.

BETTER MEDICAL TREATMENTS. Twenty years ago, one of the major reasons that older people had problems with walking and shopping was arthritis.[19] The major developments that required nursing home care were cognitive impairment, followed by heart disease and stroke. The medical profession has been able to alleviate many of these health problems. The debilitating effects of arthritis have been substantially controlled by the use of anti-inflammatory drugs.[20] Joint replacements, which roughly doubled from the 1980s to the 1990s, are also a major innovation.[21] In terms of heart disease and stroke, the use of hypertension medication also rose in the late 1970s and early 1980s, which may explain the decline in incidence of stroke in recent years.[22] It appears that much of the improvement has come from earlier diagnosis and improved treatment of those who develop the condition rather than from a reduced onset of conditions in the first place, although the age of onset remains an unsettled question.[23]

LESS CHILDHOOD EXPOSURE TO INFECTIOUS DISEASE. The current elderly were also less exposed to disease in childhood. The medical and epidemiological literature provides many examples of the possible linkage between early life infectious disease and chronic disease and cognitive disorders late in life.[24] For example, individuals who had acute rheumatic fever as a child were likely to experience a recurrence of attacks following streptococcal infection. Other infectious diseases, such as measles, syphilis, typhoid fever, and malaria, can also cause heart problems in later life.[25] The decline of infectious diseases has likely contributed to the reduced disability of today's 65-and-over population.

Table 2-2. *Obese Population, Ages 55–64, by Gender and Race,*
1982, 1992, and 1999[a]
Percent

Year	Men		Women	
	White	*Black*	*White*	*Black*
1982	12	17	14	33
1992	18	23	18	40
1999	29	23	23	47

Source: National Center for Health Statistics, Life Tables (2006).
a. A person is classified as obese if his or her body mass index (BMI) exceeds 30. BMI is the ratio of a person's weight (measured in kilograms) to height (measured in meters) squared.

IMPROVED LIFESTYLES. In addition to having healthier childhoods, the current elderly also evidence better behavior as adults. In 1965 more than 40 percent of men were regular smokers; in 2005 only about 25 percent of the male population smoked. Smoking is the leading risk factor for heart disease, stroke, and respiratory diseases—all precursors to a disability.[26] People have also reduced the intake of salt and fats in their diets, which may have reduced the incidence of atherosclerosis and hypertension. Diabetics are taking better care of themselves relative to earlier cohorts in terms of consumption of alcohol and foods with sugar.[27] On the other hand, the growing trend toward obesity and rising incidence of diabetes are examples of unfavorable developments (table 2-2). Among older workers, white men and black women appear to be particularly at risk. Obesity is also a serious problem among younger people, raising questions about the health of tomorrow's older workers.[28] This issue is discussed below.

FEWER OCCUPATIONAL HAZARDS. The nature of work has also become less physically demanding and less hazardous.[29] First, employment has shifted from manual jobs to white-collar work. This is an important development because economists document that, even controlling carefully for education and income, those in manual occupations have worse self-reported health and experience more rapid declines in their health with age than their white-collar counterparts.[30] Manual workers also have less control over their work schedules, face repetitive tasks, and hold jobs where prestige is often low, which can cause psychological problems. Second, within manual jobs, regulations have substantially reduced occupational hazards by limiting workers' exposure to many dangerous conditions, including dust, fumes, and gases that can cause lung diseases.

HIGHER EDUCATIONAL ATTAINMENT. The improvement in educational attainment among those 65 and over could also have led to improved health. People with more education have a 50 percent lower disability rate than those with less education.[31] The share of the elderly with a college degree more than doubled from 1980 to 2006, and the share without a high school diploma dropped sharply.[32] Some contend that education inevitably stands for more than years in the classroom. That is, it is a broad measure that reflects access to medical care, patterns of medical care use, as well as exercise, diet, and smoking patterns and access to devices when disability does occur.[33] One study, however, attempts to disentangle education from these other factors and finds that, even controlling for income and wealth as well as other reasons why education might matter (past health behaviors such as smoking and drinking, job-related hazards, early life economic environment, and parental education and health), education remains an important explanatory variable.[34] One possible reason is that more-educated people will follow what can be complicated regimens and better manage their diseases.[35] This discipline may reflect an improved understanding of how current actions can affect future events, an understanding that comes with more education. In short, now that we have eliminated many of the huge disparities between rich and poor in terms of exposure to infectious diseases and even in terms of food and shelter, the impact of education on health has become increasingly important.[36]

The improvement in the condition of older Americans has been both recent and dramatic. The explanation for the timing may be twofold. First, improvements in medical care, reductions in occupational stress, changes in lifestyles, increases in education and income all occurred in a short period of time. On the medical side, Medicare, which was enacted in 1965, may well have encouraged treatment innovations for the elderly through teaching hospitals and clinical research.[37] Second, the life experiences of different population cohorts differed significantly. As described by Dora Costa,

> Those who were 70 in 1980 were born in 1910, when infectious disease rates were still high and when incomes were low, and spent their prime years in relatively dangerous jobs. In contrast, those who were 70 in the year 2000 were born in 1930, when infectious disease rates, while still high by today's standards, had fallen. They enjoyed higher incomes, improvements in food distribution that allowed them to eat a more balanced diet, more education, less dangerous jobs, and improved medical care.[38]

Figure 2-4. *Activity Limitation of Men, Ages 45–64, 1967–2004*[a]

Percent

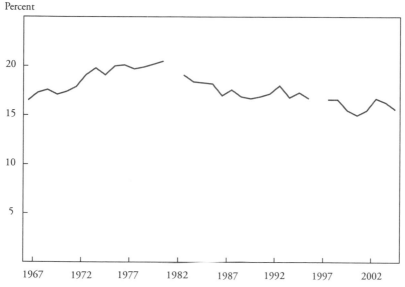

Source: National Center for Health Statistics, Current Estimates (1967–2004).

a. From 2002 to 2004, the figure shows work limitation for all persons instead of males only.

Trends in Disabilities among the Working-Age Population

The fact that the health of older Americans has improved would lead one to conclude that the health of the older working-age population was also getting better. But for a long time such a conclusion was not obvious. The major survey that tracked disabilities among the working-age population—the National Health Interview Survey (NHIS)—shows the percentage of this population with disabilities increasing from the mid-1960s through the early 1980s (figure 2-4). (The NHIS is an annual cross-sectional survey of 100,000 noninstitutionalized civilians conducted by the U.S. Centers for Disease Control and Prevention.) Decennial census data also show an increase in the fraction of both men and women ages 45–64 unable to work during the 1970s.[39] And a major survey of the evidence, undertaken in the wake of the 1983 increase in the Social Security full retirement age, concludes that the worsening of health seen over the previous twenty years would continue into the future.

Skeptics of the increasing disability story contend that the trend during the 1970s may, at least in part, reflect social factors, such as earlier detection and diagnosis of chronic diseases and greater availability of disability insur-

Figure 2-5. *Men with a Work Limitation, Ages 55–64, 1981–2005*

Percent

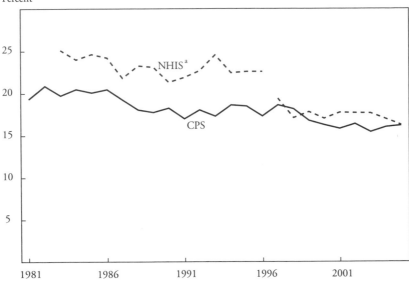

Source: Authors' calculations using National Center for Health Statistics, Current Estimates (1983–2005) from the National Health Interview Survey (NHIS) and U.S. Census Bureau and Bureau of Labor Statistics (1981–2005) the Current Population Survey (CPS).

a. The NHIS was redesigned in 1997. A change in the survey question accounts for the large drop between 1996 and 1997.

ance.[40] Thus the trend in the prevalence of disabilities during the 1970s remains controversial.[41]

Since the early to mid-1980s, however, it is clear that the percentage of older working-age men with an activity limitation has declined, according to the NHIS. Unfortunately, the survey questions have been revised every ten to fifteen years, making it impossible to construct a series over a long period of time. Nevertheless, consistent data are available from the years 1967–82, 1983–96, and 1997–2004.[42] For the period 1983–96 the survey asked, "Does any impairment or health problem now keep [person] from working at a job or business? Is [person] limited in the kind or amount of work [person] can do because of any impairment?" A person who answered yes to either question was considered to have a work limitation.[43] As figure 2-5 shows, the percentage of those ages 55–64 with a limitation declined from the early 1980s and through the mid-1990s. Between 1997 and 2005 a similar question produced a more stable trend. The NHIS data thus show work limitations declining to a level at least comparable to that in the mid-

Figure 2-6. *Working-Age Men in Fair or Poor Health, 1974–76, 1994–96, and 2004–06*

Percent

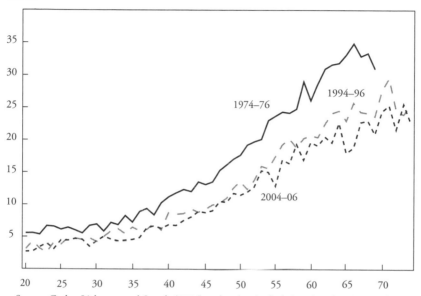

Source: Cutler, Liebman, and Smyth (2006) and authors' calculations based on National Center for Health Statistics, Current Estimates (2004–06) from the National Health Interview Survey.

1960s,[44] but that 15 to 20 percent could still have serious difficulty working into their mid-60s.

Another source of data on work limitations is the Current Population Survey (CPS). The CPS is also a large annual cross-sectional survey (about 150,000 noninstitutionalized civilians). Unlike the NHIS, the CPS was not designed to track health trends but rather to gather employment and income data for the U.S. population. Nevertheless, beginning in 1981 the March supplement has asked a question about work limitations: "Does anyone in this household have a health problem or disability which prevents them from working or which limits the kind of work they can do? [If so,] who is that? Anyone else?" And unlike the NHIS, the survey question has remained unchanged over twenty-five years. The trend since the early 1980s is one of declining disabilities (figure 2-5). The figure shows that the average level of work-based disability was higher in the NHIS data than in the CPS data. The NHIS might elicit a higher rate of reported disability because it is a health-based survey.[45] But both surveys show a downward trend in the 1980s and early 1990s.

Figure 2-7. *Men with a Work Limitation, Ages 55–64, by Household Income Tercile, 1981–2005*

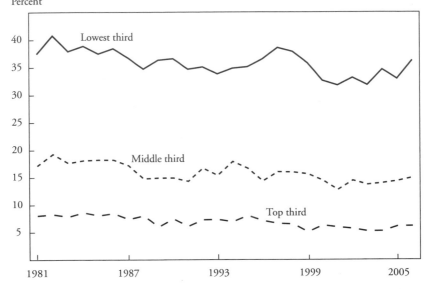

Source: Authors' calculations using U.S. Census Bureau and Bureau of Labor Statistics, Current Population Survey (1981–2005).

The evidence on work limitations is consistent with self-reported health assessments presented in figure 2-6. Since the early 1970s, the NHIS has asked the question: "Would you say your health in general is excellent, very good, fair, or poor?" A response of fair or poor is an indication of serious problems and is highly correlated with subsequent mortality.[46] The data pooled were for three time periods, 1974–76, 1994–96, and 2004–06.[47] The results show that the percentage of men at each age reporting fair or poor health in recent years was below that in the mid-1970s.

It is important to note, however, that the health of older workers is strongly related to income. Figures 2-7 and 2-8 show the incidence of work limitations of men and women ages 55–64 by household income. The incidence among men declined in each tercile since the early 1980s. Among women, health limitations became somewhat less common in the highest income tercile and were essentially unchanged in the middle and lower terciles. Most striking, however, is the large and persistent difference, among both men and women, in the incidence of health-related limitations by household income. Such limitations are far more common in the middle as opposed to the highest income tercile and are dramatically higher in the lowest income tercile. The lines of causation between health and income clearly

Figure 2-8. *Women with a Work Limitation, Ages 55–64, by Household Income Tercile, 1981–2005*

Percent

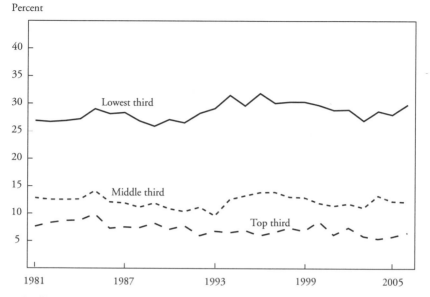

Source: Authors' calculations using U.S. Census Bureau and Bureau of Labor Statistics, Current Population Survey (1981–2005).

move in both directions. Health limitations impair the ability to work and generate income from earnings. Low income impairs access to health care if not an adequate diet and a health-promoting environment. The net result is a concentration of health-related work limitations among low-income older workers.

In short, the health of older workers began to improve in the 1980s and continued to improve since then. It makes sense that improved disability and health trends would show up earlier among those ages 55–64 than for those 65 and over, since the younger cohort was less exposed to infectious diseases in childhood, worked in less hazardous jobs, and enjoyed higher education and incomes. Note, however, that the same data that indicate improvement show that 15–20 percent of older men have a disability that limits their ability to work. These limitations, moreover, are concentrated among workers at the bottom of the income distribution.

Trouble Ahead?

One further note of caution may be in order. Some researchers report that the baby boom generation may be less healthy than its predecessors, that

Table 2-3. *Self-Reported Health Status of Men and Women, Ages 51–56, by Birth Cohort*
Percent

Self-reported health status	Male			Female		
	Original cohort (born 1936–41): 1992	War babies (born 1942–47): 1998	Early baby boomers (born 1948–53): 2004	Original cohort (born 1936–41): 1992	War babies (born 1942–47): 1998	Early baby boomers (born 1948–53): 2004
Excellent or very good	57	54	50	57	52	50
Reporting:						
Pain	17	23	29	24	30	33
Chronic problem	53	54	60	58	59	65
Psychiatric problem	8	17	21	12	27	28
Alcohol problem[a]	21	23	28	7	11	12

Source: Soldo and others (2006).

a. Respondents were coded as having a potential drinking problem if they responded positively to more than one of the following: ever felt should cut down on drinking, ever criticized for drinking, felt bad or guilty about drinking, or ever taken a drink first thing in the morning. A score greater than 1 is used clinically to screen for alcoholism (Mayfield, McLeod, and Hall 1974).

older Americans are much less healthy than older Britons, and that disability among younger people appears to be increasing.

One analysis uses data from the Health and Retirement Study (HRS) to examine the health status of those ages 51–56 from three cohorts: the original HRS cohort, which was born between 1936 and 1941; the so-called war babies, born 1942–47; and the early baby boomers, born 1948–53. Despite enormous advances in diagnosis and treatment, war babies and early baby boomers are much less likely to assess their overall health as excellent or very good. These cohorts also suffer more than the original HRS sample from pain, chronic diseases, psychiatric problems, and alcohol issues (table 2-3). And the deterioration appears to be increasing with each cohort.

Confirmation that older working-age people in the United States are facing serious health problems comes from a study that compares the self-reported rates of several chronic diseases related to diabetes and heart disease, adjusted for age and health behavior risk factors, of non-Hispanic white individuals ages 55–64 in the United States and the United Kingdom.[48] The results show the U.S. population is less healthy on the basis of the incidence of diabetes, hypertension, heart disease, myocardial infarction, stroke, lung disease, and cancer. Within each country, health problems increase as socioeconomic status declines, and the health disparities between the two countries are largest at the bottom of the education or income distribution. These results indicating relatively poor health in the United States hold even controlling for differences in behavioral factors, such as, smoking, obesity, and alcohol drinking. These differences are not due to biases in self-reporting disease because biological markers of disease exhibit exactly the same patterns.[49] And they are not solely driven by the bottom of the socioeconomic distribution; with many diseases, the top of the distribution is less healthy in the United States as well.

A final study looks at whether the young in the United States are becoming more disabled.[50] Using consistent data from the National Health Interview Study, the authors find substantial growth in reported rates of disability in the population younger than 50, even though, as discussed above, no such trend is evident for older individuals.[51] This growth becomes even more pronounced once the incidence of disability is adjusted for changes in the composition of the population in terms of age, sex, education, and so on. Indeed, disability appears to be increasing for whites and nonwhites, people in and out of the labor force, and people at all educational levels. The authors suggest that the rise in obesity could be one reason for the deterioration in health. Indeed, the rate of disability is much higher in the obese than the nonobese, and diabetes, which is closely linked with obesity, is a small but rapidly growing source of disability. There is also evidence that obesity exacerbates back problems, the leading source of disability for the nonelderly.[52]

What should we make of these pessimistic studies? The authors themselves suggest some reasons for calm. One is the failure of success discussed earlier. That is, technological advances in medicine have postponed death for frail individuals, lowering the proportion of deceased people in a cohort but raising the proportion of the disabled. In this case, increased disability could be consistent with overall improvements in health and welfare. Another explanation is that people are becoming more sensitized to even minor health problems as they are barraged by ads for prescription medications and as standards of good health increase. The final explanation relates to the U.S. disability program, which has become more attractive to low-income workers in recent years. Several researchers find that low-skilled workers are filing for disability insurance more often, even if they have not become more disabled.[53] These explanations are plausible. But if these reports of increased disability prove accurate, the story of improving health for older workers could reverse for coming generations.

Conclusion

Numerous studies show that health and work are related. Those reporting poor health are less likely to work than those in good health. Although the trends in the 1970s remain controversial, the NHIS data indicate a rise in work limitations among men ages 45–64 from the mid-1960s to the mid-1980s. This development occurred at the same time that the average retirement age for men fell from 66 to 63. The expansion of the nation's retirement income system—Social Security, Medicare, and employer pensions—clearly contributed to this decline in the average retirement age. But declining health could be part of the explanation.

Now that the retirement income system is contracting, workers need to remain employed longer to gain the same level of retirement income security. The evidence suggests that the health of older workers is at least as good today as it was forty years ago. Moreover, jobs are much less physically demanding than they were in the past. Thus physical limitations should not inhibit the bulk of Americans from working into their mid- to late 60s.

The data also make clear that, despite a positive trend, 15–20 percent of the population could find it virtually impossible to work at those ages. Studies suggest that improvements in health may have, at a minimum, stalled. Moreover, many of those who need to work longer, particularly low-wage workers dependent on Social Security, are precisely the individuals who have onerous jobs that stress their health and who lack the education to manage their care. Thus the working-longer prescription must be administered with caution.

3

Will Older Men Want to Work Longer?

This chapter summarizes what is known about the labor supply of older men, defined as those 55 and over. As discussed in the introduction, a greater proportion of older individuals will need to work than do at present, because retirement income systems are contracting and life expectancy is increasing. Working longer is the best way for most—especially for the baby boomers, who have little time to boost their saving—to ensure financial security in old age. The topic is also of great interest because older individuals will compose a much greater portion of the population, so their labor supply will have a significant impact on national output, tax revenues, and the cost of means-tested programs. This chapter focuses on men, because women's work patterns reflect the increasing participation of cohorts over time as well as the factors that affect retirement behavior. The next chapter discusses the labor supply of women.

The first section reports on the long-term decline in labor force activity among older individuals and the increase in wealth and retirement incentives that contributed to that trend. The second section describes the recent turnaround in the labor force activity of older men and the changes in Social Security, pensions, and other factors that likely led to that reversal. The third section explores whether the labor supply of older workers will continue to increase. On the one hand, the Social Security, pension, and other incentives that likely led to the recent turnaround will persist. And if, in addition, older men respond to the income effect caused by the contraction of the retirement income system described in the introduction, they should work longer. But risks exist. Specifically, in the last twenty years work patterns of older men have changed in ways (more mobility and less tenure) that make their job situations much less secure. And employers seem resistant to flexible employment arrangements. The following section discusses a major structural impediment to remaining in the workforce, namely, the availability of Social Security benefits at age 62. The final section concludes that, despite the obstacles, labor force participation rates of older men may well exceed official projections that forecast little change but are unlikely to duplicate 1960s levels.

Long-Term Decline in Employment Rates

The notion of retirement as a distinct and extended stage of life is a recent innovation. Up to the end of the nineteenth century, people generally worked as hard and as long as they could. In their prime they put in sixty hours of work each week. And at the end of life they had only about two years of "retirement," often due to ill health. Productive capacity declined with age. So they took on less taxing jobs or worked fewer hours. But they generally stopped working only when no longer able.[1] Beginning around the end of the nineteenth century the percentage of the older male population at work began to decline quite rapidly (figure 3-1).[2] The employment rate among men aged 65 and over fell from about 76 percent in 1880, to about 43 percent in 1940, and to 18 percent in 1990.

People retire for three basic reasons. First, poor health makes it impossible for them to keep working. Strength, eyesight, hearing, and mental agility decline with age, and the incidence of debilitating conditions and illnesses rises. Second, as the real or perceived productivity of older workers ebbs, employers find it unprofitable to employ them at a wage the older worker finds acceptable. Third, people acquire enough wealth to forgo earnings from work. That is, as their productivity declines and ailments raise the disutility of work, older people can choose to quit. As discussed in the previous chapter, though, health has improved, not deteriorated. Thus in terms of explaining the trend toward longer periods of retirement, increasing wealth and the attitudes of employers must be the primary drivers.[3]

Economic growth has been dramatic throughout the twentieth century. Despite the Great Depression, GDP per capita in 1940 was 2.3 times the

Figure 3-1. *Workforce Participation Rates of Men Aged 55–64 and 65 and Over, 1880–2000* [a]

Percent

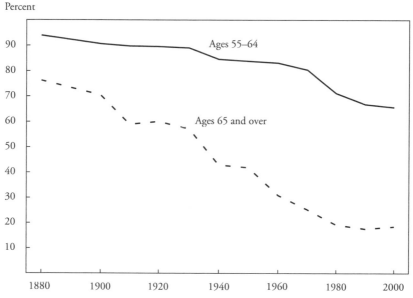

Source: Ruggles and Sobek (2004).

a. Work rates during 1880–1930 are any reported gainful occupation. In the period 1940–2000, work rates are labor force participation rates, defined as working or seeking work.

level in 1880. Workers used some of this increased affluence to reduce their work burden. The length of the work day fell sharply between the 1880s (when the typical worker labored ten hours a day, six days a week) and 1940 (when the typical work schedule was eight hours a day, five days a week).[4] But retirement requires more than rising incomes and a decision to consume more leisure. People can retire only if they have a source of income once their earnings cease.

In the preindustrial era, family farms and handicraft businesses were natural vehicles for accumulating wealth as part of a worker's normal routine, and many elderly were able to retire from active labor by selling or leasing these assets. But industrialization separated the process of gaining a livelihood from the process of acquiring income-producing property. As a result, industrial workers had to consciously set aside a portion of their earnings and invest those funds. But the saving and investing process requires a good deal of foresight, discipline, and skill. People need to predict their earnings over their lifetime, how long they will be able to work, how much they will earn on their assets, and their life expectancy. Surveys suggest that, even today, people are not very good at planning for retirement. Moreover, at the turn of the century most people had little reason to save for retirement since most died early.[5]

Instead of saving for retirement, an unexpected and substantial stream of income for the elderly appeared at the end of the nineteenth century in the form of old-age pensions to the large number of Union Army Civil War veterans. A comprehensive study finds that veterans eligible for these pensions had significantly higher retirement rates than the population at large.[6] It is important to note that these pensions did not require workers to retire; beneficiaries could collect while remaining employed. That Union Army pensions produced an upsurge in retirements clearly illustrates the impact of increased wealth on labor supply, workers choosing to consume a portion of that increased wealth in the form of more retirement.

Work rates in the United States did not return to their previous levels as the veterans died off in the early decades of the twentieth century. Instead, the percentage of the older population at work remained at about the same reduced level. Various analysts argue that this trend reflects the growth of worker incomes.[7] But employer attitudes were also becoming more important. The U.S. workforce was rapidly shifting from self-employment, most notably as farmers, to employees of large enterprises. Employers increasingly introduced mandatory retirement ages for their employees. And they were reluctant to hire older workers, especially during the Great Depression.[8]

Enactment of Social Security

The next big decline in the work rates of older people occurred after World War II. One obvious factor was the availability of Social Security benefits. The legislation was enacted in 1935, and Old Age Assistance welfare benefits were paid almost immediately. Social Security's retirement benefits began in 1940. Although benefits were seriously eroded by wartime inflation, the critical 1950 Social Security amendments substantially expanded coverage and restored benefit levels. Replacement rates—benefits relative to preretirement earnings—equaled 30 percent for the average worker.

Ultimately, the low levels of earnings replacement in Social Security were judged inadequate, given the widespread acceptance of retirement as a legitimate period of rest after a lifetime of work, the relative poverty of the elderly population, and the recognition that employer pensions would never fill the gap. In response, Congress enacted Medicare in 1965 and in 1972 sharply increased Social Security benefits to roughly a 40 percent earnings replacement rate for the average earner. It appears that workers chose to consume a portion of their new-found Social Security wealth in the form of more retirement.

Figure 3-2. *U.S. Private Sector Workers Covered by Employer Retirement Plans,*
1880–2000

Percent

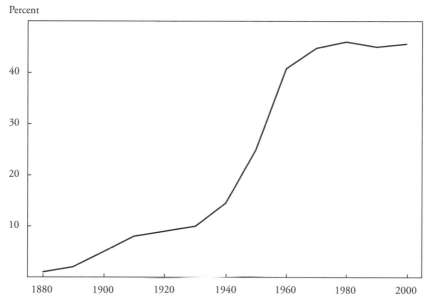

Sources: Skolnik (1976), U.S. Department of Labor (1999, 2006), and authors' estimates.

The uptick in retirements was probably also due to key features of Social
Security design: the retirement earnings test and the take-it-or-leave-it character of Social Security benefits. The earnings test meant that workers could
not collect benefits if their earnings from work were more than a trivial sum.
The take-it-or-leave-it character meant that benefits would not rise if beneficiaries delayed claiming. The effective earnings of workers who did not retire
at age 65 were their compensation less their Social Security benefit (and other
taxes and work expenses). Social Security thus decreased the value of remaining at work vis-à-vis retirement, and this substitution effect contributed to
the decline in participation. Employer pension plans had similar features and
similar effects. They required retirement for a worker to collect and offered
no increase in benefits if a worker stayed on.

Expansion of Employer Pensions

The postwar period also saw the expansion of employer pensions (figure 3-2).
Employer pensions had evolved over the course of the nineteenth century.
Large U.S. employers, which came to have huge numbers of permanent

employees, introduced pensions as instruments for shaping their relationship with their workforce. Pensions helped develop career white-collar employees and managers, to whom large employers increasingly delegated authority to oversee their operations. Such workers had to invest in organization-specific skills and relationships, make decisions in the best interest of the organization, and do so with limited oversight. Pensions paid a comfortable benefit, pegged to salary and years of service, to those white-collar workers who remained with the employer to the specified retirement age. Workers who left early typically got only a return of their own contributions. The pension thus functioned as an incentive to remain with the organization, do good work, and rise in the ranks.

Pensions also proved valuable in shaping relationships with blue-collar workers. Organizations in industries such as railroads, urban transit, and manufacturing employed very large numbers of blue-collar workers to operate their capital-intensive, high-throughput operations. These employers typically paid high market wages to attract better workers, win their loyalty, and fend off unions. But beyond a certain point, employers found it more effective to provide industrial insurance rather than ever-higher wages. This insurance protected workers and their families against the loss of earnings due to accident, death, illness, or age.

Finally, by the end of the nineteenth century, many large employers saw their offices, machine shops, and locomotives increasingly staffed by older workers whose productive abilities had clearly declined. So beginning at the turn of the century, large employers began to mandate retirement at a specified age. To remove older workers without damaging relations with the rest of the workforce, or the public at large, they retired these workers on pensions. By 1930 employer pension plans had become standard in mature big businesses and covered about 15 percent of the nonagricultural workforce. They were critical personnel tools for strengthening, then severing, relationships with workers.

The drivers of the postwar expansion in employer-sponsored plans were threefold. First, employer-sponsored, defined benefit plans had become an essential component of corporate personnel systems, so coverage grew as corporate big business blossomed.[9] Second, the special tax treatment of employer pensions became significantly more valuable in the face of mass income taxation.[10] And third, unions, which had gained powerful collective bargaining rights, made pensions a standard component of labor agreements throughout the unionized sector in the 1950s. The availability of benefits from employer-sponsored plans, with no incentive to work beyond the full retirement age, clearly encouraged retirement.[11]

By the early 1970s the combination of Social Security and employer-sponsored plans provided long-service workers with a secure and comfortable retirement. In the wake of these developments, labor force participation rates for men 65 and over declined from 33 percent in 1960 to 16 percent in 1985.

Retirement Incentives for Those under 65

While the focus of discussion has been on men 65 and over, labor force participation rates of those 55–64 also declined in the postwar period. The decline was very gradual until the early 1960s. In 1961 Congress lowered Social Security's earliest eligibility age (EEA) for men from 65 to 62, after lowering the EEA for women in 1956.[12] The reduction of the EEA for men was primarily in response to a recession that left many older workers without employment. These early retirement benefits are actuarially adjusted and thus involve no clear increase in retirement wealth. But numerous empirical studies, showing spikes in retirements around the key Social Security ages of 62 and 65, support the notion that the availability of benefits at 62 was an important factor in reducing the labor force participation rate of men ages 55–64.[13]

In addition to the availability of early Social Security benefits, many traditional employer-sponsored defined benefit plans in the 1970s began to offer significant subsidies for early retirement. The subsidy arises because companies offer benefits at an early retirement age, such as 55, that are not adjusted sufficiently to reflect the fact that retirees will receive benefits for ten years longer than if they retired at age 65.[14] The subsidy implicit in the less-than-actuarially fair reduction then gradually declines and disappears entirely at the full retirement age.[15] By decreasing the value of remaining at work vis-à-vis retirement, this pattern produces a strong incentive to retire early.

In the wake of these significant incentives to retire early, the labor force participation rate of men ages 55–64 declined from 83 percent in 1960 to 67 percent in 1990.[16]

The Recent Reversal

The decline in labor force activity of men 55–64 and 65 and over ended in the mid-1980s, and rates actually started to move higher in the 1990s (figure 3-3).[17] Important explanations for this reversal include changes in Social Security and employer-sponsored pensions.[18] But a number of other factors may also have played a significant role, including the increased education of the workforce, the shift to less physically demanding and more rewarding jobs, the rise in the labor force participation of women resulting in joint decisionmaking at retirement, and soaring health care costs.

Figure 3-3. *Workforce Participation Rates of Men Aged 55–64 and 65 and Over, 1962–2006*

Percent

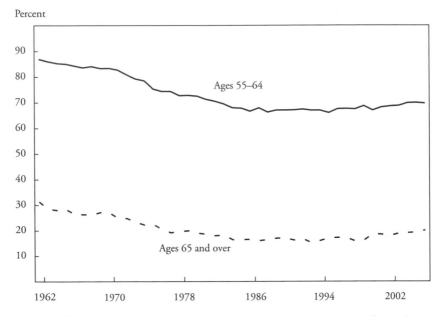

Source: U.S. Census Bureau and Bureau of Labor Statistics, Current Population Survey (1962–2006).

Changes in the Social Security Program

Social Security benefits available at any given age have become less generous, and incentives for early retirement have been reduced or eliminated.

Two changes enacted in 1983 reduced benefit amounts. First, the legislation made up to half of Social Security benefits taxable for people with earnings above a certain threshold.[19] For higher-income beneficiaries, the percentage was increased to 85 percent in 1994. Subjecting benefits to taxation is equivalent to a benefit cut for higher paid workers. Second, the 1983 legislation gradually increased the full retirement age from 65 to 67, which is equivalent to an across-the-board benefit cut. Once the increase is fully phased in, those retiring at age 62 will receive 70 percent, as opposed to the original 80 percent, of full benefits.

In addition, the changing nature of the workforce has led to a reduction in household replacement rates. The percentage of one-earner couples has fallen significantly, and one-earner couples have higher replacement rates than two-earner couples or single households. Higher benefits for one-earner couples are virtually inevitable in a system that provides a 50 percent spouse's benefit.[20] As women go to work, they increase the family's preretirement earnings but often fail to increase the couple's Social Security benefit in retirement. Thus the average Social Security replacement rate for one-earner couples in 2004 was 58 percent, compared to 41 percent for two-earner couples.[21] The increase in the portion of households receiving the lower rate has gradually reduced household replacement rates as women flooded into the labor force.[22]

The expected income effect of such benefit cuts is an increase in labor supply, with workers responding to this decline in wealth in part by consuming less while working, in part by consuming less in retirement, and in part by working longer. While much of the reduction in the couples' benefits has already occurred, the impact of the other changes primarily lies in the future. The full retirement age only began rising for those turning 62 in 2000, and that year the benefit reduction was small.[23] The increased taxation of benefits will also affect a much larger share of the population in the future, as more retirees have income above the unindexed thresholds in the tax code.

More likely candidates for contributing to the increase in participation since the mid-1980s are changes to the Social Security program that made work more attractive vis-à-vis retirement. The first is the liberalization and, for some, elimination of the earnings test. Since Social Security was initially conceived as insurance against a loss of earnings due to disability, death, or old age, the government conditioned benefit receipt on a loss of earned income. The earnings test encouraged large numbers of people to retire early, because it seemed like a tax. Most beneficiaries were unaware that the reduction in benefits while working triggered an increase in benefits later.[24] In recent years, Congress increased the exempt amount for all beneficiaries subject to the earnings test. And for beneficiaries above the full retirement age, it first reduced the benefit loss for each dollar earned and then eliminated the test altogether beginning in 2000. For those between age 62 and the full retirement age, the test allowed about $13,500 of earnings in 2008 before reducing benefits by $1 for each $2 of earnings. Most studies suggest that the earnings test has a substantial impact on the work effort of older people, while some conclude that the test has little effect on labor supply, at least among men.[25]

The delayed retirement credit, which increases benefits for each year of delay in claiming between the full retirement age and age 70, has also improved incentives to keep working. When introduced in 1972 the credit increased benefits by 1 percent a year for each year of delay between the full retirement age and age 72. In 1983 the age was lowered to 70, and the adjustment was raised to 3 percent and scheduled to increase to 8 percent in

2008. When fully phased in the credit will be roughly actuarially fair. Studies suggest that the delayed retirement credit may well have been an important factor in raising labor force participation among workers 65 and over.[26]

End of Mandatory Retirement

In the early 1970s about half of all Americans were covered by mandatory retirement provisions that required they leave their jobs no later than a certain age, usually 65. In 1978 the earliest legal age for mandatory retirement was increased from 65 to 70. In 1986 mandatory retirement was eliminated entirely for the majority of workers. As nearly all workers in 1986 and after were out of the labor force by age 70, however, this legislation probably had little to do with the subsequent rise in the labor supply of older workers.

Changes in Employer Pensions

Various changes in the structure of employer-sponsored retirement income plans have also reduced incentives to retire early. As noted above, in the early 1980s about 85 percent of those with pensions were covered by a defined benefit plan; by 2004 this percentage had declined to 37 percent. In contrast to the early retirement incentives in defined benefit plans, 401(k) plans work like savings accounts and contain no incentives to retire at any particular age. Studies document that workers covered by 401(k) plans retire a year or two later on average than similarly situated workers covered by a defined benefit plan.[27] As more and more workers on the cusp of retirement depend on defined contribution pensions, the labor supply effect of the shift from defined benefit to defined contribution plans will increase over time.[28]

Another likely change, albeit poorly documented, is a shift since the mid-1980s away from subsidized early retirement benefits in traditional defined benefit pension plans. Some experts argue that the desire to eliminate such benefits was a primary motive behind the conversion of a large number of plans, covering over 20 percent of participants in defined benefit plans, to cash balance formats.[29] From the perspective of workers, cash balance plans are much like defined contribution plans.[30] They neither subsidize nor penalize retirement at any given age. In addition, many early retirement sweeteners in the past were offered in special one-time windows. If the conversion to cash balance formats does reflect a shift away from early retirement subsidies, one would expect a comparable shift away from such one-time offers.[31]

Increased Education

Men with higher levels of education have greater labor force participation rates, and over the last quarter century the educational attainment of the

Table 3-1. *Educational Attainment of Men, by Three Age Groups,*
1983 and 2006
Percent

	1983			2006		
Education	*25–34*	*55–64*	*65 and over*	*25–34*	*55–64*	*65 and over*
Less than high school diploma	13	38	55	15	13	24
High school and some college	60	44	33	58	54	50
College degree or more	27	18	12	27	33	26

Source: U.S. Census Bureau and Bureau of Labor Statistics, Current Population Survey (1983, 2006).

population has increased significantly. In 1983, 38 percent of men ages 55–64 had not graduated from high school (table 3-1). By 2006 that figure had declined to 13 percent. Over the same period, those who had completed at least four years of college increased from 18 percent to 33 percent. Moreover, the differential on educational attainment of younger versus older workers vitually disappeared. Changes in the educational attainment for those 65 and over, while somewhat less dramatic, show the same pattern.

The differences in workforce participation by level of education are stunning, and for men ages 55–64, the gap increased significantly. As shown in figure 3-4, all educational groups had rates of participation in the 80–90 percent range in the early 1960s. By the early 1980s, the precipitous decline in labor force activity of those with less than a high school diploma had resulted in a gap of thirty percentage points. With little subsequent rise within educational categories among men ages 55–64 and 65 and over (figure 3-5), it is the movement of large numbers of men up the educational ladder that explains the increase in the overall participation rates of older men between 1985 and 2005 (figure 3-6).

Less Physically Demanding, More Rewarding Jobs

The nature of employment has changed dramatically in the last twenty years. As manufacturing declined, the service sector exploded. This expansion, and especially the expansion of knowledge-based employment, reflects the growth in jobs often thought to have significant nonpecuniary rewards, in places such as universities and hospitals and in occupations such as software development, management consulting, and graphic design. Even within manufacturing the nature of jobs has changed, as firms have automated or outsourced production and now employ more managers, engineers, and technicians.[32] Generally, jobs now involve more knowledge-based activities, which put less

Figure 3-4. *Workforce Participation Rates of Men Aged 55–64, by Education, 1962–2006*

Percent

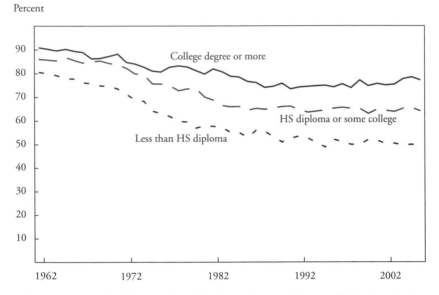

Source: Authors' calculations based on U.S. Census Bureau and Bureau of Labor Statistics, Current Population Survey (1962–2006).

strain on older bodies and provide more satisfaction for workers of all ages.[33] Less physical strain and more nonpecuniary rewards raise the value of remaining at work vis-à-vis retirement, thereby raising the supply of labor. A good portion of the increase in labor force participation since the mid-1980s may be due to such changes, especially among workers ages 65–69, who saw the most dramatic gains.

Joint Decisionmaking

Another factor that may be encouraging later employment is the movement of married women into the labor force. When only the husband was working, retirement decisions could be based on his wages, value of leisure, and retirement benefits and how continued employment would affect those benefits. With wives working, the decision has become more complicated. Now couples need to consider how the decision to stop working will affect both spouses. Studies suggest that husbands and wives like to retire together.[34] Since husbands are, on average, three years older than wives, the increased labor force participation of wives would be expected to lead to later retirement by husbands. That is, if wives want to wait at least to age 62 to qualify

Figure 3-5. *Workforce Participation Rates of Men Aged 65 and Over, by Education, 1962–2006*

Percent

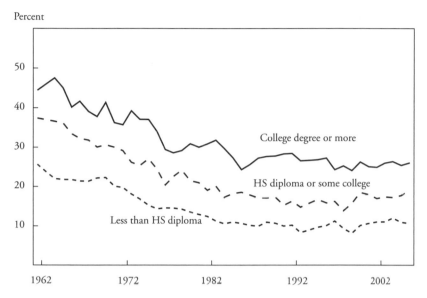

Source: Authors' calculations based on the U.S. Census Bureau and Bureau of Labor Statistics, Current Population Survey (1962–2006).

for early Social Security benefits, that pattern would push their husband's retirement date toward age 65.[35]

Decline in Postretirement Health Insurance

A final factor affecting the labor force participation rates for men at older ages is related to changes in employer-provided health insurance. Health insurance coverage among the working-age population may be declining, but it is declining very slowly. In contrast, employer provision of health insurance after retirement has dropped dramatically. According to the Kaiser Family Foundation, the percentage of firms with 200 or more employees offering retiree health insurance fell by half between 1988 and 2005. This drop dramatically changes the incentives facing workers in their late 50s and early 60s. If they stay with their employer, they will continue to receive health insurance. If they leave before 65, when they qualify for Medicare, they will be uninsured and forced to purchase insurance on their own, a very expensive undertaking. Combine the decline of retiree health insurance with the rapid rise in health care costs, and workers have a strong incentive to maintain their current coverage until they qualify for Medicare.[36]

Figure 3-6. *Workforce Participation Rates of Men Aged 50–74, 1970, 1985, and 2005*

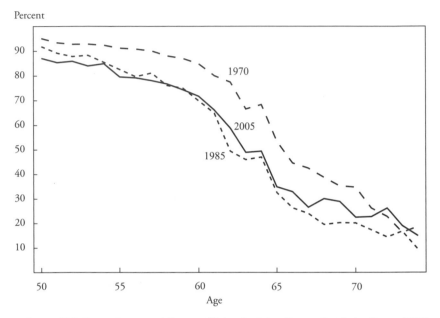

Source: U.S. Census Bureau and Bureau of Labor Statistics, Current Population Survey (1970, 1985, 2005).

In short, a large number of factors could explain the increase in labor force participation among older workers since the mid-1980s. Substantial changes in Social Security and employer retirement plans have raised the value of work vis-à-vis retirement, which increases work rates via a substitution effect. That the increase in participation occurred mainly after age 65 suggests that Social Security changes, primarily the increase in the delayed retirement credit and the end of the retirement earnings test after the full retirement age, might have been quite important.[37]

On the other hand, a study focusing on this older workforce suggests that nonpecuniary considerations might also play a significant role.[38] Older workers tend to be among the more educated, the healthiest, and the wealthiest elderly. The wages they earn are lower than those earned by their younger counterparts and lower than their own past earnings. This suggests that money may not be their prime motivator.[39]

The key question is whether the current trend toward later retirement will continue and, specifically, whether workers will respond to the contraction of the retirement income system by remaining in the workforce longer.[40]

Boomers certainly claim that they will want to work longer, but will they follow through with their plans?[41] The following section discusses the forces that will likely lead to increased work and identifies some of the risks created by changes in the labor market for older workers.

Will the Increase in Labor Force Participation Continue?

Several factors argue that the answer is yes. All the shifts in incentives that help explain the recent reversal in labor force participation rates will remain in place. Social Security benefits are actuarially increased between ages 62 and 70 if claiming is delayed, and the earnings test above the full retirement age is permanently gone. Jobs are less physically demanding and older workers are better educated. Two-earner couples are on the rise, perhaps leading more husbands to delay retirement so they can coordinate with their wives. Moreover, defined benefit plans, with their bonus for early retirement, will cover a declining share of workers; an increasing share will have just a 401(k), which has no early retirement incentives. Health care will also get increasingly expensive, encouraging more and more workers to postpone retirement until they qualify for Medicare. All of these developments make work more attractive vis-à-vis retirement.

The really big question is whether older men will respond to the income effect created by the contraction of the retirement income system. Social Security, the basic source of income for the bulk of the nation's elderly, will replace a smaller share of preretirement earnings at any given age, as the full retirement age continues on its scheduled increase from age 65 to 67. Medicare premiums are slated to take a bigger chunk out of the Social Security check. Taxes on Social Security benefits will rise. The replacement rate for married couples will also continue to fall as working wives increase the household's preretirement earnings more than its Social Security benefits. In addition, pension coverage in the private sector has shifted from defined benefit plans to 401(k) plans, and the median balance for household heads approaching retirement is only $60,000.[42] If people recognize this contraction and respond, the response would boost the labor force participation rate of men.

But there are risks. Those risks include the move away from career employment, the likely decline in the relative wage of older workers, and employer resistance to part-time employment. These risks may explain why year after year (1993–2007) in the Employment Benefit Research Institute's Retirement Confidence Survey workers say they plan to retire at 65 but year after year retirees say that they retired at 62.[43]

Figure 3-7. *Years of Tenure on Job of Employed Men, by Age Group, 1973–2004*

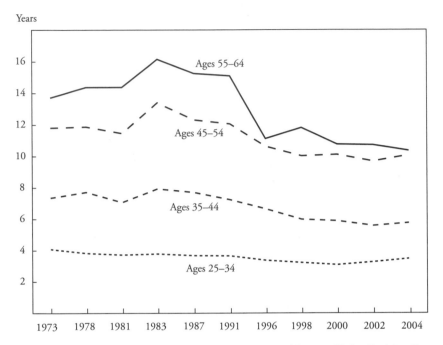

Years

Ages 55–64

Ages 45–54

Ages 35–44

Ages 25–34

1973   1978   1981   1983   1987   1991   1996   1998   2000   2002   2004

Source: Authors' calculations based on U.S. Census Bureau and Bureau of Labor Statistics, Current Population Survey (1974–2005).

The Move Away from Career Employment

One way to see the move away from career employment is to look at how long the typical older worker has been on the job. Data on the median tenure of employed males, taken from the Current Population Survey (CPS), are presented in figure 3-7.[44] The results are interesting in two respects. First, before 1990 the median years of tenure are virtually flat for every age group. These data confirm much of the earlier work on mobility that showed very little change during the 1970s and 1980s.[45] Second, beginning in 1990, after a decade of 401(k) plans, the median tenure for men at older ages starts to decline.[46] If the shift in pension coverage were to have an effect on labor supply, this is where and when one would expect to find it. Pension accumulations under defined benefit plans are very small at younger ages and never really impeded mobility. So the shift in the type of pension coverage would affect the mobility only of older workers.[47] Similarly, the effect would not be expected to become evident until a significant percentage of older workers were covered by 401(k) plans, which did not happen until the 1990s.

Table 3-2. *Men Aged 58–62, by Employment Status and Education,*
1983 and 2004
Percent

Education	Full time with age-50 employer		Full time with different employer		Part time		Not working	
	1983	2004	1983	2004	1983	2004	1983	2004
Less than high school diploma	36	19	13	23	4	3	46	54
High school and some college	46	26	17	31	4	5	34	38
College degree or more	60	35	16	33	3	6	21	25
All	45	28	15	31	4	5	36	36

Source: U.S. Census Bureau and Bureau of Labor Statistics, Current Population Survey (1983, 2004).

An even more direct way to show the decline in career employment is to see how many workers at the cusp of retirement are still with the employer they worked for when they were age 50.[48] Among men ages 58–62 in 1983 and 2004 the portion not working or working part-time was virtually identical (table 3-2). But the distribution of full-time workers changed dramatically. In 1983, 45 percent of all men ages 58–62 were working full-time with their age-50 employer (70 percent of all employed men); in 2004 this figure was only 28 percent (44 percent of all employed men). Further, the shift away from career employment is consistent across educational groups.[49]

The old notion that men settle into some form of lifetime employment by middle age and stay there through retirement no longer holds for the majority of men.[50] This change is important because older workers are likely to have an easier time staying employed and earning higher wages if they remain with their long-term employer rather than scurrying about the labor market trying to find a new job in their 50s and 60s.[51] A key question is whether this job switching at older ages is voluntary. That is, do workers move of their own volition or are they laid off?

One measure of layoffs is displacement rates as measured by the Displaced Worker Survey, which reports the number of workers who have lost their jobs through no fault of their own.[52] Displacement rates for older workers have always been lower than for younger workers.[53] The theory is that employers who have invested in these workers are reluctant to let them go.[54] Displacement rates, while cyclical, show no discernible upward or downward trend

Figure 3-8. *Work Displacement Rates, by Age Group, 1984–2004*

Percent

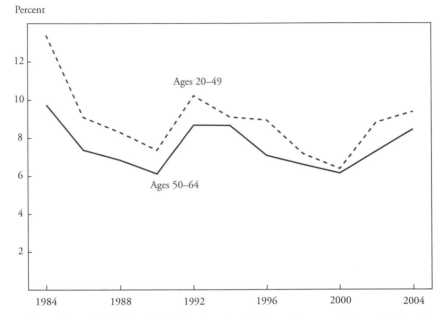

Source: Munnell and others (2006b) based on the U.S. Census Bureau and Bureau of Labor Statistics, Current Population Survey (1984–2004) and Displaced Workers Survey (1984–2004).

over the period 1984–2004 (figure 3-8). This would suggest that the dramatic rise in worker separations from their age-50 employer is largely due to quits, not layoffs—that is, to decisions made by workers, not employers.

There is no historical series on quits, comparable to the Displaced Worker Survey, to verify that this is the case. The distinction between layoffs and quits, moreover, is not always clear. Employers can reduce a worker's compensation or increase job demands. Workers can also feel insecure in their current job due to technological change or increased competition, especially from overseas. If workers quit in response to such pressures they would be leaving of their own volition. But the decline of career employment, if the result of such voluntary quits, could not be characterized as a positive development. That is, it would not reflect the emergence of attractive opportunities with other employers but rather the decline in the attractiveness of their current situation.

The basic way to evaluate these transitions, and what the decline in career employment means for older workers, is to observe the change in compensation. Separations from long-term employment relationships involve a loss of

Figure 3-9. *Percentage of Full-Time Male Workers Aged 58–62 Not Working for Their Age-50 Employer and the Ratio of Their Wages to Wages of Workers Still with Their Age-50 Employer, 1983–2004*

Percent

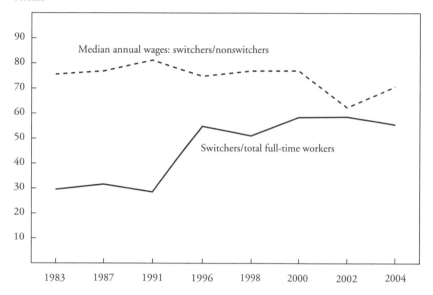

Source: Authors' calculations based on the U.S. Census Bureau and Bureau of Labor Statistics, Current Population Survey (1983–2004).

firm-specific human capital. They also involve a loss of seniority-based protections that shield older workers from the consequences of skill erosion and market competition. Thus a shift to a new employer would seem to suggest a fall in wage and benefit compensation. On the other hand, one would expect the compensation of a worker who quits in order to take a new position would rise.

A simple comparison of wages for full-time workers who switch jobs with those who do not reveals that over the period 1983–2004 the wages of switchers averaged about 75 percent of that for full-time workers who remained with their age-50 employer (figure 3-9). This suggests that the decline in career employment marks a transition to a more difficult labor market for older workers.

A study used the Health and Retirement Study to explore the effect of different types of job change on wages, benefits, and job satisfaction of older workers between 1986 and 2004.[55] Most transitions occurred among work-

Table 3-3. *Effect on Wages and Benefits of Men Who Did Not Stay with Age-50 Employer, by Reason for Leaving*
Percent

Reason for leaving	Hourly wage loss	Those losing pension	Those losing health benefits
Retired	53	76	26
Laid off	25	40	24
Quit			
Involuntarily	23	37	21
Voluntarily	13	31	14

Source: Authors' calculations based on Johnson and Kawachi (2007).

ers ages 51–60. Retirements accounted for about one-third, layoffs for about one-third, and voluntary and "involuntary" quits (quits due to health, family reasons, personal problems, and so on) for the remaining third. Intuitively, one would expect that the biggest decline in compensation would occur in the case of retirement, because the purpose of leaving is to work less hard. The second biggest decline would occur in the case of layoffs, because displaced workers usually face a costly search process and end up in an inferior position. The next biggest decline would occur among those who quit for personal or health reasons. Finally, one might expect an increase for those who quit voluntarily, presumably for "better jobs" with higher compensation or more nonmonetary rewards.

The results of the study confirm the expected ordinal pattern (table 3-3). However, all four groups of workers who left a long-term employer, even those who quit "voluntarily," saw a decline in both wages and benefits. The one silver lining is that all groups report an increase in the nonpecuniary rewards of employment. Workers say their new jobs are less stressful, less physically demanding, and more enjoyable than their old jobs. These findings nevertheless confirm the results of the simple comparison of CPS wages. The decline in career employment means that the wages and benefits earned by older workers—the primary economic rewards from continued employment—will be significantly less than had they stayed with their age-50 employer.

Adverse Cohort Effects

The second reason that the labor market situation for older workers will become more difficult is that they will constitute a significantly larger share of the U.S. labor force. Workers ages 55–64 rose from 9 percent of the workforce in 1990 to nearly 14 percent in 2006 and are projected to exceed 18

Figure 3-10. *Size of Male Workforce Aged 55–64 and Their Wages Compared with Size of Male Workforce Aged 64 and Under and Their Wages, 1962–2006*

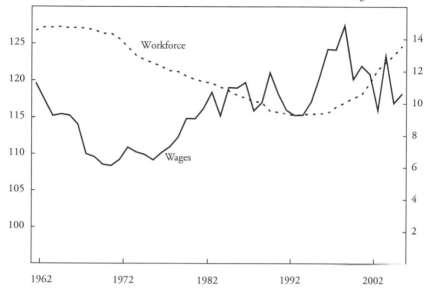

Source: Authors' calculations based on the U.S. Census Bureau and Bureau of Labor Statistics, Current Population Survey (1962–2006), and U.S. Bureau of Labor Statistics (2007b).

a. Wages are for those who graduated from high school.

percent in 2020.[56] Theory suggests that the age distribution of the workforce affects the wage structure. The notion is that workers with different amounts of labor market experience are imperfect substitutes for each other. More experienced workers generally perform different tasks and play different roles within the organization. As the supply of workers with a given level of experience grows, the wages of that group will decline relative to the rest of the workforce. The magnitude of the decline will depend on the extent to which workers with different degrees of experience can substitute for each other. The relative wages of older workers appear to be inversely related to older workers as a share of the labor force (figure 3-10).

A number of studies examine how the relative wages changed as the baby boom generation entered the market and as the boomers aged. A now-famous analysis, "The Baby Boom Babies' Financial Bust," finds that the wages of young white men were reduced relative to those of older men as the baby boomers started entering the labor market.[57] Another study finds that the depression of wages due to cohort crowding follows workers throughout their careers.[58] Thus it seems reasonable to conclude that the increasing share of older workers in the labor force will depress their wages relative to younger workers.

The reduction in wages and benefits created by the decline in career employment and cohort crowding can be expected to affect the labor supply of older workers in two ways. First, it will reduce the financial resources of older workers, a negative income effect. According to the standard life-cycle model, rational workers should respond by working longer. On the other hand, lower compensation will make work less attractive vis-à-vis retirement, a substitution effect. This effect is strengthened by the shift away from defined benefit pension plans, which produce large accruals at the end of a worker's career.[59] As a result, work will look less desirable for older people relative to retirement, and they may be less willing to supply their labor.

Employers' Resistance to Part-Time Employment

Another hurdle to continued employment could be the lack of opportunities for part-time employment. Older people consistently report that they want to work part time. For example, a study based on the Health and Retirement Study reports that, in 1996, 56 percent of respondents ages 55–65 said they would prefer to gradually reduce their hours as they age.[60] And older self-employed people tend to reduce hours worked as they approach retirement. But few older workers have part-time positions, and part-time employment does not appear to be increasing (figure 3-11).

Currently, part-time employment is concentrated in small establishments and in establishments in the service sector.[61] This is true even after controlling for other factors that would affect demand, such as wages, fringe benefits, seasonal fluctuations in demand, and hiring costs. It is not exactly clear why this is the case. Large firms might avoid part-time workers because they tend to have higher turnover rates than full-time employees.[62] Part-time work might be more common in the service sector because it is labor intensive and faces fluctuations in demand and because employers find it is easier to meet these fluctuations with part-time workers. While all these theories are plausible, they have not been supported by rigorous empirical studies.[63]

Without an increase in the availability of part-time employment, many older people may be unwilling to keep working. One study estimates that increased flexibility in work schedules would double the number of people entering partial retirement.[64] However, the same study suggests that an expansion of part-time employment might not make a significant contribution to retirement income security. It finds that total work would increase by

Figure 3-11. *Percentage of Workers Aged 55–70 Employed Part-Time,*
by Gender, 1980–2004

Percent

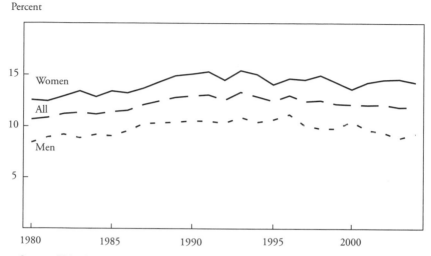

Source: U.S. Census Bureau and Bureau of Labor Statistics, Current Population Survey
(1981–2004).

only a modest amount, since half of those moving into part-time employment would have remained employed full time in the absence of the part-
time option.

Social Security Benefits at Age 62: A Major Obstacle to Labor Supply

The fact that Social Security offers benefits at age 62 is a major obstacle to
older workers' offering their services in the future. Early retirement benefits
are actuarially reduced, and the reduction is designed to be age neutral. That
is, two people with average life expectancy—one who claims benefits at 62,
the other at 66—receive equal lifetime Social Security benefits. Despite the
actuarial reduction, the vast majority of workers continue to claim benefits
well before the full retirement age. In 2005, 55 percent of the men and 59
percent of the women who claimed benefits were age 62 (table 3-4). The
claiming pattern for benefits is roughly consistent with the average retirement age, which is now about 63.[65]

Social Security's retirement age for full benefits has increased from 65 to
66 for workers born after 1943 and is scheduled to rise to 67 for workers
born after 1960.[66] As a result benefits at age 62 will decline from 80 percent
of the full amount to 70 percent.[67] But people's claiming behavior and retire-

Table 3-4. *Age Distribution of Men and Women Claiming Social Security Benefits, 2005*
Percent

Gender	Age				
	62	*63*	*64*	*65*	*66 and over*
Men	55	9	10	22	4
Women	59	8	10	17	6

Source: U.S. Social Security Administration (2007b).

ment decisions appear more sensitive to the availability of benefits than to benefit amounts, so age 62 may well remain an important benchmark.[68] Maintaining 62 as the earliest eligibility age not only diminishes the willingness of workers to remain in the labor force, it also reduces the willingness of employers to retain or hire older workers. One survey asked employers about the impact of various characteristics that could affect the productivity of older workers.[69] A major negative factor was the perception that older workers will be on the job for only a short time. To the extent that the likely departure date can be pushed forward, employers would be more willing to hire, train, and promote older workers. In short, little progress can be expected in the continued employment of older workers as long as the earliest eligibility age remains at 62.

Conclusion

Greater labor force participation by older workers could dramatically improve retirement income security as well as increase national output and government tax receipts. Some indication that people might be willing to work longer comes from the fact that the century-long downward trend in the labor force participation of older men has clearly ceased and that participation has actually been rising since the mid-1990s. The key question is whether people behave like rational actors in the life-cycle model. Will they recognize that the retirement income system is contracting, that longevity rising, that they are healthier than workers in the past, and that work is less onerous? And will they then respond by choosing to remain in the labor force longer?

Key impediments stand in the way of such a response. First, perhaps 15–20 percent of older workers are not healthy enough to work until their mid- to late 60s. A second impediment is the decline of career employment. Older workers who leave long-term jobs lose human capital and social support networks and are exposed to the vagaries of the labor market. Extended and difficult job searches, as well as the prospect of lower compensation, may

Figure 3-12. *Workforce Participation Rates of Men, by Age Group, 1962–2006, with Official Projections to 2030*

Percent

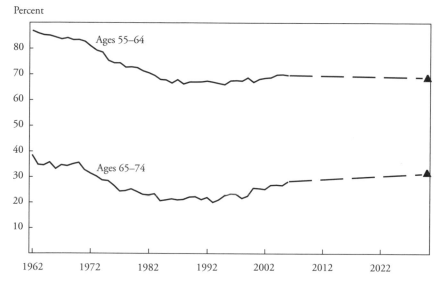

Sources: U.S. Census Bureau and Bureau of Labor Statistics, Current Population Survey (1962–2006); U.S. Bureau of Labor Statistics (2007b).

cause many to simply give up. The most important impediment could be the continued availability of Social Security benefits at age 62. Even today, with the elimination of the earnings test after the full retirement age and a nearly actuarially fair delayed retirement credit, the majority of workers essentially claim benefits as soon as they become available. Studies of retirement behavior find it relatively insensitive to changes in the level of benefits, whether provided by Social Security or an employer pension plan. The availability of benefits and early retirement incentives have been far more important influences on retirement behavior than changes in benefit levels.[70]

What's the bottom line in terms of men's labor supply? A distant upper bound would seem to be the participation rates of 1960, when men could not claim Social Security benefits before 65 and before employer pension receipt became widespread. In 1962, 87 percent of men ages 55–64 and nearly 40 percent of men ages 65–74 were working; the average retirement age was 66 (figure 3-12).

Today, approximately 70 percent of men ages 55–64 are in the labor force, up from a low of 66 percent in the mid-1990s. Among men ages 65–74, about 28 percent are in the labor force today, up from 20 percent in the mid-

1990s. The Bureau of Labor Statistics actually projects a slight decline in the younger group, to 69 percent, and an increase to 32 percent in the older group.[71] Other studies project lower participation rates.[72] Given the contraction of the retirement income system and the benefits of working longer, somewhat higher estimates seem reasonable.

Even a more optimistic projection, however, will fall short of the required change in the labor force participation rate of older workers. As indicated in chapter 1, the retirement age needs to rise at least three years, to 66, to ensure reasonably comfortable retirements. When the retirement age was 66, in 1960, labor force participation was about fifteen to twenty percentage points higher than it is today for workers ages 55–70. The economic dynamics currently in play, in other words, are unlikely to provide today's workers with economic security in their old age.

4

Will Older Women Want to Work Longer?

The previous chapter explores the extent to which men are likely to remain in the labor force longer and thereby offset the effect of the contracting retirement income system. On the one hand, elimination of incentives for early retirement, rising labor force participation of married women, improving health, better education, and the shift from goods- to service-producing industries should increase the likelihood of continued employment. On the other hand, a decline in job stability among older men and the lower wages they may face may discourage employment. Much of the recent upsurge in labor activity among older men involves the most educated and healthiest of the population, making it unclear whether the motivation is work or pleasure and whether the labor force participation of older men will indeed expand as the retirement income system contracts.

As complicated as the picture may be for men, the outlook for women is even more convoluted. Women are subject to many of the same forces buffeting men. But projecting their future behavior is complicated by the fact that women's labor force participation has been rising dramatically in each successive generation. Women also face different financial incentives and have different family responsibilities.

But women could have a lot to gain by working longer. Today nearly 30 percent of elderly nonmarried women, who represent a majority of households at older ages, are classified as poor or near poor. Some of these women were nonmarried and poor as they entered retirement; others were married and suffered a large drop in income when their spouse died. Thus women would be better off if they had stronger Social Security earnings records and their own employer pension benefits. Moreover, given the importance of joint decisionmaking for couples, the continued employment of married women may be the best way to keep their husbands working, thereby ensuring the largest Social Security benefit for their husband and the largest widow's benefit for themselves.

The question is, What determines women's labor force activity at older ages and when they retire? Only by understanding these levers is it possible to make changes that are likely to encourage stronger labor force participation, and thus greater retirement security, for women.

As a prelude to exploring the determinants of work and retirement for older women, the first section explores the labor force trends for women, which differ significantly from those for men. The second section shows how the different labor force experience of women plus specific aspects of the retirement income system affect the well-being of women in retirement. The third section then describes the financial incentives, family considerations, and demographic characteristics that are likely to influence decisions about work and retirement. The following section reports results from the Health and Retirement Study on how these factors affect the probability of older women's being in the labor force, their planned retirement ages, and the likelihood of retiring earlier than expected. The final section concludes.

The bottom line is that both the cohort and incentive effects suggest that labor force participation rates for women in their 50s and 60s will increase from their current levels. But whether women will respond further to fully offset the contraction in the retirement income system is unclear.

The Long-Term Trend in Employment Rates

The short story is that single women have always worked and that married women, until recently, have not (figure 4-1). Married women have traditionally accounted for between 65 and 80 percent of all women (table 4-1). The labor supply of married women has been the subject of an enormous body of research, fundamentally because married women are more interesting than single women or men. Some married women go to work and some don't, and the variability in their labor force activity provides grist for analysis. More-

Figure 4-1. *Workforce Participation Rates of Women Aged 35–44, by Marital Status, 1900–2000*

Percent

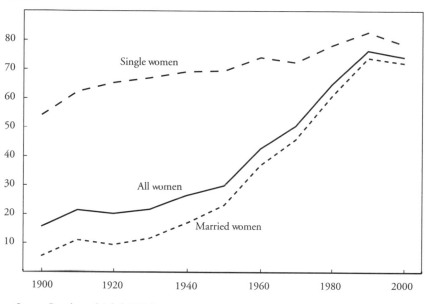

Source: Ruggles and Sobek (2004).

over, the labor force activity of married women has increased dramatically over the last hundred years, reflecting shifts in the supply curve and revealing the importance of looking at labor market decisions in a family context.

The increasing labor force activity of married women during their prime years, defined here as ages 35–44, has pushed up the participation rates for

Table 4-1. *Marital Status of Women, by Two Age Groups, Selected Years 1900–2000*

Percent

	Married		Never married		Widowed		Divorced	
Year	35–44	50–65	35–44	50–65	35–44	50–65	35–44	50–65
1900	79.1	64.2	11.5	6.8	8.7	28.5	0.7	0.5
1920	80.8	64.7	11.1	8.7	7.1	25.7	1.0	0.8
1940	81.3	66.6	10.2	8.8	5.8	22.8	2.6	1.7
1960	84.5	67.5	5.9	7.9	3.0	18.9	3.8	3.8
1980	76.7	69.5	6.0	4.9	2.1	15.6	11.3	7.7
2000	67.2	65.0	13.4	5.8	1.3	9.8	14.4	17.0

Source: Ruggles and Sobek (2004).

older women. That is, women reaching their late 50s and early 60s today have had much higher participation throughout their career than women born in earlier decades. The sweeping changes in the work activity of women over the last hundred years present a fascinating story. Goldin provides the most comprehensive and elegant overview.[1] She divides this history into four periods.

—Late nineteenth century to the 1920s. Some young, nonmarried women worked as piece workers in manufacturing or as laundresses or maids. But virtually no married women were in the labor force. Because work was generally very disagreeable, a huge social stigma was attached to wives' working outside the home. Only a poor provider would force his wife to take on a dirty, dangerous, and boring job that often involved long hours. For most of this period, less than 10 percent of married women ages 35–44 were in the labor force, and these tended to be those with the lowest incomes. Economists estimate income and substitution effects associated with women's labor force activity over time: that is, how responsive the wife's labor supply is to the household's income, typically the husband's earnings, and to the wage she can earn in the labor market. During this period the income effect was very large and negative; as the husband's income increased above fairly modest levels, the likelihood that a married woman would work declined substantially. The substitution effect was small; an increase in the wage was unlikely to coax additional work activity on the part of women.

—1930s to 1950. Between 1930 and 1950 the labor force activity of prime-age married women rose from 10 percent to 25 percent, principally because it became more acceptable for them to work. The jobs got more respectable: nicer and shorter-hour office jobs rather than dirty and long-hour manufacturing jobs. And the option of working part time arose in the 1940s and became widespread in the 1950s, an option attractive to women who were primarily responsible for home and children. Estimates of the female labor supply equation find that the income effect declined with the reduction in the stigma associated with the employment of married women. And the substitution effect increased, as labor-saving household appliances, such as refrigerators and washing machines, made working outside the home less costly in terms of foregone household amenities.[2]

—1950s to 1970s. During this period the labor force participation of prime-age married women rose from 25 percent to almost 50 percent. Appliances made housework less time consuming; husbands did not object to their wives working; and the demand for labor was strong. Women worked as secretaries, schoolteachers, and nurses. They came fully trained to these positions, did not expect advancement, and treated their work as a job, not as an element of their identity. Yet they ended up spending a substantial portion of their life employed. In terms of the labor supply equation, the income effect became much less important and the substitution effect increased as women became more responsive to wages.

—1970s to the present. Young women growing up in the 1960s could see that they would spend most of their lives employed.[3] In response, they invested in their education. They went to college in increasing numbers, majored in career-oriented subjects, and went on to professional schools. The advent of the contraceptive pill allowed many to postpone marriage and establish themselves professionally.[4] Many placed career on equal footing with marriage. Income and substitution effects changed once again. The labor supply of married women was influenced even less than before by their husband's earnings.[5] And women were less responsive to changes in wages. In short, their labor supply equations looked increasingly inelastic, like those of men.[6]

This transformation of women's employment—particularly the increased labor force participation of married women—has had a profound effect on the labor force activity of older women, the topic of this chapter. Each cohort of women has spent more time in the labor force than the previous cohort because of women's changing role, increasing the likelihood that they will be working at older ages. At the same time, however, older women confronted many of the same incentives as men did to retire early. They became eligible for Social Security benefits at age 62 in 1956. They faced a stiff Social Security retirement earnings test and lost lifetime benefits if they worked beyond age 65. They benefited from the enactment of Medicare in 1965 and the sharp increase in Social Security benefits in 1972 to roughly a 40 percent replacement rate for the benchmark average earner. In contrast to men, because fewer women are covered by traditional defined benefit plans, their labor supply decisions were not significantly affected by the early-retirement subsidies such plans offered.

These conflicting forces may help explain the pattern in the labor force participation of women ages 55–64 (figure 4-2). Until 1950 less than 20 percent of women in this age group were in the labor force. Between 1950 and 1970, the percentage doubled to more than 40 percent. But then in the 1970s, just as the male rate began to decline noticeably, older women's labor force participation leveled out, possibly the result of the offsetting cohort effects that increased participation and incentive effects of Social Security and pensions that encouraged retirement. A smaller percentage of women 62 and over was working in 1985 than in 1970 (figure 4-3). These are the ages that would be most affected by the increase in Social Security replacement rates and the incentives to claim early.

Figure 4-2. *Workforce Participation Rates of Men and Women, by Age Group,*
1880–2000

Percent

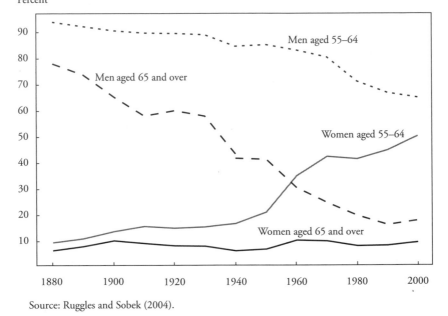

Source: Ruggles and Sobek (2004).

In recent years the labor force participation of women ages 55–64 has
renewed its upward trend. By the end of the century, more than 50 percent
were in the labor force. Part of this increase may reflect the shift in incentives
in Social Security, such as the increase in the delayed retirement credit and the
relaxation of the earnings test (and its elimination for those over the full retirement age), the declining importance of the early retirement incentives in
defined benefit plans, and the need to work until eligible for Medicare, given
the decline in employer-provided retiree health insurance and the rapidly rising costs of health care. But the largest increases occurred among women
under 60, while most of these changes in the retirement income system tend
to encourage work at older ages (figure 4-3). This suggests that the cohort
effect—that is, the increasing participation of women at younger ages—has
played an important role. Historically, the relationship between the percentage
of prime-age (35–44) women in the labor force and the percentage of women
55–64 working twenty years later has been fairly close (figure 4-4). The share
of prime-age women in the labor force peaked in 1990 at 76 percent, and this
level is likely to be reflected in higher labor force activity for women at older
ages in the future. So both incentive and cohort effects may be driving the
recent push in the labor force activity of those 55–64.

Figure 4-3. *Workforce Participation Rates of Women Aged 55–74, 1970, 1985, 2005*

Percent

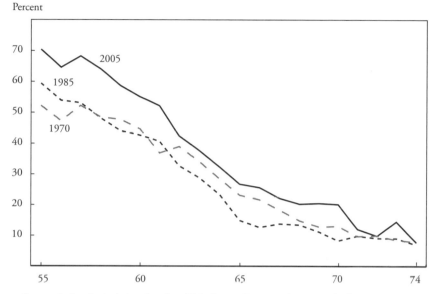

Source: Authors' calculations based on U.S. Census Bureau and Bureau of Labor Statistics, Current Population Survey (1970, 1985, 2005).

The labor force activity of women 65 and over is a much less exciting story. The proportion working was 10 percent in 1900, and it was 10 percent in 2000. The transformation of the labor force over the hundred years appears to have had virtually no impact on the activity of this group. The most likely reason that the labor force participation of older women has not increased is joint decisionmaking by married couples with regard to retirement. Studies suggest that husbands and wives like to retire together. Since wives are, on average, three years younger than their husbands, the dramatic drop in participation rates for men 65 and older, which have been below 20 percent since 1980, may well have held down work rates for older women.

Women's Work Patterns and Retirement Security

Although women's labor force participation has increased dramatically and is approaching that of men, their pattern of work differs significantly from that of their male counterparts. They are more likely to work part time, they spend fewer years in the labor force, and even women who are employed full time earn about 20 percent less than men. As a result, women in 2005 made up 46 percent of the workforce but received only 37 percent of earnings.

Figure 4-4. *Workforce Participation Rate of Women, by Age Group, 1860–2000*

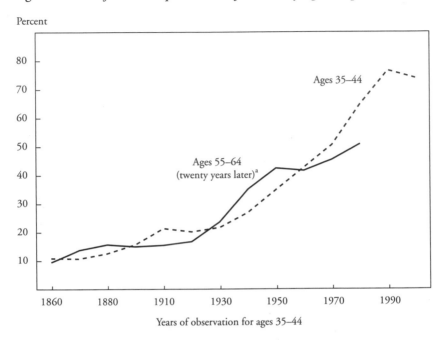

Percent

Source: Ruggles and Sobek (2004).
a. Data for ages 55–64 are for the same cohort observed twenty years later.

Since the retirement income system in the United States is based on earnings, women with their typically lower earnings receive lower benefits. Those married women who depend primarily on their husband's Social Security and pension benefits tend to outlive their spouses and experience a significant drop in income when their husbands die. As a result, these women tend to end up single and financially stressed in old age. In 2004, 17 percent of non-married women fell below the poverty line, and 11 percent were classified as near poor, which means that they had an income of less than 125 percent of the poverty threshold. Thus 28 percent of single older women are either poor or near poor.[7]

Women's Work Patterns

Women's lifetime work patterns are important because their attachment to the labor force during their prime working years will affect the retirement income benefits they earn as well as their desire and ability to work in their 60s.

Women, in particular married women, are far more likely than men to work part time, either for their entire work lives or for a part of their careers. In 2006 about 25 percent of married women in the labor force ages 25–54 worked part time, compared to only 5 percent of men. Part-time work was more prevalent among both male and female workers ages 55 and older. But older working women are more likely than men to work part time. Workers in part-time jobs not only work fewer hours but also earn less per hour than workers in full-time jobs.[8] Thus while part-time work may make it easier for women to participate in the labor force, its lower wage provides less of a reward for doing so.

In addition to the depressing effect on earnings of part-time work, women who work full time earn less than their male counterparts. Although the gender gap has narrowed, in 2006 the median earnings for women full-time workers were 80 percent of that for their male counterparts.[9]

Women also have fewer years in the labor force than men. Among workers who claimed Social Security retirement benefits in 2003, women had on average thirteen years with zero earnings (measured from age 22 to the year before first collecting retired worker benefits), compared to six years on average for men.[10]

Finally, women work in different occupations and sectors of the economy than men. Some aspects of this pattern should make it easier for women to work longer. For example, more than half of all women are employed in industries with sales, office, or service occupations, where jobs should be more available at older ages. Less than 10 percent work in physically demanding jobs, such as construction and manufacturing. So the physical requirements of the job should not be an impediment to continued employment. On the other hand, women are also much less likely than men to be self-employed and, therefore, less able to gradually reduce their work effort as they age (figure 4-5).

Women's Career Patterns and Retirement Security

Women's career patterns have a somewhat muted impact on their incomes in retirement. Because of their lower wage and less time in the labor force, women workers aged 62–64 claiming benefits received an average monthly Social Security benefit of $741 in 2005; their male counterparts received $1,084.[11] But only 40 percent of women received benefits based solely on their own earnings record; the remaining 60 percent were entitled, in whole or in part, based on their husband's earnings (figure 4-6).

Similarly, because women have less attachment to the labor force and earn less, they are less likely to end up with an employer-sponsored pension.

Figure 4-5. *Self-Employed as a Percentage of Workers, Men and Women, by Age Group, 2006*

Percent

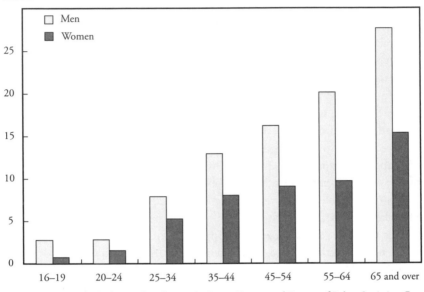

Source: Authors' calculations based on U.S. Census Bureau and Bureau of Labor Statistics, Current Population Survey (2006).

When they do, that pension benefit is likely to be smaller than a man's. In 2004, according to the Health and Retirement Study, of individuals ages 65–74, only 43 percent of women had a pension compared with 65 percent of men. Women's median annual income from a defined benefit plan was significantly smaller than men's ($9,600 versus $15,600 in 2004 dollars), and women's median balances in 401(k) accounts were less than half of men's ($16,200 versus $37,700 in 2004 dollars).

Married women, who share in their husband's benefits, fare much better than single women. Whereas only 9 percent of married persons age 65 and over are either poor or near poor, 28 percent of nonmarried women are either poor or near poor. If women could stay married throughout retirement, they might do reasonably well. But women live longer than men: a life expectancy at 65 of 19.7 years, compared to 17.2 for men.[12] As married women are typically three years younger than their husbands, most married women end up widowed. When their husband dies, two things happen to their retirement income. First, the couple's Social Security benefit is cut by between one-third and one-half. Second, the couple's private pension benefit either disappears

Figure 4-6. *Basis of Entitlement to Social Security of Women Aged 62 and Over, 1960–2005*

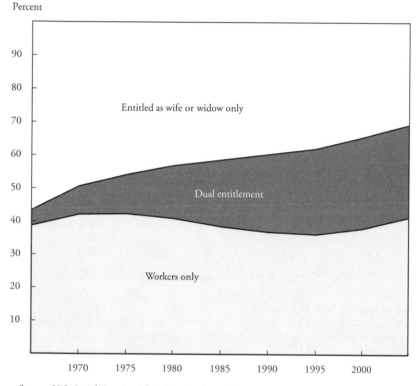

Percent

Source: U.S. Social Security Administration (2007b).

completely or is reduced. In many instances, the household's wealth is also significantly diminished by medical and related expenses incurred at the end of the husband's life.[13]

With the reduction in Social Security benefits, the reduction or cessation of employer-sponsored pension benefits, and the drain on the household's financial resources, women often suffer a severe decline in their income when their husbands die. Figure 4-7 shows the income situation of two groups, one in which married couples remain intact, the other in which the husbands die. Income is measured in terms of the family's income relative to the poverty line. Intact couples maintain an income-to-poverty ratio which hovers around three. For widows the income-to-poverty ratio falls below two.

In short, poverty among women in old age is directly attributable to the interaction of a retirement system based on earnings and a pattern of no and

Figure 4-7. *Ratio of Income to Poverty Line, Married Couples and Widows*[a]

Ratio

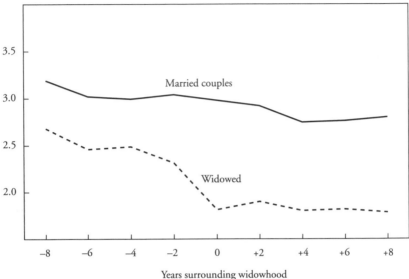

Years surrounding widowhood

Source: Karamcheva and Munnell (2007).

a. Ratio is total income relative to the poverty line. For married couples, the time period is the entire period of the study; for widows it is the years surrounding widowhood.

low earnings on the part of women. Married women often rely on their husband's Social Security and employer-sponsored pension benefits. It is clear that women profit most by having their husbands stay in the labor force as long as possible in order to ensure the largest possible widow's benefit under Social Security.[14] Women, both married and unmarried, will also have a more secure retirement income if they work longer, both to strengthen their earnings records and the retirement benefits based on that record and to shorten the length of retirement those benefits must support. The question is, what are the financial, family, and demographic factors that influence the work and retirement decisions of older women.

Financial, Family, and Demographic Factors Facing Older Women

Women face a different array of costs and benefits than men when considering employment and retirement. Their financial incentives to work are often less attractive. Family responsibilities may also affect the likelihood that

Table 4-2. *Employment Status of Women Aged 58–62, 1983 and 2004*
Percent

Employment	1983	2004
Not working	60	48
Working full-time with age-50 employer	21	21
Working full-time with different employer	13	23
Working part-time	7	7

Source: Authors' calculations based on U.S. Census Bureau and Bureau of Labor Statistics, Current Population Survey (1983, 2004).

women will remain in the labor force. Finally, women's health, education, and divorce prospects may also affect their employment outlook. Understanding the unique situation of older women is critical to crafting effective strategies for encouraging them to work at older ages.

Financial Incentives to Work

Women face different financial incentives than men when considering whether to work or not. This generalization applies to the wages they earn before taxes, the taxes applied, pension coverage, and the rewards from working under Social Security.

WAGES. Despite improvement in the ratio of female-to-male earnings, as noted earlier, women still earn less than men even when they work full time. This pattern holds at every level of education and across occupational categories. Moreover, as discussed above, a much higher proportion of women than men work part time, and the hourly rate for part-time workers is less than for those working full time. Therefore, as women assess the work-leisure decision, they face less of a reward from entering or staying in the labor force than their male counterparts.

The wages of older women have also been adversely affected by reduction in job tenure. Older women, like older men, are much less likely to be with their career employer as they approach retirement. In 1983 almost two-thirds of women ages 58–62 working full time were with the same employer as at age 50; by 2004 that proportion had declined to less than half (table 4-2). As noted in the previous chapter, once older workers leave a career job they have a difficult time finding new employment, and when they do find a job they generally earn less in wages and fringe benefits. This increased churning among older women further reduces the incentive to remain in the labor force.

TAXES. In addition to earning less, family dynamics often result in married women's facing higher tax rates than men or single women. The U.S. personal income tax is progressive, with 2008 marginal rates ranging from 10 percent for couples with incomes of less than $16,050 to 35 percent for couples with incomes over $357,700.[15] Even though the status of women has changed dramatically in the last forty years, the man is usually considered the primary breadwinner. This perception more or less comports with reality, in that in families where both the wives and husbands work, only 25 percent of wives earn more than their husbands.[16] Because the man is usually the primary breadwinner, within the family his employment is often considered fixed and his earnings taxed at the lower marginal rates. The woman, as the secondary earner, has her income stacked on top of her husband's and taxed at the higher marginal rates.

Of course, the alternative arrangement is equally possible, with the woman's income on the bottom and the husband's income on the top. But in most instances when the woman considers working, the couple usually views her income as subject to the higher marginal tax rates. The higher tax rates faced by married women, together with the lower wages that women receive, make their financial return from work significantly less than that for men.[17] Add the cost of child care to the equation, and women often barely break even.

PENSIONS. Pensions also affect the retirement decision, and pensions have changed in two important ways over the last twenty-five years. First, pension coverage has shifted from traditional defined benefit plans, in which the worker receives a lifetime benefit based on years of service and final earnings, to 401(k) plans, which are like savings accounts. Second, pension coverage has declined for men over the same period and increased for women. At this point, men and women have the same coverage rates, and the rate of coverage for full-time women is actually higher than that for full-time men.[18]

Traditional defined benefit plans have penalties for delayed retirement and often a subsidy for early retirement, while 401(k) plans provide no incentive to retire at a particular age and reward continued work with increased retirement wealth. Women have been less affected by defined benefit incentives than men because women have been less likely to have any pension coverage and much less likely to be covered by a defined benefit plan. However, now that women are more likely to be covered, generally by a defined contribution plan, they might be enticed to work longer in order to build up their 401(k) accounts. On the other hand, a growing percentage of covered women will have a nest egg of their own and the resources to stop working earlier than they otherwise would (see box 4-1).[19]

Box 4-1. *Implications for Women of a Changing Pension System*

For women, the shift from defined benefit to 401(k) plans is a good news–bad news story. When women are employed and accruing retirement income benefits, the news is good. One key difference between traditional defined benefit plans and 401(k) plans is what happens to benefits when people move from job to job or in and out of the labor force. Basically, workers with 401(k) plans can take their full accumulations when they leave, while workers with traditional defined benefit plans suffer a loss when they shift jobs. As a result, 401(k) plans are better for short-tenured workers, and women are more likely than men to have short tenures. Therefore, more women are likely to end up with more benefits, and their benefits are likely to be larger.

The bad news arrives when women retire. As women tend to live longer than men, their 401(k) balances must provide an income stream over a longer stretch of time. Should they wish to annuitize a portion of their 401(k) accumulations at retirement, they will find that insurance companies compensate for women's longer life expectancy by providing them with smaller monthly benefits than men. In defined benefit plans, men and women with comparable work histories get the same monthly benefit.

Women who rely on their husbands' earnings and pension benefits are also affected by the shift from defined benefit plans to 401(k)s. Under traditional defined benefit plans, the government requires that the worker receive a joint-and-survivor annuity at retirement, unless the spouse specifically waives the requirement. This provision gives the wife a legal claim on her husband's pension benefits. No such automatic claim exists with 401(k) plans.

The bottom line is that women will benefit from 401(k)s to the extent they are workers and lose to the extent they are dependent on their husbands' earnings.

SOCIAL SECURITY ACCRUALS. Individuals can improve their monthly Social Security benefits by working longer in two ways. They can augment the earnings record that Social Security uses to calculate lifetime benefits, and they can spread those benefits over a shorter retirement span by claiming at a later age. Social Security benefits are based on the thirty-five years of highest earnings, indexed to reflect the increase in wages. Working an additional year allows participants to replace a year of low earnings with a year of the higher earnings likely to be earned later in life. This opportunity can be particularly important for women who may have been out of the labor force to care for children and therefore have many zeros in their earnings history. In this regard, Social Security provides women with a greater incentive to stay in the labor force than it does men. They can also raise their monthly benefit by retiring later. They can avoid Social Security's reduction for retirement before the full retirement age and receive a delayed retirement credit for each year of delay thereafter. These adjustments are designed to be actuarially fair, so that lifetime benefits based on a given earnings record do not depend on when benefits are claimed. However, the later the age of retirement, the greater the monthly benefit.[20]

On the other hand, some women may not improve their Social Security outcome through additional work. These are married women whose lifetime earnings are so low that they qualify for the spouse or survivor's benefit. Despite women's increased labor force participation, as noted earlier, only 40 percent of women 62 and over receive benefits based solely on their own earnings. That is, most women receive benefits based in whole or in part on their husband's earnings records and would gain little from further work.

AVAILABILITY OF SOCIAL SECURITY BENEFITS. The existence of Social Security's earliest eligibility age means that women, like men, have an important choice to make once they reach age 62: claim reduced Social Security benefits right away or delay until some further date and receive a larger benefit. In 2005, 59 percent of women and 55 percent of men who claimed benefits were age 62.[21] As discussed in the last chapter, the availability of these benefits is a major obstacle to the continued employment of older workers both women and men.

Family Considerations

Within the family, women often play the role of caregivers, and married women function as part of a joint decisionmaking unit regarding the work-retirement decision. These factors are likely to affect women's ability and desire to stay in the labor force.

CAREGIVING. At younger ages, women tend to have the primary responsibility for child care. The notable reduction in family size should be a contributing factor to the increased workforce participation of women at younger ages. And the ability to work when young is likely to have a positive impact on participation later in life.

At older ages, women generally have the responsibility for caring for elderly parents or older relatives.[22] More than three-quarters of America's family caregivers are women, and these responsibilities affect their work lives. According to one survey, 84 percent of caregivers had to make informal adjustments to their work schedule, and 64 percent had to make formal adjustments.[23] As the need to care for spouses and parents rises with age, such responsibilities limit the ability of older workers, primarily women, to continue working. The fact that women are having children later, however, could work in the opposite direction, as the rising financial burden of paying for college shifts to older ages.

JOINT DECISIONMAKING. Married men and women generally coordinate their withdrawal from the labor force. A significant proportion of husbands and wives retire within one or two years of each other.[24] Studies show that spouses tend to retire together because they want to spend time together.[25] Economists have been unable to find any support for competing hypotheses for this tendency to retire together, such as husbands and wives' having the same taste for work and leisure or that they face the same financial incentives.

A few studies explore how wives respond when their husbands retire for health reasons. The response could go either way. The wife could stay at work, or enter the labor force if not currently employed, to make up for her husband's lost earnings. In fact, standard labor supply models predict such a response to avoid a major fall in household consumption. Alternatively, the wife might leave the labor force or work fewer hours to spend time with, or to take care of, her husband. Such a response would be consistent with the joint retirement pattern seen among healthy retirees but would have serious financial implications for the family. The data tend to show that wives are less likely to retire with their husbands when the husband is forced into retirement because of health problems or loss of a job.[26]

Joint decisionmaking has major implications for women. If men continue to retire early, then older women will continue to withdraw from the labor force at a relatively young age, tapping their 401(k) plans prematurely, facing a period before Social Security kicks in, and then claiming actuarially reduced benefits at 62. On the other hand, joint decisionmaking may provide an important path to a more secure retirement for couples. If wives insist on working at least until age 62, when they become eligible for Social Security, they could encourage their husbands, who are on average three years older, to work to 65. Wives have every interest in keeping their husbands in the labor force as long as possible, since the larger the husband's Social Security benefit, the larger is the widow's benefit.

Demographic Characteristics

In addition to the financial incentives and family responsibilities, some of women's basic characteristics have changed dramatically in the last several decades, and these should have a profound affect on their ability and desire to work and their ability to postpone retirement.

Figure 4-8. *Workforce Participation of Married Women Aged 55–64, by Education, 1962–2006*

Percent

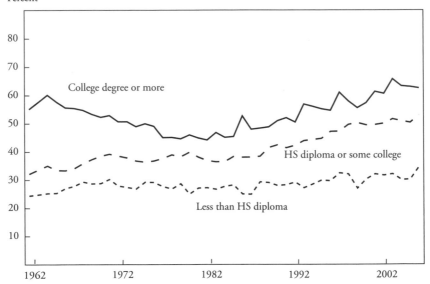

Source: Authors' calculations based on U.S. Census Bureau and Bureau of Labor Statistics, Current Population Survey (1962–2006).

HEALTH.   Health status, as discussed in chapter 2, is likely an important determinant of a person's labor force activity. Having poor health makes it harder to fulfill work responsibilities and limits job opportunities. However, health status has improved among women as well as men. For example, the share of women ages 45–64 reporting activity limitations dropped from 23 percent in 1980 to 16 percent in 2005.[27] Improving health conditions should allow older women to stay in the labor force longer.

EDUCATION.   A higher level of education means more job opportunities and generally more satisfying careers. As a result, labor force participation rates have always been much higher for both married and nonmarried women with a college education or more and much lower for those who have not finished high school (figures 4-8 and 4-9). The percentage of women receiving college degrees has increased significantly. As recently as 1970, only 8 percent of women aged 25 and older had a college degree. By 2006 this share had increased to 27 percent. Most jobs that require a high level of education do not require physical effort or excellent health and often provide significant

Figure 4-9. *Workforce Participation of Nonmarried Women Aged 55–64, by Education, 1962–2006*

Percent

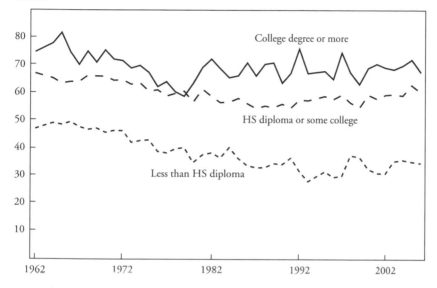

Source: Authors' calculations based on U.S. Census Bureau and Bureau of Labor Statistics, Current Population Survey (1962–2006).

nonpecuniary rewards. Rising educational attainment thus allows older women to stay in the labor force longer and makes them happier to do so.

DIVORCE. Divorce, either as a theoretical possibility or an actual occurrence, may also affect a woman's decision about whether to work and for how long.[28] From the mid-1960s to the mid-1970s the number of divorces per marriage nearly doubled, from one in four to one in two, and has remained high since then. The dramatic increase in the probability of divorce between the mid-1960s and mid-1970s may explain, in part, the increase in female labor force activity during this period. The risk that marriage might end in divorce may encourage more married women to build a career of their own.[29] When divorce does occur, the loss of the husband's earnings often forces the woman to enter the labor force.

In short, financial, family, and demographic factors all play into women's decisions to work or not work. The following section describes the results of some regression analyses that measure the effect of the factors described on the employment and retirement decisions of older workers.

Work and Retirement Decisions of Older Women

The following analysis explores three questions. What factors affect the probability that older women will be employed? What factors affect their expected retirement age? And what factors affect the probability that they will retire earlier than expected? The data come from the Health and Retirement Study, a nationally representative data set that began in 1992, with subsequent interviews every two years.[30] The original survey interviewed people ages 51–61 (born 1931–41) and their spouses. War babies (born 1942–47) were added in 1998, and early baby boomers (born 1948–53) were added in 2004, bringing the total sample to more than 22,000.[31] The study contains detailed information on education, job history, health, and many other demographic and economic factors that could affect women's decisions about working and retirement. The regressions presented in the appendix to this chapter attempt to identify the effect of such factors on women's work and retirement decisions. Other specifications are clearly possible—and reasonable. So the results should be seen as suggestive. The following discussion summarizes the key results.[32]

What Factors Affect the Probability That Older Women Will Be Employed?

For women to be able to continue working into their 60s, they generally need to be employed in their 50s. Therefore an important question is the extent to which the financial, family, and demographic factors discussed above affect the likelihood that older women will be working.

COHORT EFFECT. Early baby boomer married women (born 1948–53) have a whopping 14 percentage points greater likelihood of being employed in their 50s than the original HRS cohort (born 1936–41), even after controlling for the effect of greater education, rising divorce, and other factors that affect employment (figure 4-10). In 2008 these women are ages 55–60; they will be more likely to be working in their 60s than earlier generations. The boomer cohort represents a big change from even the war babies (born 1942–47), where married women had only a six percentage point greater likelihood of being employed than their original HRS counterparts. Surprisingly, even among nonmarried women, who have experienced steady high rates of employment with little variation from one cohort to another, early boomers had a six percentage points greater likelihood of working than the original HRS sample.[33]

Figure 4-10. *Cohort and Demographic Effects on the Probability of Women Ages 51–56 Being Employed, by Marital Status, 1992, 1998, and 2004*

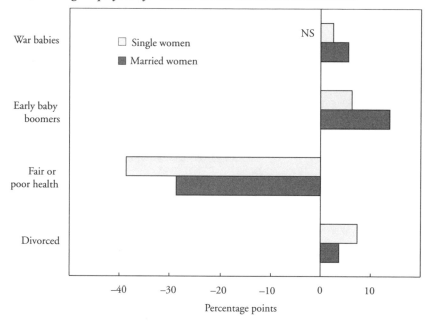

Source: Authors' estimates based on University of Michigan (1992–2004).

FINANCIAL INCENTIVES. Higher wages, lower taxes, and the ability to improve their Social Security benefits appear to be the major factors that encourage older women to work (figure 4-11). Higher wages would be expected to encourage more work. But with a sample that includes some people working and some not, wage information is not available for everybody, so education serves as a measure of wages.[34] The results show that having a college education (and presumably higher wages) increases the likelihood of work for both single and married women.

To test the impact of tax incentives, the analysis includes a measure for when the wife's education is greater than her husband's. The notion is that if a woman's education exceeds that of her husband, she is less likely to be viewed as the marginal earner facing the higher marginal tax rates and more likely to work. Holding other factors constant, married women who are more educated than their husbands are 4 percent more likely to work than women who are less educated.

Figure 4-11. *Effects of Financial Incentives and Education on the Probability of Women Ages 51–56 Being Employed, by Marital Status, 1992, 1998, and 2004*

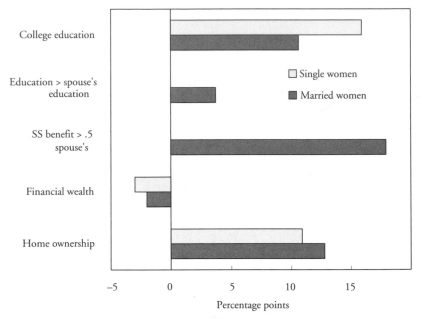

Source: Authors' estimates based on University of Michigan (1992–2004).

To test the impact of Social Security's spousal benefit on work incentives, the analysis compares women whose full retirement age benefits are projected to exceed 50 percent of their spouse's benefit with women whose benefits are projected to be at or below 50 percent. Women in the first group should be more likely to work, since they can improve future benefits through employment. In fact the results are consistent with this hypothesis: holding other factors constant, women whose Social Security benefits are projected to exceed 50 percent of their husband's benefits are significantly more likely to work than women with lower projected benefits.

Having substantial financial resources means there is less of a need for paid employment, and the results indicate that an additional $100,000 of financial assets decreases the probability of working for single and married women.[35] Homeownership may work either way. As a measure of financial wealth, it would indicate less need to work. On the other hand, meeting monthly mortgage payments may require both members of a couple to be employed. The results show that home ownership is positively related to work for women, suggesting that the need to cover mortgage payments outweighs the additional financial wealth that a house represents.

FAMILY CONSIDERATIONS.   Family caregiving responsibilities can include care for a child, a parent, or a spouse. Any of these activities can interfere with a woman's ability to work. But in this analysis the only activity that appears to reduce work effort is caring for a parent by single women, which decreases the probability of working by about 10 percentage points.

As discussed earlier, married women appear to make their employment decisions jointly with their husbands. This study finds that joint decision-making appears alive and well. Having a working spouse increases the probability of working by 13 percentage points for married women. At the same time, the more the husband earns the less need there is to work for pay. The analysis tests for this effect as well but finds that the husband's income has no effect on the probability of a married woman's working. As shown below, the fact that women coordinate their activity with their husbands is a major explanation for their early retirement.

In short, the results confirm that all the factors discussed earlier involving the labor force participation of women are relevant. The cohort matters, incentives matter, and joint decisionmaking is important. Early baby boomer married women, who are currently in their late 50s, are much more likely to be working than earlier cohorts. This finding means that, as early boomers enter their 60s, the female labor force participation rate for that age range should be higher than it has ever been in the past. Higher education, and therefore presumably higher wages, increases the probability of being in the labor force. Being the higher earner and therefore taxed at lower marginal rates and having the ability to increase one's Social Security benefits also increases the probability of working. Decisions are made jointly by married couples. Having a husband working increases the probability of an older woman's being in the labor force. Caregiving appears to serve as an impediment to working only for single women.[36]

What Factors Explain Expected Retirement Ages?

The focus of this chapter is the labor supply of older women, so various factors that affect the likelihood of their being in the labor force were reviewed. The second step is to identify the factors that determine women's retirement plans. Specifically, this next equation identifies the factors that affect the expected retirement age for older single and married women who were working in 1992, 1998, and 2004.[37]

COHORT EFFECTS.   The expected retirement age for married women reveals a significant swing by cohort. Married war babies plan to retire three-quarters of a year earlier than the original sample, who were born 1936–41, while married early baby boomers have an expected retirement age about half a year later than the original sample. Putting the two results together suggests that early baby boomer married women plan to retire a year and a quarter later than the war babies immediately preceding them. That is a stunning increase in expected retirement ages over a relatively few years. As one would expect, nonmarried women, who have shown steady employment patterns, do not have statistically significant different expected retirement ages than the original HRS cohort.[38]

FINANCIAL INCENTIVES. The main financial incentives affecting the retirement plans of older women currently in the labor force are the same as those affecting men (figure 4-12). Having a defined benefit pension, either as the employee's only plan or in combination with a defined contribution plan, reduces the expected retirement age by about one year for single and married women. Women, both single and married, with access to postretirement health insurance expect to retire about one year earlier than those without access. Owning a home also reduces the expected retirement age by about one year.

Several factors important in the work decision do not appear to be important in plans for retirement. Wages, education, and financial wealth do not affect working women's expected retirement age. And the incentive variables for married women that play a significant role in the employment equation—education greater than spouse's and a Social Security benefit greater than 50 percent of spouse's—do not have a statistically significant effect in explaining expected retirement age.

FAMILY CONSIDERATIONS. Joint decisionmaking by couples is evident in that married women whose spouses are in the labor force plan to retire later, although the effect falls slightly below the cutoff for statistical significance. The health of the spouse appears to have no independent effect, and the spouse's income has only a very small negative effect on the expected retirement age of married women. The most dramatic impact of family considerations arises again in the case of single women. Those who have to care for a parent expect to retire more than a year earlier than those not faced with such a responsibility.

On balance, the information on expected retirement age of older women reflects the same factors as those discussed in the earlier chapter on men.[39] Being covered by a defined benefit plan and the availability of employer-provided retiree health insurance lead to earlier planned retirement. Both of these benefits are on the decline, however. Increasing numbers of women will find themselves reliant on 401(k) plans, with no early retirement incentives,

Figure 4-12. *Effects of Financial Incentives on Women's Expected Retirement Age, by Marital Status, 1992–2004*

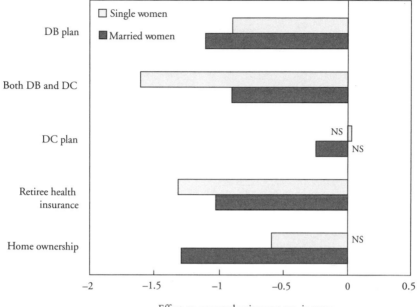

Effect on expected retirement age, in years

Source: Authors' estimates based on University of Michigan (1992–2004).

and more will find themselves without employer-provided health insurance and will feel compelled to wait until age 65, when they qualify for Medicare. The big news, where the outlook for women differs from that for men, is the cohort effect. Early baby boomer married women say they plan to retire half a year later than the original HRS sample and a year and a quarter later than their immediate predecessors, the war babies. Will these plans pan out?

Probability of Earlier-than-Planned Retirement

Having been determined above as to what affects the likelihood of older women's being in the labor force and what affects their expected retirement age, the final question is what can make retirement plans go awry. Surveys consistently show that women—like men—plan to retire around age 65, but the median actual retirement age is 62.[40] The question is why some women retire earlier than expected.

This sample starts with all older women working in 1992 and identifies those who retired earlier than expected.[41] The explanatory variables include initial variables and new shock variables.[42] Four shock variables have a signif-

Figure 4-13. *Effects of Shock Variables on Women's Probability of Retiring Earlier than Planned, by Marital Status, 1992–2004*

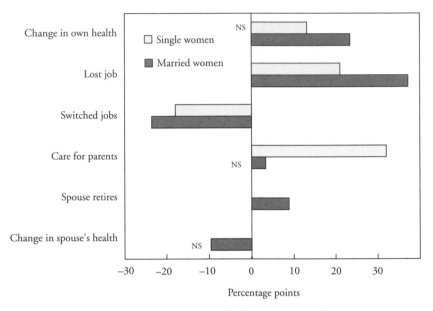

Percentage points

Source: Authors' estimates based on University of Michigan (1992–2004).

icant impact on the probability of retiring earlier than planned (figure 4-13). A decline in health status from good to bad significantly increases the probability of retiring earlier for married women but is not statistically significant for nonmarried women. Having been displaced greatly increases the probability of retiring unexpectedly early for both single and married women. On the other hand, having switched jobs significantly reduces the probability of retiring earlier than planned. One possible explanation for this result is that women who leave their main job may switch to a job that better fits their lifestyle as they approach retirement, allowing them to stay in the workforce longer. Another explanation is that the new job pays less in wages and benefits, and the worker remains in the labor force longer to offset the loss. Finally, finding oneself caring for a parent increases the probability of retiring earlier than expected for nonmarried women.

The results for married couples confirm the importance of joint decision-making. Married women retire earlier than expected if their spouses retire. In fact the probability of retiring early increases by nine percentage points. The results also suggest that married women are less likely to retire early if their spouse's health deteriorates.[43] The latter result is consistent with other studies that suggest that women respond to a husband's illness by taking over the role of breadwinner.

This final equation offers a note of caution about the optimistic retirement plans of the early boomers. Things do go awry and lead people to retire earlier than planned.

Conclusion

Given the pressures on retirement programs and the enormous increase in life expectancy, it will not be possible for people to continue to retire at age 62 and support themselves for twenty or thirty years in retirement. Women are particularly vulnerable to these trends, in that even today many end up in poverty. The reason is that retirement income programs are based on earnings, and women generally have low earnings. Women depend on their husbands for retirement income, and when their husband dies they often suffer a sharp drop in living standards or even fall into poverty. Women can take two steps to improve their retirement security. First, they can encourage their husbands to work as long as possible, which will ensure that they receive the largest possible Social Security widow's benefit. Second, they can enhance their own retirement incomes by continuing to work in their 50s and 60s.

In determining whether or not more work is possible, it is important to remember that women face different financial incentives and family responsibilities than men. Women earn lower wages than men, even when they work full time. Married women are likely to be viewed within the family as the secondary earner and face higher marginal tax rates under the personal income tax, which may well discourage employment at later ages. Their Social Security benefit often will be based on their husbands' earnings. Nearly all women's survivor benefits will be based on their husbands' earnings, and continued employment generally will do nothing to enhance these payments. Finally, societal norms make it more acceptable for women not to work since they continue to be the primary caregivers.

When it comes to retirement, joint decisionmaking means that wives tend to retire when their husbands stop working. Since women are on average three years younger than their husbands, they withdraw from the labor force at an early age. Thus extending women's careers requires one of two changes—either husbands retire later or wives decide that joint retirement may not be best for them in the long run. Husbands retiring later is the far better option for women and could be the key for most women to a more secure retirement. And one of the best ways to get the husband to work longer is for the woman to remain in the workforce!

In some ways, the work prospects for older women look bright. The labor force participation of women in their prime years has risen significantly. Increasingly their work decisions and careers look more like those of men. And early baby boomer married women claim they are going to retire more than a year later than their immediate predecessors. Indeed, the changing incentives in the retirement income system should encourage more employment for both men and women. But good plans go awry. Given their weaker attachment to the labor force, smaller financial incentives, tendency to coordinate retirement with their typically older husbands, the challenge for women to stay in the labor force is greater than that facing men.

Appendix 4A

Statistical Appendix

Table 4A-1. *Marginal Effects from Equation Explaining the Probability of Older Women's Being Employed, HRS Cohorts in 1992, 1998, 2004*

	Single women		Married women		Men	
Item	*dF/dx*	*z statistic*	*dF/dx*	*z statistic*	*dF/dx*	*z statistic*
Financial incentive						
Financial wealth[a]	−0.030	−2.220	−0.020	−4.940	0.000	−1.940
Home ownership	0.109	4.480	0.128	4.920	0.086	5.360
College education	0.159	4.820	0.106	5.120	0.059	4.100
Degree greater than spouse's degree	n.a.	n.a.	0.037	3.420	−0.016	−1.040
Social Security benefit greater than half of spouse's	n.a.	n.a.	0.179	10.370	0.020	0.870
Family consideration						
Number of biological children	−0.008	−1.370	−0.004	−0.990	0.002	0.770
Care for parents (≥ 500 hours a year)	−0.113	−2.180	−0.007	−0.210	−0.041	−1.250
Spouse working	n.a.	n.a.	0.125	6.500	0.056	3.640
Spouse's income	n.a.	n.a.	−0.003	−1.540	−0.009	−3.050
Spouse health fair or poor	n.a.	n.a.	0.017	0.86	−0.046	−2.68
Married	n.a.	n.a.	n.a.	n.a.	0.06	2.17
Demographic						
Age	−0.005	−0.8	−0.013	−2.91	−0.012	−3.61
Nonwhite	−0.041	−1.68	0.04	1.79	−0.052	−3.62
Fair or poor health	−0.386	−15.21	−0.286	−14.41	−0.33	−20.73
Divorced	0.073	2.53	0.037	2.09	−0.018	−1.4
Widowed	−0.011	−0.34	n.a.	n.a.	n.a.	n.a.
Warbaby	0.025	0.85	0.055	3.16	0.035	2.47
Early baby boomer	0.062	2.31	0.139	6.76	0.055	3.41
Social Security benefit missing	n.a.	n.a.	0.044	2.14	0.038	1.69
Pseudo *R*-squared	0.189		0.1046		0.1628	
Sample size	1,770		4,468		4,888	

Source: Authors' estimates based on University of Michigan (1992–2004).

n.a.: Not applicable; HRS: Health and Retirement Study.

a. Financial wealth is measured in $100,000 increments. The results might be slightly off, as this variable was measured in $10,000 increments in the original probit regression.

Table 4A-2. *Coefficients from Equation Explaining Expected Retirement Age for Older Women, HRS Cohorts in 1992, 1998, 2004* [a]

	Single women		Married women		Men	
Item	Coeff.	t statistic	Coeff.	t statistic	Coeff.	t statistic
Financial incentive						
Wage	0.009	0.22	–0.002	–0.85	–0.001	–3.47
College education	0.330	0.60	0.070	0.24	1.094	4.50
Home ownership	–0.593	–1.81	–1.290	–3.52	–1.087	–4.00
Retiree health insurance	–1.314	–4.07	–1.030	–5.38	–0.516	–2.72
Degree greater than spouse's degree	n.a.	n.a.	0.262	1.20	–0.388	–1.79
Social Security benefit greater than half of spouse's	n.a.	n.a.	0.126	0.64	–0.144	–0.59
Financial wealth[b]	0.560	1.09	–0.260	–3.90	–0.140	–2.98
Defined benefit	–0.901	–2.20	–1.110	–4.03	–1.979	–7.28
Defined contribution	0.031	0.08	–0.247	–0.92	–0.417	–1.57
Both DB & DC	–1.606	–3.19	–0.907	–2.82	–2.078	–7.16
Family consideration						
Married, spouse working	n.a.	n.a.	0.380	1.53	0.670	2.78
Spouse health fair or poor	n.a.	n.a.	0.280	1.06	0.291	0.97
Care for parents (≥ 500 hours a year)	–1.361	–2.40	–0.328	–0.78	–0.491	–0.93
Spouse's income	n.a.	n.a.	–0.056	–2.11	–0.101	–1.84
Married	n.a.	n.a.	n.a.	n.a.	0.369	1.00
Attachment to labor force						
Part time	–0.976	–1.14	0.316	0.65	0.507	0.71
Physically demanding job	–0.286	–0.91	-0.169	–0.80	–0.031	–0.16
Hours worked	0.003	0.17	0.030	1.99	0.024	2.34
Self-employed	–0.803	–0.99	0.607	1.31	0.940	2.61
Demographic characteristic						
Age	0.135	1.55	0.181	3.26	0.259	5.09
Fair or poor health	–1.043	–2.56	0.283	1.09	–0.496	–1.87
Nonwhite	–1.524	-4.62	–0.956	–3.70	–0.623	–2.67
Divorced	0.507	1.50	0.323	1.45	0.052	0.26
Widowed	–0.675	–1.78	n.a.	n.a.	n.a.	n.a.
Warbaby	–0.623	–1.54	–0.731	–3.16	–0.354	–1.42
Early baby boomer	–0.062	–0.16	0.555	2.19	0.884	2.81
Constant	58.366	11.96	53.858	17.18	49.955	18.07
R-squared	0.1374		0.0941		0.1373	
Sample size	719		1,753		2,139	

Source: See table 4A-1.

n.a. Not applicable; HRS: Health and Retirement Study.

a. Our results are consistent with Mermin, Johnson, and Murphy's (2006) findings that early baby boomers expect to work longer than earlier cohorts did. While we analyze the expected retirement age, they compared the expected probability of working full-time past the age of 62 and age 65 by cohort.

b. Financial wealth is measured in $100,000 increments. The results might be slightly off, as this variable was measured in $10,000 increments in the original probit regression.

Table 4A-3. *Marginal Effects from Probit Equation Explaining the Probability of Retiring Earlier than Planned for Older Women, HRS Cohorts in 1992, 1998, 2004*

Item	Single women		Married women		Men	
	dF/dx	z statistic	dF/dx	z statistic	dF/dx	z statistic
Initial variable						
Age	–0.034	–4.02	–0.015	–2.77	–0.028	–5.50
Health fair or poor	0.228	2.43	0.248	3.89	0.070	1.32
College education	–0.073	–1.31	0.091	1.98	–0.010	–0.29
Self-employed	0.138	1.13	–0.002	–0.02	–0.039	–0.83
Retiree health insurance	0.070	1.41	–0.020	–0.59	–0.027	–0.84
Nonwhite	–0.054	–1.06	–0.049	–1.06	–0.043	–1.00
Shock variable						
Change in own health (from good to bad)	0.131	1.57	0.234	3.79	0.081	1.62
Lost job	0.210	2.08	0.372	4.63	0.111	1.80
Switched jobs	–0.179	–3.35	–0.236	–5.74	–0.186	–5.39
Care for parents ($\geq$ 500 hours)	0.320	2.82	0.033	0.45	–0.090	–1.03
Spouse retires	n.a.	n.a.	0.088	2.36	0.027	0.72
Change in spouse's health (from good to bad)	n.a.	n.a.	–0.096	–1.70	0.057	0.94
Change in total financial wealth[a]	0.040	1.82	0.010	1.58	0.020	3.02
Pension coverage						
Defined benefit	0.092	1.25	–0.007	–0.16	–0.073	–1.80
Defined contribution	0.114	1.36	–0.044	–0.93	–0.075	–1.75
Both	0.007	0.09	–0.052	–1.00	–0.027	–0.61
Pseudo *R*-squared	0.213		0.134		0.0960	
Number of observations	275		651		847	

Source: See table 4A-1.

n.a. Not applicable; HRS: Health and Retirement Study.

a. Financial wealth is measured in $100,000 increments. Results might be slightly off, as this variable was measured in $10,000 increments in the original probit regression.

5

Will Employers Want to Employ Older Workers?

Whether Americans will be able to work into their mid- to late 60s is not a decision they can generally make on their own. Most Americans work for an employer, not for themselves. So their employers also have a say. And employers have not shown themselves especially receptive to employing older workers.

Retirement from employment was to a significant degree the work of employers. They dismissed or eased out older employees whose strength and acuity declined; later they created retirement policies that forced workers out at a specified age. To facilitate orderly exits, large employers gave the workers they retired old-age pensions and then sweetened the benefits to induce even earlier separations. And employers rarely hired older workers except for a narrow subset of jobs.

Many observers say employer attitudes will change. Today's older workers are in many ways more capable than those of the past, and work is in many ways less taxing. The shift away from defined benefit pensions, the cost of which rises rapidly as workers age, has eliminated a major impediment to the employment of older workers. Perhaps most important, many observers say employers face the prospect of labor shortages and the loss of valuable institutional knowledge when the baby boom generation retires, which will make older workers much more attractive. On the other hand, more older workers might be unable to keep pace with the demands of a dynamic, knowledge-based economy. The rising cost of health insurance, which makes up a larger share of compensation as workers age, will make retaining or hiring older workers increasingly expensive. And there are reasons to think most employers will not face a significant shortage of labor or institutional intelligence when the baby boom generation retires.

Going forward, employers will retain or hire older workers only if it is profitable to do so—if the value of what they produce is greater than what they are paid. The first section of this chapter reviews what is known about the productivity of older workers. The following section reviews what is known about their compensation and the relationship between productivity and compensation. The third section reviews what is known about the increasingly important market for older workers. The fourth discusses how things might change going forward. The last section concludes.

Productivity of Older Workers

The value of what workers produce generally declines at older ages. While most workers remain healthy enough to be productively employed, certain physical and mental abilities drop off. More important in a dynamic, knowledge-based economy, the market value of skills acquired over the course of a lifetime tends to decline over time. Older workers can generally do what they did when younger. But shifts in the demand for goods and services, technical innovations that favor new sets of skills, and competition from younger workers, who are more productive or less expensive, tend to diminish the market value of what older workers can do.

Effect of Aging on Innate Abilities

The most apparent change in productivity that comes with age is a decline in the ability to do physical work. Physiological measures clearly show aging associated with "progressive decreases in aerobic power, thermoregulation, reaction speed and acuity of the special senses."[1] As seen in chapter 2, the health of older workers has improved, so physical limitations impair productivity much less than they did in the past. Education and wage-related disparities in health status, however, are enormous. Health declines generally arrive earlier among less educated, low-wage workers, which further reduces such workers' productivity. So while the physical capabilities of older workers are generally quite good, health issues remain a problem for a significant subset.

Figure 5-1. *Employed Workers in Physically Demanding Jobs, Selected Years 1950–1996*

Percent

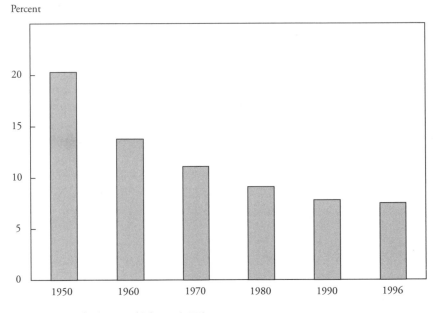

Source: Steuerle, Spiro, and Johnson (1999).

While the general health status of older workers has improved, physical capabilities have much less economic value than they did in the past. Employment has shifted from physically demanding, goods-producing industries—agriculture, mining, construction, and manufacturing—to service-producing industries and knowledge-based production. Less than 8 percent of workers currently have physically demanding jobs, down from over 20 percent in 1950 (figure 5-1). Even in such jobs, advances in automation and mechanization have relaxed the "need to push workers to their physical limits."[2] In one survey, many employers identify physical strength and stamina as a factor diminishing the productivity of older workers, especially among rank-and-file employees.[3] But essentially no employer surveyed sees the physical effects of aging as having a "very negative impact" on productivity.[4]

While physical capabilities have lost a great deal of economic value, cognitive and emotional capabilities have become critically important. As people age, some valuable cognitive and emotional capabilities improve, many are essentially unchanged, and others decline.

Aging has a generally positive effect on various emotional capabilities that enhance productivity. Human resource managers typically give older workers

Figure 5-2. *Importance of Employee Qualities and Evaluation of Employees Aged 50 and Over* [a]

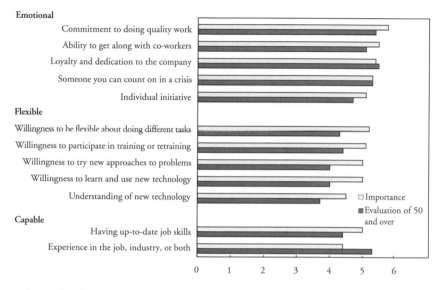

Source: AARP (2005).

a. Human resource managers were asked to rate the importance of various qualities in an employee of any age on a scale of 1 to 6: 6 = absolutely essential to 1 = not too important. The results are shown in the top bar for each employee quality. These managers were then asked to evaluate employees aged 50 and over on these qualities on a scale of 1 to 6: 6 = excellent to 1 = poor. These evaluations are shown on the bottom bar for each employee quality.

high marks for their work ethic, collegiality, loyalty, and reliability in a crisis—all highly valued attributes (figure 5-2). The picture is not uniformly positive. One study, for example, finds older workers more likely to have unfulfilled ambitions for advancement and personal achievement, which diminish work effort and impair relationships with supervisors and co-workers.[5] Nevertheless, the overall tenor of employer survey responses clearly indicates that the emotional makeup of older workers enhances their attractiveness as employees.[6]

Cognitive capabilities, however, do not hold up as well. A review of nearly 100 empirical studies of cognitive functioning reports that perceptual speed and reasoning, and thus the ability to learn and adapt, decline with age.[7] Various studies find an association between health and cognitive speed, which suggests that the long-term improvement in health status has slowed the decline in the ability to learn and adjust.[8] Current studies nevertheless show that the falloff begins quite early, when workers are in their 20s or early 30s, and continues as they age. This decline in the ability to learn and adapt affects men and women, all ethnic subgroups, and individuals at all levels of intellectual ability.[9] It is important to note, however, that researchers find a great deal of variation. Some individuals appear to maintain their mental alacrity while others lose a great deal.[10] Given the generally adverse effects of aging, it is not surprising that employers typically cite inflexibility and limitations in the willingness and ability to learn as primary shortcomings of their older employees (figure 5-2).[11]

The effect of this general decline in the ability to learn and adapt, however, should not be overstated. Many jobs are largely routine, requiring little in the way of cognitive flexibility or learning. Other cognitive abilities also hold up rather well. Older workers can generally access things already learned, and they have learned a great deal over the course of their careers. Vocabulary and verbal abilities are essentially unchanged.[12] Tacit knowledge, or knowing how to get things done, is also generally unaffected.[13] Workers tend to become domain-specific experts, with a rich but encapsulated knowledge base that often lets them function within that domain on a par with, or better than, younger workers.[14] Not surprisingly, employers typically cite job knowledge and experience as a major productive asset of older workers.[15]

While the ability to learn tends to decline as workers age, it hardly disappears. Various studies show that workers in technically dynamic industries, where the ability to learn is critically important, do tend to retire earlier than workers in less dynamic sectors.[16] But it seems to be large technical shocks, not the pace of change per se, that push workers—both old and young—out of high-tech industries. As long as the pace of change is relatively steady, workers in high-tech industries actually tend to retire later than workers in less dynamic sectors.[17] The explanation for this apparent anomaly seems to be the practice of continuous on-the-job training in high-tech industries. Even though the pace of change is brisk, older high-tech workers seem capable of absorbing what is taught. Their ability to learn, despite its decline from younger ages, is sufficient to allow them to maintain their productive value.[18]

Effect of Aging on Acquired Abilities

The importance of on-the-job training nevertheless highlights a serious challenge in maintaining the productivity of older workers. As noted above, older workers generally retain the knowledge and skills acquired at younger ages. This accumulation of knowledge and skills is the critical asset they offer employers in today's knowledge-based economy. But the passage of time tends to erode the market value of knowledge and skills acquired in the past. This is true for knowledge and skills acquired through a process of formal education or through experience in a company, industry, or occupation.

In today's knowledge-based economy, schooling is perhaps the primary source of worker productivity. The close association between earnings and educational attainment is the centerpiece of contemporary labor economics. A major analysis of the sources of U.S. economic growth over the past two centuries likewise attributes much of the productivity gains over the past hundred years to investments in education.[19] Over 80 percent of workers entering the labor market in the first decade of the twentieth century had not finished high school.[20] Today nearly 90 percent of workers entering the labor market have a high-school diploma, 30 percent have a college degree, and nearly a third of those who finished college also have a postgraduate degree.[21]

A by-product of this dramatic rise in educational attainment over the course of the twentieth century is that older workers generally had much less schooling than their younger counterparts. As a result, they were less productive. In recent decades, the expansion of trade with less developed nations, which have large pools of less educated workers, further diminished the market value of older, less educated U.S. workers. But the rise in educational attainment slowed dramatically for cohorts following the baby boom. So today's older workers, as a group, are no longer significantly disadvantaged relative to younger workers in terms of educational attainment.

An emerging problem, however, is that the schooling of older workers is generally 30–40 years old. The vintage of one's education was not a significant problem when most workers had just a high school diploma. But the market value of college and postgraduate education, and especially advanced technical education, tends to erode over time. One study finds that the earnings of workers with college and postgraduate education, but not those with a high school education or "some college," decline, relative to the national average, at older ages.[22] Another study finds that the earnings of workers with college degrees peak nearly three years earlier in high-tech as compared to low-tech industries.[23]

Experience is the other source of knowledge and skills that underlies the productivity of older workers. Surveys consistently show that employers value older workers for their experience-based job knowledge, skills, and contacts. Experience is especially valuable in large organizations, as it takes time to learn how they work, their priorities and procedures, and how to get things done. One study, which controlled for educational attainment and cohort-crowding effects, finds that productivity gains due to experience generally level off after four to ten years.[24] Staying on the job longer and gaining more experience will not make workers much more productive. Nevertheless, older, long-service workers have an asset that takes time and effort for an employer to replace.

The economic value of experience, like that of advanced and technical education, tends to erode over time. Workers gain experience in organizations, industries, occupations, and technologies that rise, evolve, and decline over time in response to shifts in demand and supply. Older workers are less responsive than younger workers to such shifts in the economic landscape. Their mobility is impaired by sunk investments in skills, organizations, and locations and by a shorter payback period to recoup new investments. So they tend to be employed in older organizations, industries, occupations, and technologies, which are growing slowly or even contracting.[25] Unless counteracted by a process such as on-the-job training, or networking that refreshes one's industry and occupational contacts, the experience of older workers will generally lose value as they age.

Productivity of Older Workers

Changes in productivity as workers age are difficult to measure quantitatively. Researchers often use wages to measure productivity, based on the notion that the market equates the price of labor with its value to employers. But wages are not well suited to evaluating the relationship between productivity and age. This is because wages are a subset of the compensation employers pay their workers and, as discussed below, tend to decline as a share of compensation as workers age. The distribution of compensation across a worker's tenure with an employer is also often influenced by institutional factors, such as unions or deferred compensation arrangements, that delink its relationship with productivity at any given age.[26] Measuring how productivity changes with age must thus rely on various indirect measures.

Piece-rate wages are a reasonably good measure of productivity. A study of piece-rate wages in nineteenth-century manufacturing, in which piece-rate systems were widely used, finds that workers in their early 30s had the highest earnings and that wages declined with age.[27] In the 1950s the U.S. Department of Labor used time-and-motion methods to measure the effect of age on productivity in similar manufacturing settings. These studies find that in some manufacturing industries workers in their 30s were again most productive but that productivity peaked significantly later in other manufacturing industries and was essentially unaffected by age in various clerical activities.[28] These studies indicate that productivity past age 55 in more physically demanding tasks at best stays level but generally turns down. That age-related productivity declines were milder in the 1950s than in the nineteenth century supports the notion that improvements in health, medical care, and machinery and the shift in employment from the production of goods to the production of services—changes that have continued to the present—have enhanced the relative position of older workers in the labor market.

While piece-rate earnings and time-and-motion studies provide fairly direct measures of productivity, they cannot be taken as representative of the effect of aging in the contemporary U.S. economy. Most workers today are salaried or paid by the hour. They are largely compensated this way because they are not employed doing repetitive tasks, so employers cannot readily measure the output of individual workers. The performance of salaried and hourly workers, however, is typically evaluated by a supervisor. Researchers use these evaluations to analyze the productivity of workers of different ages. In general, these studies find little or no relationship between productivity and age. These findings, however, must be viewed with caution. The evaluations of supervisors are influenced by personal relationships and generally thought to bias the results in favor of older, long-service workers. The finding of little or no decline in productivity as workers age thus probably needs to be adjusted downward.[29]

Another set of studies estimates the effect of age on productivity by comparing the productivity of similar establishments that employ workers of different ages.[30] These studies also have problems. Most examine manufacturing industries, in which the physical effects of aging are more important than in the economy at large. Most measure output imprecisely, by sales rather than by value added. The direction of causation is also generally unclear. As productive establishments are likely to expand and hire young workers, increased productivity will reduce the average age of an establishment's workforce, rather than a younger workforce's making an establishment more productive. Nevertheless, these studies generally evaluate a large number of establishments and control for factors that might influence worker productivity, most particularly educational attainment. They also generally report much the same finding: that older workers are less productive than younger workers.

The most damaging finding on the productivity of older workers comes from a study based on the compensation a large corporation paid to workers hired at different ages.[31] The study uses the firm's administrative records to estimate the present value of wage and pension compensation over the worker's expected career. It then uses differences in the present value of compensation of similar workers hired at different ages to estimate productivity by age. For example, if the present value of compensation of workers hired at age 35 is $50,000 more than that of workers hired at age 36, productivity at age 35 is estimated at $50,000.[32] The age-productivity profiles this method produces peak when workers are in their 40s and decline quite sharply thereafter. By the time workers are in their 60s, their estimated productivity is less than half what it is at its peak. These results, however, must also be viewed cautiously. They are based on the experience of a single corporation. The analysis is also based on a variety of strong assumptions, such as the uniform quality of workers hired and leaving at different ages and the stability of age-productivity profiles over the period under study, 1969–83. This was a time of unusual stress and transition in the U.S. economy, with the two deepest recessions since the Great Depression, the rise of serious global competition, and the entry of the baby boom generation into the labor market. Many employers were busy reducing their workforce and realigning their operations to use cheap and well-educated boomers by inducing older workers to leave.

Research on the effect of aging on productivity is thus quite varied in both methods and findings. Taken as a whole, however, the results suggest that older workers are less productive, though the productivity gap between young and old workers has likely narrowed. The effect of physical decline, which comes with age, is milder and much less important. The deficit in educational attainment has essentially disappeared. While cognitive flexibility and the ability to learn generally decline, most older workers have sufficient mental agility to learn and adapt if given the necessary training. Investments in training, however, decline sharply for older workers.[33] This is sometimes blamed on the inflexibility of older workers or discrimination on the part of their employers. Rational considerations, however, are also present. Older workers are approaching retirement. The sooner they expect to retire, the shorter the payback period to recoup an investment in upgrading their skills. If the expected retirement age rises, so should investments in training, which would allow workers to remain productive longer.[34]

Cost of Older Workers

Employers can expect the productivity of older workers to at best remain level but in all likelihood fall as they age. They can expect the cost of such workers to be just the opposite—to at best remain level but in all likelihood rise. This means the financial gain from employing older workers tends to decline, and employers at some point are likely to face a productivity compensation deficit.

Effect of Aging on Wage and Benefit Costs

Wages, the largest component of the compensation employers pay employees, tend to be "sticky downward." Employers generally avoid cutting wages, as it creates a variety of personnel management problems, from quits by the

Figure 5-3. *Average Pay, by Years of Service, Fortune 1000 Companies, 2003*

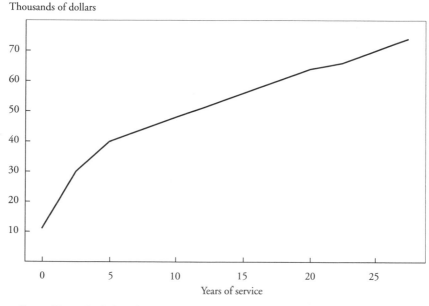

Thousands of dollars

Years of service

Source: Towers Perrin (2005).

firm's better workers to a reduction of effort by those who remain. The wages of long-service workers are also often protected by seniority rights, explicitly in unionized settings and implicitly in nonunionized settings.[35] This is illustrated in figure 5-3, which shows wages of workers by tenure, using a sample of Fortune 1000 companies.[36]

That the wages employers pay older workers are basically flat or ratcheting higher while their productivity is basically flat or falling creates a productivity compensation deficit as these workers age. This led employers to introduce mandatory retirement, typically at age 65. Many employers that introduced mandatory retirement added a defined benefit pension plan to help ease workers out.[37] Once in place, these defined benefit pension plans raise the cost of employing older workers even more.

The cost of providing a defined benefit pension rises sharply with age for two reasons. First, such plans typically promise an annuity based on final pay and years of service, say 1.5 percent of final pay for each year of service (figure 5-4). As wages rise—even just to keep pace with inflation—the increase raises the value of benefits earned in the past. As workers age and accumulate more years of service, this increase in a worker's pension due to wage growth

Figure 5-4. *Private Defined Benefit Plan Accruals as Percentage of Earnings for Workers Starting at Age 25*[a]

Percent

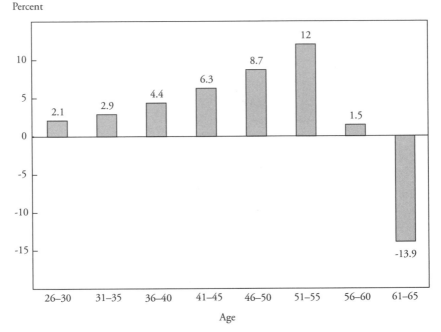

Source: Penner, Perun, and Steuerle (2002).

a. The analysis is based on a sample of 340 salary-based defined benefit plans in the private sector. Accrual estimates assume that workers join the firm at age 25 and leave at the age that maximizes the present discounted value of pension benefits (or at age 70). The analysis assumes that wages grow at the average age-specific rate for college-educated male workers with defined benefit plans. The real interest rate is set at 3.0 percent and the inflation rate at 3.3 percent. Estimates are weighted by firm size.

becomes increasingly large relative to current earnings. The second reason that pension costs rise with age is that each dollar of future pension benefit becomes more expensive as workers approach retirement. The employer's pension contribution has less time to sit in the pension fund and accumulate investment income, so employers must contribute more to fund each dollar of future pension benefit.

The introduction of defined benefit pensions thus dramatically raised the cost of retaining or hiring workers at the end of their careers. Employers with such plans, however, did not purchase labor by the hour or the year. They generally adopted a career employment personnel management system that purchased a career's worth of work. Compensation in such personnel management systems was distributed over the employee's entire career to accommodate employer investments in human capital and the delegation of authority to employees who were difficult to monitor closely. They paid workers more than the value of what they produced at the beginning of their careers (when investments were made); less than what they produced in the middle of their careers (when investments were reaped and authority delegated); more at the end (as a reward for loyal and diligent service); and called a halt to the overpayment at the mandatory retirement age.[38]

Most plans allowed workers to retire before the plan's full retirement age on an actuarially reduced benefit. To induce retirements at an earlier target age, many employers in the 1970s and 1980s sweetened these early-retirement benefits. Employees who remained beyond that target age had their compensation in effect reduced by an amount equal to the forgone sweetener. The initiative thus raised the cost of employing workers approaching the target retirement age and reduced the cost beyond that age. But as most employees retired on cue, these sweetened benefits were a major contributor to the decline in the average retirement age.[39]

The shift from defined benefit pensions to 401(k)s is a dramatic move away from this age-based compensation profile and the career employment model it supports. The employer's cost in a 401(k) is mainly the matching contribution, which is generally the same percentage of pay for young and old workers. More older workers tend to participate in a plan, creating some age-based cost differential. But it is dramatically smaller in a 401(k) than in a defined benefit pension plan. The shift to 401(k)s has thus removed a major factor that drove up the cost of employing older workers.[40]

As the cost of providing retirement benefits is becoming essentially age neutral, health insurance has taken its place as the major factor that drives up compensation costs as workers age. Unlike retirement benefits, the cost of providing health insurance is quite sensitive to a worker's age but is essentially unrelated to the wages a worker is paid. The 2003 cost of insuring workers in their early 60s was $7,600, which was $3,500 more than the cost of insuring workers twenty years younger (figure 5-5). The differential is especially significant for low- and average-wage workers covered by an employer health insurance plan, since the cost of health insurance is so large relative to their earnings.[41] The age-related rise in the cost of health insurance is thus a major increase in the cost of older workers. Not surprisingly, researchers have found that health insurance costs are an important factor in reducing employment opportunities for older workers.[42]

Effect of Aging on the Attractiveness of Employees

Employers can be expected to employ older workers if the value of what they produce exceeds what they are paid. The quantitative studies of productivity

Figure 5-5. *Medical Claims of Employees and Dependents, by Age of Employee, 2003*

Dollars

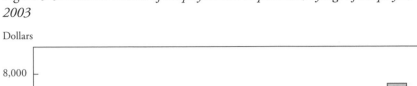

Source: Towers Perrin (2005).

discussed above generally show productivity declining as workers age. The studies cited also measure compensation and generally find it rises with age. Older workers might not be paid more than the value of what they produce; these studies nevertheless indicate that most employers would find it more profitable to employ younger workers.[43]

Less educated older workers in particular have trouble keeping the value of what they produce greater than what they are paid, leading to especially high rates of "retirement" at relatively young ages. Early exits by low-wage workers is a pattern seen throughout the industrial era, even before the enactment of Social Security and reflects a decline in employer demand for workers whose labor market value was low even in their prime working years.[44] Cyclic and sector-specific downturns in demand are often the proximate cause of such early exits, as shown in a study of employment declines among older workers by industry, state, and educational attainment since the mid-1960s.[45] Exits from the labor force spike when the demand for labor turns down in recessions and in states where employment in a worker's industry declines.

Employers, when surveyed, generally express a somewhat optimistic view of their older employees. In one survey employers tended to characterize workers aged 55 and over as more costly but also more productive and, on balance, as attractive as younger workers in similar positions. Older managers and professionals score somewhat better than older rank-and-file workers. Large employers, which are more likely to have career employment personnel systems that undercompensate middle-aged workers and overcompensate older workers, are less positive toward older white-collar employees. Small employers and employers in goods-producing industries are less positive toward older rank-and-file workers. But on the whole, employers are reasonably comfortable with the productivity compensation trade-off for employees aged 55 and over.[46]

Confirming this positive employer perspective on the attractiveness of older workers is their relatively low risk of displacement. As discussed in chapter 3, employers are more likely to lay off their younger employees. But age might not be the factor that protects older workers. Using data from the Displaced Workers Survey, one study shows the probability of being laid off actually increases with age once other factors are taken into account.[47] Older workers have relatively long tenure with their employer, and that is what has reduced their risk of layoff. Were it not for their greater tenure, their age would actually put older workers at greater risk of displacement than younger workers (figure 5-6). As discussed in chapter 3, the tenure of older workers with their current employer has declined substantially since the early 1980s. Offsetting the effect of declining tenure, however, is the rapid increase in the educational attainment of older workers and the employment shift from goods to services. Older workers, as a result, continue to have lower displacement rates than younger workers.

That employers are comfortable with their older employees and are less likely to displace them does not mean they are keen on retaining employees past their traditional retirement age. One survey asked employers to estimate how many employees currently in their 50s would lack the resources needed to retire at their traditional age; employers were then asked how many such workers they expected would want to stay on the job two to four years longer than workers have in the past. Employers thought that about a quarter of their employees currently in their 50s would be unable to retire and would want to stay on. Most employers in the survey had a traditional retirement age of 65, so staying on two to four years longer meant working to 67 or 69. Employers were then asked to estimate the likelihood that they would accommodate at least half of their employees who would want to work longer. On a scale from 1 (unlikely) to 10 (likely), the median response was a

Figure 5-6. *Factors Influencing the Probability of Displacement, 1996–2004* [a]

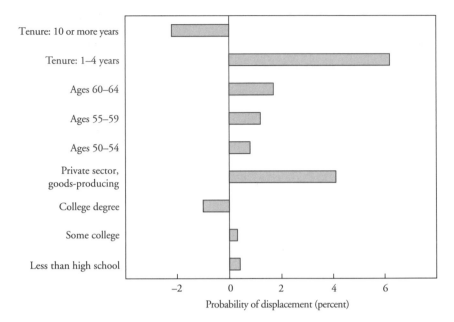

Probability of displacement (percent)

Source: Authors' calculations based on Munnell and others (2006b) and U.S. Census Bureau and Bureau of Labor Statistics, Displaced Workers Survey (1996–2004).

a. Coefficients are relative to workers aged 40–44 with a high school diploma, five to nine years of tenure, and employed in the private services sector for the three-year period ending in 2000. The displacement rate for such benchmark workers is 7.4 percent.

lukewarm 6. So while employers are reasonably comfortable with the productivity-compensation trade-off on older workers they currently employ, they are not keen on retaining even half who want to stay on to age 67 or 69.[48]

Market for Older Workers

The discussion up to now largely focuses on factors that influence employer decisions to retain older employees. The decision to hire older workers is more complex. It is also increasingly important. As discussed in chapter 3, most workers aged 50 will change employers before retirement. That is, the typical 50-year-old worker is no longer in a career employment job, one that provides employment for the remainder of his or her career. And if work lives are to be extended, an increasing share of workers aged 50 and over will change employers before retirement.

The decline in career employment does not seem primarily due to employers's dismissing a greater share of their older workers. Despite the widespread sense that jobs have become less secure, dislocation rates for older workers have been remarkably stable over the past quarter century.[49] Quits, for health and family reasons as well as for traditional economic considerations, outnumber layoffs.[50] And despite the increase in labor market transitions, the same percentage of men aged 58–62 is employed today as in 1982. So employers are hiring older workers. The critical question is, For what types of positions?

Traditional Market for Older Workers

Historically, the range of job opportunities tends to narrow dramatically as workers age. Most employers, according to a survey conducted in the mid-1960s, had explicit age limits when hiring, typically 45 or 55.[51] Even after such policies were outlawed, older job seekers could find employment in many fewer industries and occupations than younger job seekers or than currently employed older workers.[52] The available jobs were less strenuous, stressful, and responsible and paid less in wages and benefits than jobs held by older, long-tenured workers.[53]

Older job seekers could not expect an employment situation comparable to that of older, long-tenured employees. The older employees would be more productive due to their experience in the organization, accumulation of firm-specific human capital, and buildup of employer-employee trust over many years of service. Many if not most older employees were also at the end of a career employment relationship, with back-loaded compensation profiles that now paid them more than the value of what they produced. Given the productivity differences and the workings of entrenched personnel management systems, older job seekers could not expect to be compensated at a similar level.

Nor could older job seekers compete effectively for most available career employment positions. Compared to younger job seekers, they tended to be less educated. Nor were they as strong or physically agile. Perhaps most important, filling a career employment position is a forward-looking decision.[54] When comparing older and younger applicants, the productivity-compensation trade-off tended to become increasingly unfavorable to the former going forward. Older workers do have generally lower turnover rates, a plus for employers with low retention rates.[55] But employers could expect a younger hire, with stronger learning skills, to adapt to the organization more quickly. Once up to speed, a younger hire could be there for the long haul, while the older hire would be approaching retirement. Younger applicants have much more potential to sell, and employers cite promotion potential as an important consideration when hiring.[56]

Employers have also been accused of passing over older job seekers out of prejudice. Accusations of such age-based discrimination are quite widespread. In one survey of older workers, two-thirds said they "personally witnessed or experienced age discrimination on the job."[57] Researchers have verified the existence of age discrimination in hiring decisions by sending prospective employers resumes essentially identical except for the applicant's age.[58] Surveys of employers outside the United States, where age discrimination laws are less stringent, find that many refuse to hire workers above a certain age.[59] It is difficult, however, to disentangle the importance of prejudice as opposed to economically based discrimination. While employers typically express much more interest in younger applicants, economic reasons might be driving their decision. Evidence of prejudice does emerge, however, in surveys that ask employers to compare younger and older employees. All else equal, younger employers have a significantly poorer opinion of older workers than older employers. It is unclear whether this difference reflects prejudice against older workers by younger employers or prejudice in favor of older workers by older employers. But it does show that noneconomic factors affect employer evaluations of older workers.[60]

Market for Older Workers Today

There are reasons to think older job seekers might have more success in the marketplace today than they had in the past. Manufacturing, where physical capabilities are relatively important, employs a declining share of the labor force. Older job seekers are now better educated, with no significant deficit relative to younger applicants. The aging of the workforce also means that more of the hiring is done by older managers and supervisors, who have a better opinion of older job applicants. And while the cost of health insurance has become a more serious impediment, especially for lower-paid workers, the cost of retirement benefits is increasingly age neutral.

In some respects, however, the labor market has become more challenging. In a knowledge-based economy, skills acquired in the past tend to lose value, and older workers have greater difficulty acquiring new skills and in justifying the investment needed to do so. Older workers have also been relatively scarce since the mid-1960s, when the baby boomers entered the labor market. As old and young workers are to some extent complementary, the relative scarcity of older workers enhanced their value to employers. But the aging of the baby boom generation over the past decade has made older workers relatively abundant, depressing their value to employers.[61]

An additional problem for an older job seeker is the difficulty in finding a suitable match. Because today's older workers are better schooled and have worked for more types of employers, they bring unique combinations of education and experience to market. They need jobs that use a good portion of their bundle of acquired skills to continue their careers—and to be compensated accordingly. There are signs that employers today are more willing to fill high-value positions externally. There is even a brisk market for CEOs, with a third of all appointments filled externally, compared to 15 percent in the 1970s.[62] But finding the right match in the labor market is a costly process.[63] Many employers thus still prefer to fill high-value positions by promoting from within and recruit young, ambitious workers whom they can train and monitor over time to assume more senior positions.

One study illustrates the difficulty older workers face following a layoff.[64] For displaced workers in their early 50s it took a year before half had found another job. For workers in their late 50s, it took two years before half had been reemployed. The new job almost always had lower pay and benefits. Many of the matches were also short-lived. Where the matches lasted and workers became more productive through experience gains, they tended to remain with their new employer and retired at older ages than workers who never left their original employer. This is what one would expect of workers suffering a financial loss: working longer to offset the loss resulting from their unemployment and lower compensation in their new position. But the study shows the difficulty displaced workers have in finding such an opportunity.

On balance it is difficult to conclude that the position of older workers in the labor market has improved. The wages of workers who switched employers after age 50, relative to the wages of those who remained with their initial employer, are much the same today as they were in the early 1980s. Throughout the transition away from career employment, full-time workers who switched employers earned about 75 percent of the career employee's wage.[65]

A study of job switching among older workers finds that most move to a new occupation or industry, that benefit losses are even greater than wage losses, but that stress, physical strain, and managerial responsibilities also decline.[66] Many of these transitions no doubt reflect a desire on the part of workers to downshift and take more enjoyable and less stressful jobs. But the overall pattern gives little evidence that employers are hiring workers in their 50s for significantly more productive and well-compensated positions than they did in the past. And older workers in the past had few productive and well-compensated opportunities.

How Things Might Change Going Forward

If working longer is to emerge as an effective response to the nation's retirement income challenge, employers will need to significantly increase their demand for older workers from where it is today. Despite changes in the labor market that would seem to make older workers more attractive, such as the shift in employment from the production of goods to the production of services, the rise in educational attainment, and the decline of defined benefit pension plans, employers do not seem more interested in employing older workers. They are not retaining nearly as many of their workers aged 50 and over as they did in the past. Nor are they eager to retain the employees they do keep an additional two to four years past their traditional retirement age. Nor do they seem terribly interested in hiring older workers for productive and well-paid positions.

Many observers in business and government, however, claim that this will change over the next ten years.[67] They say employers will face labor shortages and a loss of institutional intelligence when the baby boom generation exits the labor force, and these developments will push employers to seek out older workers.

Will Employers Face a Labor Shortage?

The notion that employers will face a labor shortage is based the fact that the population ages 25–54, the traditional prime working-age population, will essentially stop growing as the baby boom generation begins to retire.[68] This is because succeeding cohorts are of roughly similar size. Labor force participation rates among those under 55 are unlikely to rise very much. So for the economy to expand at its historical rate of growth, employers would need alternate sources of labor. Older workers, along with immigrants, are the obvious candidates.

There are three difficulties with this line of reasoning. The first is the notion that the economy will grow at its historical rate. Employers would clearly need to scramble to find enough workers if this were the case. But there is nothing magical about the historical rate of economic growth—whether of GDP or GDP per capita—that ensures its continuation into the future. One should expect that the abrupt slowing of labor force growth, to a rate well below that of population growth so that the dependency ratio increases, will dampen the rise in both total and per capita GDP. The expansion of per capita economic output is driven by the growth of factor inputs, essentially labor and capital, gains in productivity, and changes in the dependency ratio. The rapid deceleration in labor force growth and the rise in the dependency ratio, without an offsetting rise in capital stock or productivity, will reduce the rate of growth in per capita output. The economy would clearly need more workers to grow at its historical rate. But the economy has no homeostatic mechanism that will produce those workers, or create a demand for those workers, to maintain that rate of growth.

Such a decline in the growth of per capita GDP does not necessarily imply a slowdown in the growth of living standards as measured by consumption per capita. As a greater share of the population moves into retirement and the growth of the labor force slows, one would expect a decline in saving (as retirees dissave to support their standard of living) and investment (as a slower growing labor force needs less new plant and equipment). A greater share of GDP would thus be devoted to consumption, and consumption per capita could continue to rise at its historical rate. Unfortunately, we have not saved and invested enough for the baby boom generation to retire—at least at the same ages as workers have in the past—without affecting the growth of consumption per capita. It is possible that this decline in living standards could trigger some mechanism, be it political or economic, that would increase national output and thereby the demand for labor. But the nature of this mechanism is hardly clear.

One mechanism that could increase demand for workers as labor force growth decelerates is a rise in the amount of capital per worker. A review of the literature on how saving and investment respond to demographic change suggests that capital-to-labor ratios will indeed increase.[69] The study reports that saving has generally been more stable than investment demand in response to demographic swings. Both saving and investment demand should fall as the growth of the labor force slows. But saving will likely decline more slowly, resulting in more capital chasing fewer workers. This effect, however, is unlikely to create a major labor shortage.

The second difficulty with the labor shortage notion is that U.S. employers increasingly operate in a global economy and respond to swings in the global, more than the domestic, supply of labor.[70] As the baby boom generation retires, labor force growth will slow throughout the advanced industrial world. But the dramatic expansion of the global economy over the past 10–15 years far offsets this effect. Educational and infrastructure advances in developing nations, from Brazil to Indonesia, are rapidly enlarging the effective global labor supply. Most striking, however, is the entry of China, India, and the former Soviet Union into the world trading system, which has doubled the size of the labor force potentially available to U.S. employers (figure 5-7). The magnitude of this expansion in the global labor supply clearly swamps any shortage created by the retirement of the baby boomers

Figure 5-7. *Workers from Developed Countries, Developing Countries, China, India, and the Former Soviet Union, circa 2000*

Millions of workers

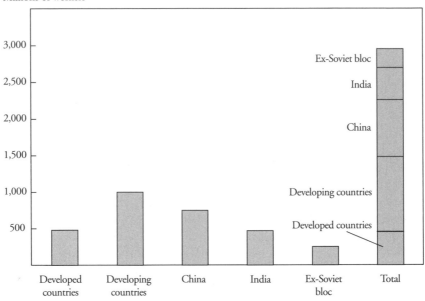

Source: Freeman (2006).

and the slowdown of U.S. labor force growth. Rather than a shortage of labor and a glut of capital, U.S. employers are likely to face precisely the opposite conditions.

The third difficulty with the labor shortage notion involves the location of older workers in the U.S. economy. Older workers tend to be in older industries and occupations, where employment is growing slowly or even declining. Young workers seek employment in fast-growing sectors; old workers tend to be employed in sectors that were fast growing when they were young but might not be growing any more. A study of occupations with a disproportionate share of workers finds that many, such as farming, tool and die making, and clerical and railroad employment, are projected to decline.[71] Rather than contribute to an economywide labor shortage, the impending wave of retirements in such occupations should bring staffing levels closer to equilibrium levels.

Some industries and occupations with a disproportionate share of older workers will face significant labor shortages as the baby boom generation retires. By far the most important in terms of the number of workers affected

Figure 5-8. *Factors with a Positive Effect on the Likelihood an Employer Will Retain Older Workers*[a]

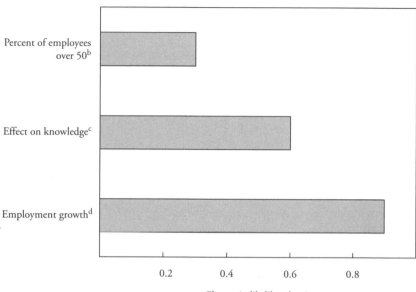

Factor

Change in likelihood rating

Source: Eschtruth, Sass, and Aubry (2007).

a. "Retaining older workers" is defined as creating job opportunities for at least half of workers who wish to work two to four years longer than the firm's traditional retirement age. The effects shown are the effect of a swing from the 20th to the 80th percentile value of each factor.

b. "Percent of employees over 50" is the effect of the employer's having 50 percent or more of its workforce aged 50 and older versus 10 percent of the workforce aged 50 and older.

c. "Effect on knowledge" is the effect of having a "highly positive" effect on the company's knowledge base if a significant number of workers stay past the organization's traditional retirement age as opposed to a "neutral" effect on the company's knowledge base.

d. "Employment growth" is the effect of "significant" expected employment growth as opposed to "not much change" in expected employment levels.

are K–12 public education and state and local government.[72] Most workers in these public sector activities, however, are covered by defined benefit pension plans. And these plans act as powerful impediments to the retention or recruitment of older workers.

The generally limited importance of replacement demand, or labor demand created by the retirement of current incumbents, is reflected in a survey that asked employers (all from the private sector) how likely they would be to create opportunities for employees to stay two to four years past their traditional retirement age (figure 5-8). Employers with half of their workforce aged 50 or over were only slightly more likely to create such opportunities than those with just 10 percent of their workers aged 50 or over. In terms of filling future staffing needs, expected employment growth was far more important than replacement demand. Employers expecting "significant growth" in employment were much more positive about retaining older workers than those expecting "not much change."[73]

Will Employers Face a Loss of Institutional Intelligence?

The second claim that employer demand for older workers will expand going forward is based on the notion that older workers are the repositories of institutional intelligence. So when the baby boom generation retires, organizations will simply refuse to lose so much of this precious asset.

There is clearly some logic in this claim, especially for organizations in which a large share of the managerial and professional staff will be retiring. On the other hand, the economy now has many more older workers than it had just a decade ago and soon will have many more. In 1995 just 12 percent of the labor force was 55 years of age or older. That figure was 17 percent in 2005 and is expected to rise to 25 percent by 2025 (figure 5-9). Many employers will thus have an abundance, not a shortage, of institutional intelligence within their organizations.

The shift away from career employment also suggests a decline in the value that employers place on institutional intelligence. They have been willing to see an increasing share of their older, long-tenure workers leave. Most have also abandoned defined benefit pension plans, instruments designed to keep such workers from leaving before their target retirement age. Employers do recognize that older workers are repositories of institutional intelligence: two-thirds say that retaining workers two to four years past their traditional retirement age would have a "somewhat positive" or "highly positive" impact on the organization's knowledge base. However, this does not significantly increase their interest in extending tenures past the traditional retirement age. Even employers that characterize the effect on the knowledge base as "highly positive" are only slightly more interested in extending careers past their traditional retirement age than employers that characterize the effect as "neutral."[74]

Some employers no doubt need to retain older employees to maintain institutional continuity. But given the large number of older workers in most organizations, and the apparent decline in the value employers place on the contribution of long-tenure employees, it seems unlikely that employers will significantly increase their demand for older workers, when the baby boom generation retires, to prevent a loss of institutional intelligence.

Figure 5-9. *Civilian Labor Force Aged 55 and Older, 1965–2035*

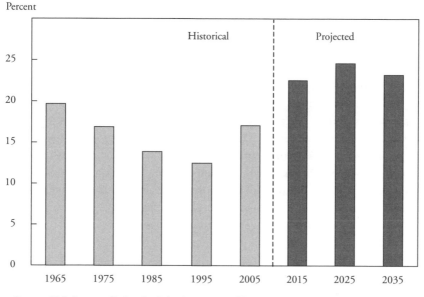

Sources: U.S. Bureau of Labor Statistics (2007a, 2007b).

Conclusion

Employers in the past have not been eager to retain or to hire older workers, and there is little indication that attitudes have significantly changed. The productivity of older workers can be expected to at best stay level but will likely turn down, while their compensation will at best stay level but will probably rise. These patterns make older workers, whether existing employees or potential hires, relatively unattractive.

Older workers today should be more attractive to employers than they were in the past. They are better educated, with no significant educational deficit relative to younger workers. Employment has shifted away from activities that require physical strength and stamina. And employer retirement income programs are no longer an escalator of compensation costs as workers age. Nevertheless, there is little indication thus far that the employment prospects of older workers have significantly improved. The decline in career employment suggests that employers are less inclined than they were in the past to retain employees as they age. The eroding value of acquired skills in today's knowledge-based economy, combined with the age-related decline in flexibility and learning ability and the general lack of training for older workers, is especially corrosive of the market value of higher-wage workers. The high and rising cost of employer-provided health insurance is especially damaging to the labor market prospects of lower-wage workers. And where a decline in market value for a higher paid worker could mean employment at a lower wage, for a lower-paid worker it more likely means "retirement" at a relatively young age.

It is possible that employers will become more interested in employing older workers going forward. There could be an uptick in demand when the baby boom generation retires if capital-labor ratios rise or if employers need to retain older workers to maintain institutional intelligence. But notions that employers will significantly increase their demand for older workers in response to a serious shortage of labor or threats to their knowledge base are overblown at best.

6

What Can Be Done?

Americans will need to work two to four years longer than they do at present to ensure a reasonably comfortable old age. As the average retirement age for men has been 63 for the past quarter century, they must now remain employed until their mid- to late 60s. In many respects, this is a reasonable objective. Most men worked to at least age 66 as recently as 1960. The physical demands of work have since declined. Work has also become much more personally and socially rewarding.

There are signs that Americans will indeed stay in the labor force longer. Most Americans say they want to continue to work even after they retire. Employment rates among persons age 55 and over are rising.[1] And employment rates of older women should become similar to those of men as the baby boom cohort matures. The rise in employment rates seems due, in part, to the increased attractiveness of work. It also seems due to changes in the design of retirement income programs. The shift from traditional defined benefit pensions to 401(k)s, the liberalization of the Social Security earnings test, and the increase in the adjustment to Social Security benefits if a worker claims after the full retirement age all encourage employment at older ages.

But not all signs are positive. Employment rates among men in their early 50s have actually declined. This trend is especially pro-

Figure 6-1. *Workforce Participation Rates of Men, 1985 and 2005, and Hypothetical Target for Average Retirement Age of 66*

Percent

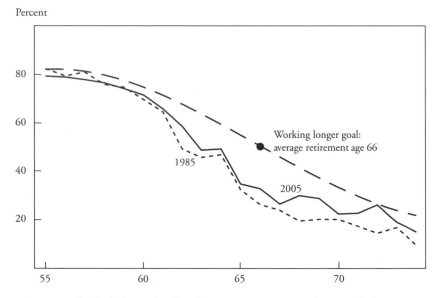

Source: Authors' calculations based on the U.S. Census Bureau and Bureau of Labor Statistics, Current Population Survey (1985, 2005).

nounced among less educated, low-wage workers.[2] Such workers are heavily dependent on Social Security for their retirement income, and the share of pre-retirement earnings Social Security replaces is falling for benefits claimed at any given age. If current employment patterns persist, such workers would have very low incomes both at the end of their working years and in retirement.

The positive signs—primarily the rising employment rates among people aged 55 and over—have also been far too mild to provide a sense of comfort. One can expect participation rates to increase somewhat further as educational attainment rises, as Social Security benefits decline, and as more workers approach retirement with meager balances in their 401(k)s. But no extrapolation of recent trends produces an additional two to four years of employment.[3] Labor force participation rates for men in their 50s and 60s would have to rise substantially to attain an average retirement age of 66, where average is defined as the age at which 50 percent of men are no longer in the labor force (figure 6-1). So more must be done if working longer is to emerge as a viable response to the contraction of the nation's retirement income system and our ever-rising longevity.

This chapter lays out an agenda for each of the three actors that influence employment rates of older individuals: the workers themselves, their employers, and government. The first section discusses what workers should do in response to the contraction of the retirement income system, rising longevity, and the decline of career employment. The second section discusses what employers should do in response to the aging of the U.S. labor force and the desire of many workers to remain employed to older ages. The final section discusses what government could do to push back the work-retirement divide to lessen the pressure on the nation's overstressed retirement income system and strengthen retirement income security.

What Workers Can Do

The first thing workers must do is take stock of their financial situation going forward. If they are well prepared for retirement, and secure in their job until they retire, they can direct their attention elsewhere. But most workers will find that they are not so well situated. Social Security and employer-provided defined benefit pensions will replace a far smaller share of household earnings than these programs did for their parents. Their 401(k) balances are unlikely to make up the difference. The 401(k) drawdown process, over retirements that could easily last three decades, is also fraught with risk. Nor can most workers comfortably assume that they will remain in the same job from age 50 to retirement.

Most workers will conclude after such a review that they must remain employed until their mid- to late 60s or risk a significant reduction in living standards in retirement. Most will also conclude that remaining employed that long will be challenging. But only by overcoming those challenges can they improve their retirement income security.

The most important thing workers can do to extend their careers is to keep their skills up to date and remain responsive to employer needs. Human resource managers, in one survey, identify flexibility and the mastery of needed technical skills as the employee capabilities with the greatest discrepancy between the needs of their organization and the characteristics of older workers (see figure 5-2, chapter 5).[4] Remaining flexible and responsive is a question of attitude, of thinking "young." Keeping one's skills up to date, however, requires investments of time, effort, and perhaps even money for tuition. And the further out of date one becomes, the harder it is to catch up should the need arise. Workers should also note that they will have more time to recoup such investments if they remain in the labor force longer.

The second most important thing workers can do is to make sure their employer knows their target retirement age (that is, mid- to late 60s) and their commitment to keep their skills and contacts up to date. This communication can take many forms. But demonstrations of flexibility and investments in skills along with conversations with supervisors are likely to be most persuasive. Given the lack of clarity about when workers will retire, and whether their productivity can be sustained to that age, such messages will strengthen the standing of older workers in the eyes of their employers. It could even help workers whose productivity-compensation surplus is slipping, as their employers will have a reasonable expectation about when the relationship will end.

The labor market value of older workers is generally greatest with their current employer. Using data from the Health and Retirement Study, one recent study of older workers who switched employers finds that even those who quit generally earn lower wages and benefits in their new job.[5] But if their employer, industry, occupation, or geographic location is in decline, remaining in place might not be the best option going forward. Changing jobs, let alone industries, occupations, or geographic locations, is difficult, especially at older ages. But switching could well be the best decision for workers who need to remain in the labor force for another ten, fifteen, or even more years. And the earlier workers make a transition, the more "future" they offer a prospective employer.

Discussions of older workers often focus on their preference for part-time work and less intensive employment. Downshifting to a less intensive job could be fine if it keeps workers in the labor force and pays the bills until their target retirement age. Such a pattern might even emerge as the norm in response to the decline of career employment, the rise of job shifting after age 50, and a reduction in the market value of what many older workers can produce. Part-time work might also be appropriate for workers at the cusp of retirement or already retired. But workers in their mid-50s, with a target retirement age in their mid- to late 60s, should be extremely cautious about opting for anything other than regular, full-time employment.

Changing jobs is risky, even to more enjoyable and less stressful positions. A recent study finds that only a third of all workers who want to downshift and only a quarter who want to change the type of work they do are able to do so.[6] It is also hard for workers to reverse course and return to their initial higher-intensity and higher-wage employment—say, if the stock market crashes and they need to rebuild their 401(k) balances. The risk is magnified by the fact that the market typically crashes in recessions, when labor demand is also weak. So workers in their 50s and even early 60s might need to live with frustrations on the job and pass up the allure of more comfortable and less intensive employment, much like they did when they were middle-aged.[7] So workers and their families must be prepared to absorb the emotional stress that comes with more years of employment at their current job.

Workers will also need to stay healthy. Age brings aches, pains, and maladies that can impair productivity and even the ability to work. Workers have no control over the onset of many of these conditions. But they are more responsible for their baseline level of health and well-being than when they were younger and their body did a better job of caring for itself. Attending to one's health will increase longevity and the need for retirement assets. But it also allows one to remain in the labor force longer, shortening the retirement span while allowing one's assets to grow. A longer and healthier life seems a reasonable trade-off for attending to one's diet, adding a bit of exercise, and remaining in the labor force to a somewhat older age.

Finally, workers must know that Americans have not been very successful in planning their retirement age. Surveys consistently find that workers plan on retiring around age 65.[8] But half of all men retire by age 63 and half of all women by age 62. So even if workers decide they must delay retirement, they must know that such plans are often overly optimistic and could well be disrupted by health and employment shocks.

What Employers Can Do

Employers in the past have not been especially eager to retain or recruit older workers. Going forward, some may expand opportunities for older workers in response to labor shortages or a loss of institutional intelligence as the huge baby boom generation retires. But others will face the opposite problem: a lack of retirements as older employees, without the resources needed to retire, stay on longer than these employers might like. As discussed in chapter 5, one survey finds employers expect a quarter of their baby boom employees will be in this position and want to stay two to four years past their traditional retirement age—the additional time workers will need to offset the contraction in the retirement income system.[9] But these employers were generally lukewarm about retaining even half of their employees they expect will want to stay.[10] Employers seeking new workers will also find that older workers make up a larger share of the available supply, with more willing to come out of retirement if they think they can land a job. But employers that are lukewarm about retaining employees past their traditional retirement age are likely to be downright cool about hiring workers approaching that age.

Thus the aging of the labor force, and the need of most older workers to remain in the labor force longer, will present employers with a new set of challenges. Only as they successfully respond to these challenges is the employment of older workers likely to expand significantly. As in the case of the rapid expansion in the supply of other types of workers, such a response will require innovations in employer production and personnel management systems. For example, employers responded to the influx of married women by expanding employment in various service occupations, as a disproportionate share of women are office and clerical, service, and sales workers and relatively few are laborers, operators, and craft workers, and by making greater use of part-time employment. More dramatic was the response to the influx of highly educated workers, with the expansion of professional service and high-tech industries, a focus on the development of new technologies and businesses, and the use of personnel management systems that delegate significant initiative to employees and project teams.[11]

Various studies indicate that most employers have not even begun to address the opportunities and challenges that an aging workforce presents. They have not even taken the first step, which is gathering information on the age structure of their workforce and identifying where older workers are concentrated, whether the organization is more likely to face a surge of retirements or a dearth of retirements, and what production and personnel management innovations are needed in response.[12] Most see the aging work force as "an issue to be dealt with, not an opportunity to be leveraged."[13] Given the significant increase in the share of older workers in the available pool of labor, employers seeking new workers also need to consider how best to access this large and generally underutilized resource. As in the case of women and highly educated workers, employers that successfully utilize this expanding resource will gain a competitive advantage in the marketplace.

Innovations in the Production System

The aging of the workforce could induce employers to change what they produce and how they produce it. This is because older workers have different skill sets and often want to supply their labor differently from younger workers.

Older workers bring different capabilities to the workplace than younger workers. They generally have better judgment and a stronger work ethic and are better in dealing with people. With thirty or more years of experience, they tend to be much more productive than young workers. But they are generally less productive than middle-aged workers, due to the vintage of their education and declines in health, strength, stamina, and the speed at which they learn. Many employers with an aging workforce will thus find that they have a competitive advantage in different types of production than they had in the past. They will be more adept in activities requiring judgment, diligence, people skills, and depth of experience and less in activities requiring strength, stamina, rapid learning, or youthful good looks. Given the dramatic expansion of the global economy, work requiring strength, stamina, and rapid learning will likely move to emerging economies in other parts of the world.[14] So U.S. employers have an added impetus to refocus their domestic operations toward activities more suited to an older workforce.

In addition to offering a different set of skills and experience, many older workers want to downshift. They want to reduce their hours of work or intensity of effort or shift to a job that offers more nonpecuniary rewards, even though it means lower wages and benefits. Given the expanding share of older workers in the available pool of labor—both current employees and prospective hires—many employers will find it advantageous to expand such downshifted employment options that older workers prefer. As has been widely noted in the current discussion of older workers, this could be an effective way for employers to address staffing shortages or institutional intelligence challenges created by the retirement of the baby boom generation. Expanding downshifted opportunities could also be an effective way for employers to address a dearth of retirements. By allowing full-time workers to shift to less intensive or part-time jobs they could reduce the effective supply and cost of labor. Note that this would enhance retirement income security only if it allowed workers to remain in the labor force longer—if the alternative to downshifting is to be laid off or quit—and workers could thereby push back the age at which they claim Social Security or access their employer pensions or 401(k)s.

Expanding the use of part-time work or nonpecuniary rewards can be expected to change what employers produce and how they produce it. Discrete, routine, and self-contained tasks, such as some types of clerical or professional work, and activities that cater to demand spread unevenly across the day and week, such as retailing, restaurants, and other personal services, are more amenable to part-time employment than team-based managerial and manufacturing activities.[15] The expanded supply of older workers seeking part-time work should thus induce employers to expand the former and contract the latter. Nonpecuniary rewards are typically greater in activities such as social service, graphic design, and recreational instruction than in ditch digging, long-distance trucking, and high-pressure sales. The expanded supply of older workers should thus induce employers to adjust what they produce and how they produce it and to redesign jobs in activities such as ditch digging, trucking, and sales to reduce stress and enhance nonpecuniary rewards.

Finally, employers can often modify their production system, at relatively low cost, in ways that allow older workers to continue in their jobs despite a functional decline. For example, the introduction of mechanized hospital beds extended the careers of older nurses, and replacing heavy hand-held tools with tools suspended from the ceiling did the same for older factory workers.[16] Declines in functionality such as eyesight, which is classified as a disability and must be reasonably accommodated under the Americans with Disabilities Act, can often be addressed with improvements in lighting or with larger computer monitors and font sizes.[17] Initiatives that identify and address such functional declines will often be the employer's most cost-effective response to the impact of an aging workforce on its existing production system.

Innovations in the Personnel Management System

The aging of the workforce is likely to require even more innovations in personnel management—how employers supervise, compensate, and move workers through the organization. An aging workforce raises various thorny personnel management issues that essentially all employers must face.

A critical issue is the heterogeneity of today's older workforce, both in the capabilities older workers offer employers and in how intensively and how much longer they want to work. This heterogeneity had not been a significant issue in personnel management systems based on career employment. Older workers had much more uniform sets of skills and experiences, as they had spent much of their careers with their current employer. The age of retirement was also well defined, reinforced by social custom and financial incentives built into defined benefit pension plans. So whatever their individual preferences, older employees continued on the job working more or less steadily until they left the organization at the expected retirement age.

With the decline in career employment and the rise in educational attainment, many of today's older workers have acquired unique combinations of skills and experience. The physical and cognitive effects of aging are also varied, with many older workers remaining physically and mentally fit. Such workers will also make up a much larger share of the available pool of labor, given the aging of the workforce. So the odds are much greater that one of those older workers will have a combination of skills, experience, and personal characteristics that would be an especially good fit for an employer seeking to fill a staffing need. But for employers to identify what older workers can do, and match that against their needs, takes a significant amount of

Figure 6-2. *Retirement Rates by Age of Worker, Workers in Defined Contribution Plans, 1994–2002*

Percent

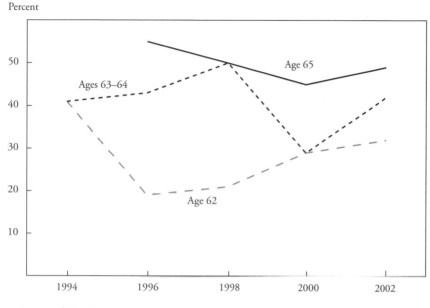

Source: Schieber (2007).

effort. This is especially so when hiring new workers, as employers initially have much less information about an applicant's capabilities. To access the expanding pool of older workers, employers will thus need to develop more effective ways to identify workers—both within their organization and in the external labor market—with the capabilities that best fit their needs.[18]

Employers must also address heterogeneity in how older employees want to supply their labor, how intensively they want to work, and when they want to retire. End-of-career work patterns have become significantly more dispersed over time. This in part is due to the evolution of different occupational career paths, the decline of career employment, and the deinstitutionalization of the retirement process.[19] Employers will thus find that some employees will want to continue working in their current capacity into their late 60s or beyond. Engineers, scientists, and academics favor such extended career paths. According to worker surveys, however, most employees would like to downshift much earlier, cutting back their hours or switching to a less intensive job with more nonpecuniary rewards. And some just want to retire

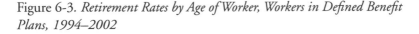

Figure 6-3. *Retirement Rates by Age of Worker, Workers in Defined Benefit Plans, 1994–2002*

Percent

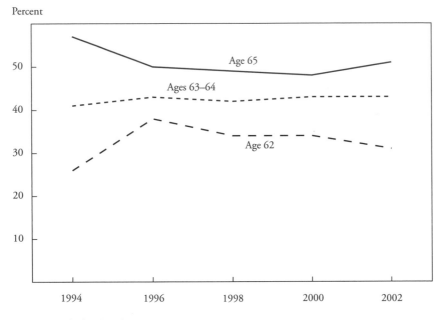

Source: Schieber (2007).

in the near future. Workers with 401(k)s, moreover, have far less reason to leave their employer at a particular age than workers covered by a traditional defined benefit pension plan, and when they will leave is much less predictable (figures 6-2, 6-3). For employers to plan their staffing, training, and succession needs, they must develop effective ways to identify and respond to such preferences.

Employers could rely on expanded career planning programs to identify the preferences and capabilities of older workers. In such programs, employees (and prospective hires) present their capabilities and preferences and, with their supervisor, define employment and performance objectives. Employees who say they want to extend their careers generally commit to activities that enhance their value down the road, such as signing up for training or taking on a new assignment. Those who want to downshift can develop a suitable career path going forward with their supervisor. The specification of performance objectives in such career planning programs provides benchmarks for assessing worker productivity, an especially important consideration in managing an older workforce.[20]

Offering downshifted employment opportunities, however, raises a variety of personnel management issues. It could suit an employer's needs in some departments and with some types of workers but rarely in all departments and for all types of worker. Phased retirement (a reduction in hours) and less intensive full-time work typically require more management and supervision per dollar of output, which should translate into lower compensation per hour. Downshifted employment also raises other thorny compensation issues, primarily related to employee benefits, discussed below. So employers have been quite cautious about offering such opportunities. They generally allow workers to go to part time only on a case-by-case basis, with the approval of the employee's supervisor.[21] The employer wants the supervisor to evaluate the contribution the worker would make, and whether the alternative is no employment or full-time employment. Many employers thus prefer a clean break in the employment relationship, with the worker re-engaged in a different capacity or on a part-time or per-project basis as an independent contractor.[22] To significantly expand downshifted employment opportunities, employers will need to develop more effective ways to evaluate their effect on the organization and to supervise and compensate workers who downshift.

An employer facing a lack of retirements (that is, too many older workers relative to its full-time employment needs) and too few downshifted options (that could reduce the effective supply of labor) could consider offering outplacement assistance. This has been traditional in Japan, where employers set a mandatory retirement age from career employment at 55–60. Employers then help these workers downshift into a less stressful second career with another organization, often a customer or supplier, or into self-employment as a small farmer or shop owner.[23] IBM introduced a somewhat similar program, offering workers an entrée into math and science teaching. Although promoted as a program addressing society's need for more qualified math and science teachers, it also offers workers a second career with significant nonpecuniary rewards.[24] Such programs could become a valued employee benefit, as they have in Japan, and could facilitate more orderly separations for both worker and employer.

Addressing the heterogeneity of older workers will also help employers deal with the problem of age discrimination. The capabilities and preferences of older workers are quite varied and cannot be painted with a uniform brush. To the extent that supervisors and co-workers are sensitized to this variation, discriminatory stereotypes are less likely to impair an employer's ability to make effective use of an aging workforce.

Innovations in Compensation

The aging of the labor force also raises significant compensation issues that employers will need to address. Perhaps most important is resisting the tendency of compensation to rise with age. Given that the productivity of older workers tends to stay flat or decline, employers will need to control compensation escalation to effectively utilize this expanding pool of labor.

Health insurance and traditional defined benefit pensions are the primary source of compensation escalation. The number of employers still offering these pensions is declining rapidly. But health insurance has become increasingly expensive and has emerged as the major factor driving up compensation costs as workers age. It is especially important in driving up the cost of lower-wage workers, as health insurance costs do not vary with wage rates and thus make up a larger share of total compensation the lower a worker's wage.

One way employers could address the escalation of health insurance costs is through a cafeteria-type employee benefit plan. Such plans offer multiple health insurance options, from expensive indemnity plans to inexpensive health maintenance organizations (HMOs), with the employer making a similar contribution to each. To the extent that older workers elect the indemnity plans with their much higher required employee contribution and younger workers the bare-bones HMO, older workers will bear much of their rising health care costs.

Phased retirement raises additional employee benefit issues. For employers with defined benefit pension plans, government regulations forbid payments to active workers younger than age 62. Workers phasing out before that age, and who want to collect their pensions, must quit and return as a private contractor. Pension benefits are also traditionally based on years of service and annual wages at the end of a worker's career. Phased retirement involves a decline in hours and wages. In calculating a worker's pension, most employers seem to ignore the lower wages earned in the phase-out period. It is unclear, however, whether they credit years of service in the phase-out period in calculating the benefit.[25]

Health insurance can be especially troublesome in downshifted employment arrangements. Coverage is quite important, and expensive, for older workers. In phased retirement, compensation per hour will rise if wage rates are unchanged and the employer continues coverage and fall if coverage ends. The change in compensation per hour could be substantial, given the high cost of insurance that needs to be spread over fewer hours of work. The change will be especially great for low-wage workers, as health insurance is a larger share of their total compensation. Continued coverage could make phased retirement too costly to offer to low-wage workers. But discontinuing coverage makes phased retirement much less attractive, as workers cannot purchase health insurance on advantageous terms. Offering a pro rata employer contribution, with a half-time worker getting half of the employer's contribution, would seem to be a viable option. A survey of phased retirement among white-collar workers nevertheless finds that most employers continue coverage, although a significant share does not. For phased retirement to become a widespread practice, employers must develop ways that minimize the effect of health insurance coverage in changing compensation rates.[26]

Innovations in the Retirement Process

Retirement is a major life transition. It marks the end of relationships and activities that are primary components of a person's identity as well as an end to work as the primary source of one's livelihood. Given these social, psychological, and economic breaks, retirement can be highly traumatic. Traditional personnel management systems contained the trauma by institutionalizing the retirement process. Social Security and employer pensions ensured an adequate income, at least through the initial retirement years. Workers generally retired of their own volition, in response to cultural and financial cues. They neither were fired nor did they quit, but they simply went with the flow.

This orderly process will not be present to organize the retirement of the baby boom generation. The decline of career employment means that workers and employers no longer have defined benefit pensions and a clear set of markers that define how the employment relationship ends. The balances in older workers' 401(k)s, and in IRAs holding balances rolled over from previous employers, are quite varied. Also quite varied are evaluations of how much is enough to finance retirement. Employers thus have no clear idea of when their workers might leave. So the retirement process is likely to be messy and unpredictable, as many workers will likely want to stay on the job longer than their employers would like. Employers in declining industries, with older workers whose skills are no longer needed, and employers with personnel systems that rely on promotions as a key motivational device will be especially cool to older workers who want to stay.

With the baby boom generation nearing retirement, employers have little time to develop a response to the severance problem. The easiest solution could be to develop employment opportunities. This could be standard full-time employment, downshifting to less demanding positions, or a phased retirement program. Employers could also explore outplacement assistance, perhaps to a job at a related employer (the Japanese model) or into a second career that offers more nonpecuniary rewards. Without such a response, many employers will be pressured to fire older workers who need the job and will not leave on their own.

What Government Can Do

Government has an important interest in pushing back the work-retirement divide, given its commitment to retirement income security and the pressures on the national retirement income system. Government can encourage workers to remain in the labor force longer by changing the provisions of Social Security and publicly subsidized and regulated retirement income programs. It can encourage employers to retain or hire older workers by reducing their cost. Government can also improve the effectiveness of the labor market in matching older workers with employers.

Encourage Workers to Remain in the Labor Force

Government exerts a significant influence on work and retirement decisions through the provisions of the Social Security program and through regulations governing private retirement income programs.

As discussed above, the government has already changed the provisions of the Social Security program in ways that encourage workers to remain in the labor force longer. Government has done that by offering "carrots" that raise the rewards of work vis-à-vis retirement—liberalizing the earnings test and increasing the benefit adjustment if a worker delays claiming benefits past the full retirement age. It is also using "sticks"—cutting benefits available at any given age and increasing the taxes retirees must pay on their benefits.

Additional carrots would encourage workers to stay in the labor force longer. The most prominent such proposal would allow older workers to opt out of contributing to the program at a specified age.[27] This would be advantageous to many, as Social Security uses only the highest thirty-five years of earnings to calculate a worker's primary insurance amount (PIA), the benefit received at the full retirement age.[28] For workers with thirty-five years of employment, remaining in the labor force and contributing to Social Security will have little or no effect on the PIA.[29] Their contributions essentially become a tax, a levy without a compensating benefit. Allowing workers with thirty-five or forty years of covered earnings to opt out of the program would exempt such workers and their employers from paying the 6.2 percent payroll tax (7.65 percent if also exempt from the Medicare tax). This would increase the reward for remaining employed. It would also make older workers less expensive, and more attractive, to employers. One study estimates that exempting both workers and employers from the payroll tax after the worker turns 62 would have a very large effect on labor supply, inducing workers to postpone retirement by as much as three years.[30]

Exempting or allowing older workers to opt out of the Social Security payroll tax would increase the program's long-run financing shortfall. The revenue loss would be relatively small, however, given the relatively low employment rates and wages earned at those ages. If the initiative expands employment, the government could also recoup some or all of the forgone revenue from additional income tax collections. But given the financial pressures on the federal government, proposals that raise employment rates without increasing outlays—that is, sticks—have a greater chance of enactment.

One such stick is raising the averaging period that the program uses to calculate benefits from thirty-five to forty years. This change would substantially increase the number of workers who could raise their primary insurance amount by working longer, providing a benefit in return for continued contributions to the program. To the extent that the change in the averaging period increases employment rates, both Social Security and federal income tax revenues would rise. It would also help Social Security's financing problem by reducing the benefits of workers with fewer than forty years of earnings.[31] The reduction would adversely affect many women and low-wage workers, who have inconsistent employment records and very low retirement incomes. There are, however, adjustments to the benefit design, such as providing credit for child rearing, that could partially protect such vulnerable groups.[32]

One stick that would advantage women, and significantly reduce the hardship that many face at the end of their lives, would be to require the spouse's permission for a worker to claim benefits before the full retirement age. Married women have a strong interest in having their husbands claim at a later age. Wives on average are about three years younger than their husbands, and their life expectancy is about three years longer. If they outlive their husbands, which is likely, they will then be entitled as survivors to the greater of their own earned benefit or that of their spouse. The earned benefit of married women is nearly always less than that of their husbands. So the great majority of married women get their husbands' benefit as widows. If their husbands claim at 66, which is the full retirement age for workers born between 1943 and 1954, the survivor benefit will be one-third greater than if their husbands claim at 62. As many married women suffer sharp drops in income upon the death of their husband and become highly dependent on Social Security, such a provision, if it results in later claiming, could significantly improve retirement income security. An alternative would guarantee survivors a benefit at least equal to their spouse's full retirement benefit, with the cost offset by further reducing benefits claimed before the full retirement

Figure 6-4. *Early Retirement Benefit Reduction to Preserve Survivor Benefit at Primary Insurance Amount, at Full Retirement Age of 66* [a]

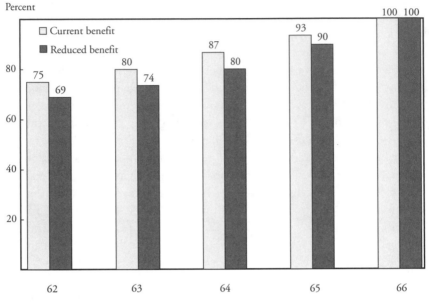

Percent

Source: Sass, Sun, and Webb (2008).

a. Estimates assume all survivor benefits are claimed after the survivor attains the full retirement age of 66.

age (figure 6-4). The husband and wife could then decide whether to offset the reduction in early retirement benefits by working longer.

The most powerful stick the government could use to encourage workers to remain in the labor force longer is to raise the earliest eligibility age (EEA) at which they can access the retirement income system. The earliest age at which one can claim Social Security old age benefits is 62, and most workers currently claim benefits and leave the labor force at 62 or 63. While the program's full retirement age, the age a worker can claim unreduced benefits, is rising from 65 to 67, the EEA will remain 62. If the EEA were raised to 64 (in line with the two-year rise in the normal age), most workers would likely remain in the labor force until at least that age, even though they would be free to use their own resources and retire earlier. According to one estimate, about 60 percent of those who currently retire at 62 would retire at 64.[33] Monthly benefits claimed at age 64 are 16 percent higher than if claimed at age 62, even with no increase in the worker's primary insurance amount (figure 6-5).[34] These higher monthly benefits would have a noticeable effect on retirement income security, as retirees tend to spend down other assets and

Figure 6-5. *Social Security Benefit, by Age Claimed, as Share of Benefit Claimed at Full Retirement Age 66*[a]

Percent

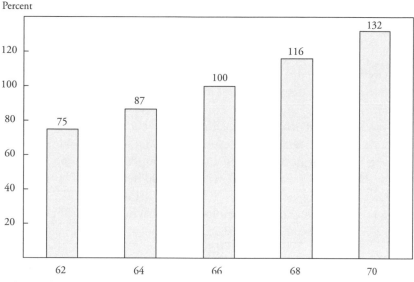

Source: U.S. Social Security Administration (2006b).

a. The benefit assumes no change in the worker's primary insurance amount (the benefit at full retirement age.)

rely increasingly on Social Security as they age. Because monthly benefits claimed at any age are declining while life expectancy is rising, shifting Social Security wealth to when individuals are truly old will become increasingly important.[35]

The same logic holds for raising the age at which workers can access tax-advantaged 401(k)s, individual retirement accounts (IRAs), and similar retirement income programs without penalty. Currently, withdrawals before the year the worker turns 59½ incur a 10 percent penalty tax. The age could be raised to the year the worker turns 61½. The government could also make a similar provision for defined benefit pensions, which currently have no such rule. Workers could still retire early, without penalty, using funds other than those benefiting from favorable tax treatment. Many if not most workers, however, would probably opt to remain in the labor force longer. Employment rates should rise and the drawdown of tax-favored "retirement wealth" would shift from late middle age to when individuals are somewhat older.

Not everyone is convinced that raising the EEA is a good idea. Withholding access to Social Security benefits until age 64 would impose a hardship on workers who are in poor health and lack the assets to support themselves until age 64.[36] An additional group might be healthy enough to work but cannot find employment. Critics also say that raising the EEA would be unfair to groups with relatively short life expectancy, such as low-wage workers and African Americans.[37]

These criticisms have merit but need to be put in perspective. Most workers who currently claim benefits early would not face significant hardship. Most are either capable of working until the new EEA or have sufficient non–Social Security resources to fill the gap.[38] Nor would raising the EEA generally reduce lifetime benefits. For most households, especially married couples, claiming later actually increases lifetime benefits.[39] In addition, the unfairness to groups with low life expectancy could be offset within a package of reforms that produced a more even overall distribution of costs and benefits. Hardships created by a higher EEA could be addressed by expanded safety net programs, such as Social Security's Disability Insurance program for those in poor health or Unemployment Insurance and Supplemental Security Income programs for those unable to find employment.[40]

An attractive alternate for addressing the objections to a higher EEA is to assign workers different earliest claiming ages based on their lifetime earnings.[41] Low lifetime earnings are highly correlated with the major risk factors associated with raising the EEA—poor health, little financial wealth, and poor employment prospects at age 62. So the EEA could remain 62 for workers with low lifetime earnings and rise to 64 for workers with lifetime earnings above a specified threshold. Preliminary estimates suggest that an "elastic" EEA could shelter a substantial proportion of the most vulnerable population—workers with little or no financial assets and whose health or employment prospects are poor (figure 6-6). As lifetime earnings are closely correlated with longevity, such an elastic EEA could also significantly reduce the fairness objection to a general increase in the earliest age of claiming.[42]

One change in the Social Security program that would not be helpful is the elimination of the retirement earnings test. For beneficiaries below the full retirement age the test reduces benefits by $1 for each $2 of earnings above a specified threshold ($13,560 in 2008). While these reductions are offset by increases in future benefits, workers seem to view the earnings test as imposing a tax on continued employment. Most researchers find the test to be a significant work disincentive, so removing it might expand employment among Social Security beneficiaries below the full retirement age. But if the goal of increased employment is to strengthen retirement income security, eliminating the earnings test would be counterproductive. This is because early claiming would also rise, resulting in lower monthly Social

Figure 6-6. *Percentage of Men in Risk Group Who Woould Have Their EEA Rise by Less than One Year*[a]

Percent

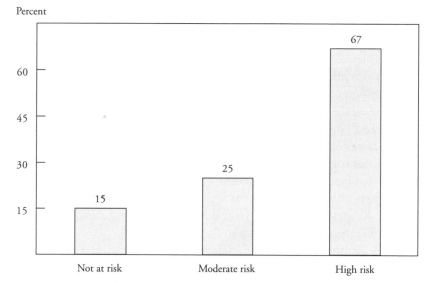

Source: Zhivan and others (2008).

a. Workers are classified as at "high risk" if they cannot support themselves without working from age 62 to age 64 and have both a health problem and a labor market problem; "moderate risk" if they cannot support themselves without working and have either a health or a labor market problem; and "not at risk" if they can support themselves without working or have neither a health nor a labor market problem. A "health problem" is defined as a self-report of "poor" or "fair" health or a work-limiting health condition. A "labor market problem" is defined as peak earnings between the ages 55 and 59 that are less than 80 percent of the national average wage at age 55. The "inability to support oneself from age 62 to age 64 without working" is defined as having financial assets less than two times the average lifetime earnings.

Security benefits and decreased income at older ages, when the elderly are significantly worse off.[43]

Encourage Employers to Retain and Hire Older Workers

The primary way government can influence employers to retain and hire older workers is to lower their cost. Such initiatives would be most important for low-wage workers, who disproportionately find themselves priced out of a job. Making such workers more attractive to employers is especially important if government raised the EEA or reduced the size of early retirement benefits, as low-wage workers disproportionately lack a source of support other than work or Social Security. The most important costs government can directly influence are the Social Security payroll tax (discussed above) and the cost of providing health insurance.

For most employers, health insurance is the major factor that drives up the cost of older workers. This is especially so for low-wage workers, as health insurance is a much larger share of their total compensation. The most common proposal for lowering the employer's cost is to eliminate the requirement that Medicare serve as the secondary payer for anyone covered by an employer plan. When workers become eligible for Medicare, at age 65, employers currently see no reduction in their health care expense. Medicare only covers costs not covered by the employer's plan. If Medicare were the primary payer, the government would pick up the bulk of the worker's health care expenses. This would increase current Medicare spending about 1.5 percent and somewhat more in the future, as the baby boom generation swells the number of covered workers age 65 and over.[44] Given the high cost of providing health care, the government is unlikely to recoup these additional costs through increased employment and higher income and payroll tax revenues. As the Medicare program faces enormous long-term deficits, the proposal is unlikely to gain much support.[45]

The Medicare first-payer proposal, moreover, only affects the cost of workers age 65 and over. Health insurance is the primary factor driving up their cost to employers well before that age. So initiatives that reduce or eliminate age-related health care costs borne by employers for workers younger than age 65 are far more critical. The U.S. health care system could undergo significant reform, as the continual increase in the share of national output that health care absorbs seems unsustainable. Such reform could reduce the age-related trajectory of health care costs. This could be done directly, through tax-financed initiatives, or indirectly, through regulatory initiatives. Reforming the health care system, however, is clearly a much bigger policy decision than the issue of employing older workers.[46]

Finally, government could lower the cost of employing older workers by allowing mandatory retirement at a specific age, say, Social Security's full retirement age. The cost of compensating older workers tends to rise with age and productivity decline. Employers can dismiss older workers who can no longer do their job, though they run the risk of an age discrimination lawsuit. But employers cannot legally dismiss older workers whose health insurance premiums have risen too high or who have expensive medical problems. Mandatory retirement would limit the employer's exposure to productivity declines and compensation escalation that typically emerge as workers age. Studies find that the elimination of mandatory retirement raises employment rates of workers above traditional mandatory retirement ages.[47] But most of these workers were in career employment jobs, and the end of mandatory retirement and the enactment of legislation prohibiting age discrimination allowed such workers to stay on to older ages. Given the decline in career employment, however, hiring decisions have become more important to the employment of older workers; and putting a lid on tenure could make hiring workers in their 50s and early 60s more attractive. This could be especially so for low- and average-wage workers with employers that offer health insurance, as the value of what they produce could well be expected to slip below what they are paid at older ages.

Strengthen the Labor Market for Older Workers

Government, primarily state government, engages in a variety of activities designed to keep the labor force productive and employed. It operates One-Stop Career Centers to help unemployed workers find new jobs. Community colleges offer training to update skills. State colleges, universities, and administrative agencies advise employers on how to improve their operations. State economic development agencies promote job creation and retention. And state and federal agencies combat age discrimination in the workplace.

Older workers primarily access such government services at the One-Stop Career Centers after losing a job; here they can get counseling, job matching, and access to publicly funded training. Many studies that review the prospects of older workers stress the importance of expanded training opportunities.[48] As in the case of employer-funded programs, older workers receive less publicly funded training than younger job seekers. The publicly funded programs, however, primarily focus on helping low-wage and disadvantaged groups enter the labor force.[49] The One-Stops also tend to direct older low-wage job seekers to the Senior Community Service Employment Program, which offers graceful exits from the labor force via placements in subsidized, minimum-wage, community service jobs. This concentration on disadvantaged and low-wage workers is due to budget constraints and the need to direct limited training funds to this high-priority need. A United Nations study finds that the United States spends a much smaller share of GDP on training (less than 0.5 percent) than any of the twenty European and North American countries surveyed: Denmark, for example, spends over 4.5 percent of per capita GDP on labor market programs, and Canada spends over 1.0 percent. The effectiveness of U.S. public training programs is also unclear, although the general impression is that success has been quite modest.[50] So as desirable as expanded and effective training for older job seekers might be, it seems unlikely to emerge any time soon.

Counseling and job-matching services, however, are less expensive than an effective training program. They could also be even more important to older job seekers, as most are reasonably skilled. Older job seekers generally need advice not just on getting a job but also on how employment (or the lack thereof) will affect their well-being in retirement. Such counseling will likely shift their reemployment objective toward remaining in regular full-time work over a longer time horizon. Job matching is also more important for older job seekers, whose skills and experiences are typically quite varied. Employers often fail to fully specify the capabilities they need and often shy away from older workers. So older job seekers need help, and encouragement, on how to identify a prospective match and then how to convince an employer to give them a job.[51]

Government can also strengthen the labor market position of older workers by advising employers on how best to use an aging workforce. As part of their public service mission, state agencies, colleges, and universities advise businesses on how they might improve their operations. Older workers represent a large and largely underused economic resource. To employ that resource more effectively, business leaders at a series of state summits on the mature workforce consistently requested "support and technical assistance in managing a more age-diverse workforce, changing attitudes about workplace flexibility, identifying and sharing best practices, and most important restructuring jobs and work flow" (box 6-1). If employers receive such assistance and employ older workers more effectively, employment opportunities would expand and workers could remain in the labor force longer.

Many states also provide economic development services (and funding) to create and retain employment. Older workers tend to be disproportionately concentrated in declining industries. They also tend to have poor reemployment prospects if they lose their job. So they and the local economy would suffer large economic losses if their employers ceased operations or significantly cut back employment. The aging of the workforce thus suggests that state economic development efforts should focus more in retaining and less on expanding employment. This primarily involves attending to the needs of existing employers for infrastructure improvements, skills training, well-designed workmen's compensation and unemployment insurance programs, and the like.

Finally, government could more actively combat age discrimination in the workplace. The federal Age Discrimination in Employment Act of 1967 prohibits such discrimination against workers by employers with more than twenty employees. Many states have similar laws that further protect older workers. This legislation has essentially eliminated overt discrimination, such as explicit age limits in help-wanted ads. But their effect on subtle forms of age discrimination is hard to gauge. Two-thirds of older workers in one survey say they have "personally witnessed or experienced age discrimination on

Box 6-1. *Recommendations from the Arizona Summits on the Mature Workforce*

Public Education and Awareness

Unanimous recommendation from all three summits that the state should launch a public awareness/public education campaign about the aging of our workforce, how it can be addressed, and what workers and businesses need to know and do.

Training and Technical Assistance

Business leaders in all three summits asked for support and technical assistance in managing a more age-diverse workforce, changing attitudes about workplace flexibility, identifying and sharing best practices, and most important restructuring jobs and work flow to accommodate the changing nature of Arizona's workforce. They also asked that skills training for mature workers be more readily available and affordable.

Linkages between Employers and Mature Workers

While nearly all of the business leaders involved recognized the value of mature workers in their operations, finding ways for businesses and mature workers to connect with each other that does not violate EEO, FLSA, and other important antidiscrimination protections is an issue. Both businesses and workers in all three summits expressed the need for a web-based mechanism where jobs and resumes could be posted that would be friendly to mature workers (that is, you don't have to be a technology whiz to use it) and efficient for businesses.

Innovations and Incentives

The participants in the three summits came up with a number of innovative ideas about how they could attract and retain mature workers, including offering cafeteria benefits/pay plans, using mature workers as mentors, providing phased-retirement options, hiring retirees back as consultants, and looking at part-year residents as an additional workforce. While implementation of most of these ideas lies in the hands of business, technical assistance, as discussed earlier, would be a critical factor.

Policy and Regulatory Changes

Of major concern was the frequent cost disincentive in health care plans when the average age of a company's workforce increases. Thus the more mature workers a business hires, the more expensive their health plans become. . . . Another expressed concern was the fear that hiring more mature workers could result in more litigation around age discrimination.

Source: Arizona Mature Workforce Initiative (2006).

the job."[52] Age discrimination is nevertheless difficult to prove: job performance is often difficult to measure, and what constitutes illegal discrimination can be ambiguous.[53] As accusations of age discrimination are also difficult to disprove, employers might react to a tough legal environment against age discrimination by avoiding older workers altogether. One study concludes that the legislation on the books has, on balance, had a positive effect on employment opportunities for older workers.[54] But another finds that older workers in states with tougher laws against age discrimination have lower employment rates.[55] So it might be difficult for the government to do much more.

Conclusion

Given the contraction of the retirement income system and the lack of saving outside this system, Americans must work into their mid- to late 60s—two to four years longer than they do at present—to secure a reasonably comfortable retirement. In many ways, this should not be a problem. Most Americans are healthy enough to work that long. Work is also less demanding and more rewarding than it has been in the past. But pushing back the work-retirement divide is not something easily done. Workers, employers, and government all have to play a part. No one actor can accomplish the goal alone.

Workers are at the core of the drama. Their work and their well-being are at stake. Workers must understand the connection between remaining in the workforce and their security in retirement. They must know that a few more years of work will translate into a large increase in monthly retirement income. And they must understand this connection well before the cusp of retirement so they can make the investments in skills and relationships that will allow them to extend their careers.

Employers are the most problematic actors in the retirement drama. Employers are not in business to supply secure retirements. Moreover, the rising share of older workers is likely to reduce their relative value to most employers. The rising share, however, will induce employers to change their production and personnel management systems in ways that make better use of older workers. As employers make such changes more older workers who want to remain in the workforce are likely to succeed.

Government has the most difficult task. The most effective change government can make to improve retirement income security is to restrict worker choice: to push back the age at which workers can access Social Security or other retirement benefits. Workers can be expected to resist, especially those who would face hardship. But raising the earliest eligibility age for Social Security, in particular, seems crucial. Only such a clear and visible act can change the work and retirement expectations of workers and employers alike. And only when workers and employers both understand that an average retirement age of 63 is a thing of the past will each make the changes necessary to raise the work-retirement divide.

7

Rounding Out the Picture

The retirement income system is contracting. Social Security will replace less of preretirement income in the future than it does today, and one-third of households are totally dependent on Social Security as their only source of retirement income. The remaining two-thirds of households have traditionally supplemented Social Security with income from employer-sponsored plans. But these plans have changed from defined benefit plans, where the employer guarantees an income for life, to 401(k) plans, where, to date at least, balances are quite modest. And households tend to save very little on their own.

At the same time that the retirement system is contracting, life expectancy is increasing. People retiring at ages 62 or 63, the typical age for women and men today, will live on average for about another twenty years. But the variation around this life expectancy is enormous. About 19 percent of men and 33 percent of women who survive to age 65 will live to age 90 or older and have to support themselves for almost thirty years (table 7-1). The arithmetic does not work. With a contracting retirement income system, households will not be able to accumulate enough retirement wealth over a forty-year work life to support themselves for twenty or thirty years of retirement.

Table 7-1. *Probability of Surviving to Given Age, Sixty-Five-Year-Old Men and Women Born in 1940*
Percent

Age	Men	Women
70	89	93
75	75	83
80	58	70
85	38	53
90	19	33
95	7	15

Source: U.S. Social Security Administration (2003).

The retirement income challenge is confounded by the rapidly accelerating costs of health care and the withdrawal of employers from the provision of postretirement health care benefits. Between 1989 and 2006 the percentage of large firms offering postretirement health care benefits dropped from 66 percent to 35 percent. This decline actually understates the extent of the cutback, because the generosity of the benefits has also been reduced. Employers have increased retiree contributions to premiums, increased retiree coinsurance or copayments, raised deductibles, and increased out-of-pocket limits.[1] Moreover, many of those providing postretirement health benefits today have terminated such benefits for new retirees.

Combine rapidly increasing health care costs and widening gaps in coverage with the contracting retirement income system and increased longevity and the result is that households face an enormous challenge in ensuring a secure retirement.

Potentially, the best way out of the box is for both men and women to work longer. And working longer does not mean working forever. An additional two to four years can have a powerful effect. These years enable households to avoid the actuarial reduction in Social Security benefits: benefits received at age 66 are one-third higher than those received at age 62. They allow workers to avoid tapping into their 401(k) balances, earn additional interest on those balances, and maybe even make further contributions. Finally, additional years of work shorten the period over which households must support themselves with accumulated retirement assets. Roughly speaking, working four more years changes the ratio of retirement years to working years from 1:2 (twenty years of retirement and forty years of work) to almost 1:3 (sixteen years of retirement and forty-four years of work). Thus the goal that emerges from the preceding analysis is that people should aim to retire at age 66, Social Security's current full retirement age.

Achieving such a goal should be possible. Age 66 was the average retirement age for men as recently as 1960. And since 1960 people have become healthier and jobs have become less physically demanding. So if people want to work and can find employment, most should be capable of performing the tasks. But those are the two big questions. Will men and women want to supply their labor? And will employers want to employ them? On both fronts, the preceding chapters suggest some positive movement but nothing of the magnitude to return the average retirement age to 66. Achieving this goal will require concerted changes on the part of individuals, employers, and government.

In addition to this broad conclusion, other important issues have arisen in the process of exploring the potential for continued employment. These issues involve the fixation on phased retirement; the risks that low-wage workers will face in the new world; the decline in employment rates of men in their 50s; the shift away from career employment; and the coming "messiness" of the retirement process. These issues are addressed briefly below.

Phased Retirement May Be a Diversion

Much of the discussion about working longer has focused on expanding opportunities for phased retirement or part-time employment.[2] Most workers aged 55–64 say they would like to retire gradually, cutting back their hours rather than retiring "cold turkey."[3] So expanding opportunities for such workers to reduce their hours has seemed a reasonable way for them to extend their careers. But if the average retirement age is going to increase to 66, most workers aged 55–64 will need to remain in regular full-time employment. Only if workers are expected to remain in full-time employment until then will workers in their 50s have enough of a future in the labor force that it makes sense to invest in skills and relationships that will keep them productive into their mid-60s.

Moreover, initiatives to expand part-time employment at the end of a worker's career might not be especially fruitful. Relatively few types of production seem suited to part-time work. Most economic activity seems far more efficient when done by teams of full-time workers who are continually present at the same location.[4] Part-time employment is also expensive in the sense that the employer must spread the costs of recruiting, training, scheduling, supervising, and evaluating workers over fewer hours of labor. Most important, expanding part-time opportunities might not result in increased employment, according to one study.[5] The study, using a structural model of labor supply, finds that some workers would delay retirement and increase employment at older ages but others would also expand part-time work at younger ages in lieu of full-time employment. The net result would be little change in either full-time-equivalent employment or retirement income security.

Low-Wage Workers Will Be at Risk

One finding that comes through at each stage of the analysis is that low-wage workers will be at risk. Begin with the most basic question of whether low-wage workers will be healthy enough to work. Survey after survey suggests that 15–20 percent of workers aged 55–64 will have a work-limiting disability. Those most likely to have such disabilities are people with less education and lower wages. Even after controlling for income and wealth as well as health behavior, such as smoking and drinking, education remains an important variable in explaining health. As discussed in chapter 2, less educated people are less able to follow complicated regimes and manage their diseases. So less educated, low-wage workers are most likely to have a health problem in their 50s and early 60s. And some studies suggest that improvements in health may have, at a minimum, stalled. The major reason for this stall is a rise in obesity and the resulting onset of diabetes. Both obesity and diabetes tend to be concentrated among the low-income population. So the future may be bleaker than the present.

The next issue is quality of jobs. While work generally has become less physically demanding, low-wage workers are more likely to have disagreeable jobs that involve either physical strain or monotonous repetition.

Moreover, the demand for low-wage workers may be low. Technological change that favors educated, high-wage workers, and competition from less educated workers overseas, has depressed the demand for less educated workers in essentially all industrial nations. As less educated workers age, this depressed demand is manifest not just in lower wages but also in lower employment rates.

Addressing this problem will not be easy. Workers with low educational attainment are difficult to train. Rising health insurance costs are a major hurdle for employment with employers that offer such plans. The one bright light is that the educational attainment of older workers is rising quite rapidly. Nevertheless, those who most may need to work longer—low-wage workers dependent on Social Security—are precisely the individuals who have onerous jobs that stress their health and who lack the education to manage their care. They will require some source of support if changes are made, such as raising the earliest eligibility age under Social Security, to spur those capable of working to remain in the labor force.

Figure 7-1. *Workforce Participation Rates of Men Aged 50–70, 1985 and 2005*

Percent

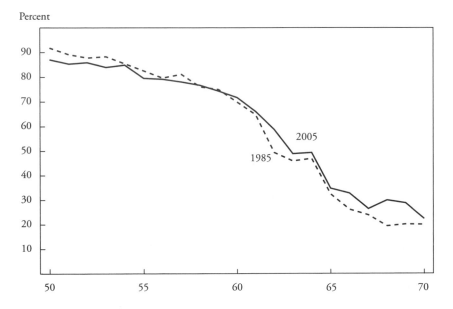

Source: U.S. Census Bureau and Bureau of Labor Statistics, Current Population Survey (1985, 2005).

Employment for Men in Their 50s Has Declined

Closely related to the issue of low-wage workers, but lost in the hoopla about the uptick in employment for older workers, is the fact that employment rates for men in their early 50s are actually down. As shown in figure 7-1, employment rates in 2005 were below those in 1985 for men aged 50–58.[6] In part, this decline is due to the depressed demand for less educated workers. But in part it is due to the availability of government benefits provided through the Social Security Disability Insurance (SSDI) program.

A survey of the literature concludes that, for low-wage workers, SSDI became more attractive over the twenty-year period 1985–2005.[7] First, SSDI benefits are kept up to date with the average wage index, which has exceeded real wage growth of low-wage workers, so SSDI replacement rates have increased. Second, administrative changes have made it easier to qualify for benefits when an individual has difficulty finding employment. Using data from the Survey of Income and Program Participation (SIPP), the authors estimate that the rate of SSDI receipt among high school dropouts increased dramatically between 1984 and 2004. In short, the United States, like other industrialized nations, has—perhaps unintentionally—expanded programs to provide a basic level of support to workers hit by declining labor force prospects in the wake of globalization. But this expansion also means that fewer men will be in the labor force in their 60s.

Examining the impact of SSDI on employment of workers in their 50s, and the subsequent effect on workers in their 60s, is beyond the scope of this book. But it is important to note that the trend for men in their 50s is down, while that for those in their 60s is up.

Job Shifting among Workers in Their 50s Is Now the Norm

If workers are to remain employed full time into their mid- to late 60s, most will do so with a different employer than they had at age 50. The market value of what they produce in such second careers will generally be less than what it had been with their career employer in their prime working years. But if they find a good match and invest in a modicum of training, most workers should be able to improve their initial productivity with their new employer through experience gains and have little or no decline in compensation into their late 60s. Indeed, as discussed in chapter 4, a comfortable job change tends to keep people in the workforce longer than they had anticipated.

Developing second career opportunities, and making such careers a well-defined stage in the work span, should be high on the policy agenda. Success will require coordinated changes on the part of workers, employers, and government. Workers in their 50s must be realistic about their employment prospects and their need to work full time into their mid- to late 60s. They must be prepared to make investments to establish themselves in a second career. They must also realize that their take-home pay could decline as they age, as rising health insurance costs take bigger bites out of their compensation. And they must be prepared to "think young," keep their skills up to date, and be amenable to working for someone the age of their children.

Employers will need to decide whether they should help their employees enter a second career with a different employer. This has typically been the case in Japan, though Japanese employers have much closer connections with customers and suppliers, a primary source of second-career employment. Employers must also figure out what second careers they themselves could offer to the large number of workers that will need one. This will involve decisions about what they produce, how they manage, develop, and compensate employees, and how they might use experienced and technically trained second-career workers as independent contractors.

Government could also play a critical role in establishing second careers as a successful and a well-defined stage in the work span. A serious retraining and job-matching program could raise the market value of what workers could produce in a second career. Government could also dampen compensation escalation, say, by controlling the rise in health insurance costs or exempting employers from paying payroll tax for workers above a certain age. Government could also advise workers and employers on how to manage second-career opportunities, services especially important while this stage in the work span is being defined. Many of these initiatives do not require significant outlays and would likely increase government revenues if second careers allow workers to remain in the labor force longer.

Retirement Will Be Messy

Finally, the shift to 401(k) plans and the increased mobility of older workers also means that retirement is going to become a much messier process than it was in the past. With mandatory retirement, both parties knew that as of a certain age the relationship would end. Employers also used traditional defined benefit plans to structure an orderly departure. No such structure exists in a 401(k) environment. Employers face the prospect of workers with declining productivity and inadequate 401(k) balances hanging on much longer than desirable.

Employers will need new tools to manage an older workforce. Without such tools, employers will avoid older workers. The tools could take the form of carrots, such as a generous retirement package, or sticks, such as some form of mandatory retirement. Of course, the latter would be extremely controversial, but it is important to recognize that, in the absence of employer-defined benefit plans, the structure that eased employees into retirement no longer exists.

Notes

Chapter 1

1. Earnings are more than 80 percent of income for those ages 55–61 but only 10 percent for those 70–74. This dwindles to only 1 percent for those age 80 and older.

2. Under legislation enacted in 1983, the increase in the full retirement age began with those born in 1938 (turning 62 in 2000) and will be fully phased in for those born in 1960 (turning 62 in 2022).

3. The premium for Medicare part B is projected to increase from 9 percent of the average Social Security benefit in 2006 to 11 percent in 2030 (Centers for Medicare and Medicaid Services 2007).

4. For married couples (and most Americans retire as part of a married couple), Social Security already replaces a significantly smaller share of household earnings than it did as recently as 1990 and will replace even less going forward (Munnell, Sanzenbacher, and Soto 2007). The reason is the dramatic increase in labor force participation by married women. As married households have increasingly relied on the earnings of working wives, these earnings have not produced a comparable increase in Social Security benefits. This is because the program provides a guaranteed spousal benefit for the wife based on 50 percent of her husband's primary insurance amount, or the benefit to which he would be entitled at the full retirement age. The increased labor force participation by married women will increase the household's Social Security benefits only to the extent that benefits based on their earnings records exceed this spousal

minimum. The average Social Security replacement rate for two-earner couples in the Health and Retirement Study is thus 41 percent, compared with 58 percent for one-earner couples (Munnell and Soto 2005).

5. The pension coverage data discussed above apply only to individual workers at any given point in time. Over a lifetime, and on a household rather than an individual basis, coverage rates are somewhat higher. For households aged 55–64, the Survey of Consumer Finances (U.S. Federal Reserve Board) shows that approximately 66 percent had some sort of pension coverage in 2004.

6. The annuity might be a dollar amount per month for each year of service, say $50; so workers with twenty years of service would receive $1,000 per month at age 65. The benefit could also be a percentage of final salary for each year of service, say 1.5 percent; so workers with twenty years would receive 30 percent (twenty years at 1.5 percent) of final salary for as long as they live. The employer finances these benefits by making pretax contributions into a pension fund; holds the assets in trust; directs the investments; and bears the risk.

7. Generally the employee, and often the employer, contributes a specified percentage of earnings into the account. These contributions are invested, usually at the direction of the employee, mostly in mutual funds consisting of stocks and bonds. Upon termination of employment or retirement, the worker generally receives the balance as a lump sum, albeit with the option to roll it over to an individual retirement account (IRA).

8. U.S. Federal Reserve Board (1983–2004).

9. A critical factor explaining the lack of offsetting balances in 401(k)s is that the entire burden of retirement saving in employer plans has shifted from the employer to the employee, and employees make mistakes at every step along the way (Munnell and Sundén 2006). In 401(k) plans, workers must decide whether or not to join, how much to contribute, how to invest the assets, when to rebalance, what to do about company stock, whether to roll over accumulations when changing jobs, and how to withdraw the money at retirement. A quarter of those eligible to participate choose not to do so. Over half fail to diversify their investments. Many overinvest in company stock. Almost no participants rebalance their portfolios as they age or in response to market returns. Most important, participants may cash out when they change jobs, and very few annuitize at retirement.

10. Munnell, Golub-Sass, and Varani (2005).

11. Delorme, Munnell, and Webb (2006). Additionally, evidence from the Health and Retirement Study shows that total pension wealth has declined from 1992–2004 (Sorokina, Webb, and Muldoon 2008).

12. Kaiser Family Foundation (2006).

13. Scholz, Seshadri, and Khitatrakun (2006) suggest that Americans are adequately prepared for retirement. This study, however, arrives at this conclusion using data on the initial cohort in the Health and Retirement Study (HRS): those aged 51–61 in 1992. Using comparable measures of adequacy, a subsequent study (Munnell, Webb, and Golub-Sass 2007) shows a large decline in preparedness

between cohorts, with the initial cohort in the HRS well prepared for retirement but the baby boom and subsequent cohorts at significant risk.

14. Penner and Johnson (2006) estimate that rising health care costs and the taxes required to cover these costs will require a moderate-income couple to work an additional two and a half years under the high-cost scenario to receive as much income in the first year of retirement—net of taxes and out-of-pocket health spending—as they would receive under the low-cost scenario.

15. Butrica and others (2006) conclude that many people could increase their consumption by more than 25 percent at older ages simply by retiring at age 67 instead of age 62.

16. The target replacement rate in this example is 80 percent of after-tax income ($47,000). Assuming a tax rate of 25 percent, this target would be equivalent to 60 percent of gross income, the more common measure (Congressional Budget Office 2004). Say that at age 62 the couple gets $20,100 from Social Security, which provides 43 percent of the target amount. If the couple works to age 66, the benefits rise to $27,600 and provide 59 percent of the couple's target retirement income. If the couple works to age 70, the benefits rise to $38,100 and provide 81 percent of the couple's target retirement income. (The assets required are the amount the couple would need at retirement to purchase an annuity from the Federal Thrift Savings Plan to reach the target.)

17. For some workers it is possible to offset the increase in full retirement age in less than two years because of increases in the average indexed monthly earnings (AIME), the base by which Social Security benefits are calculated. Working an extra year increases the AIME if earnings during the year are greater than the lowest of the individual's highest thirty-five years of indexed earnings.

18. Munnell and others (2006a).

19. The expected real return is about 3 percent a year on riskless assets and about 4.6 percent a year on a balanced portfolio. A balanced portfolio, as defined here, is composed of 50 percent stocks, 30 percent corporate bonds, and 20 percent government bonds (Goss and Wade 2002).

20. Based on Vanguard (2007) real annuity prices on August 16, 2007, a married couple who postponed the purchase of a joint life and two-thirds survivor annuity from age 62 to age 63 would increase the annual income payable over the remainder of its lifetime by 2.6 percent. The average annual increase over the age range 62–70 is 3.0 percent.

21. Raising the EEA will improve the program's cash flow in the short term, since the government can delay payments for two years to all those who would have retired early. And while a higher EEA would have little long-term impact on the finances of Social Security, studies show that it would increase income tax revenues (Butrica, Smith, and Steuerle 2006).

Chapter 2

1. Bowen and Finnegan (1969, p. 62).

2. For a survey of the literature, see Currie and Madrian (1999). An update can be found in Deschryvere (2005).

3. Also, people are more likely to report a health problem if they have sought treatment. Since people with higher incomes and more education use more medical care, they may be more likely to report certain conditions.

4. Increasingly, studies are also looking at the extent to which work affects health. These studies generally find that work has positive effects on mental and physical health. The workplace appears as an important source of friends, confidants, and social support. Most of the early studies, however, identified relationships between work and health using data from a single point in time. These cross-sectional analyses cannot establish causal relationships, because people with better health may be more likely to remain at work. One study (Calvo 2006) controls for previous well-being by including the respondent's initial "health" status and then evaluates the extent to which work leads people to deviate from their own baselines, controlling for healthy behaviors and for demographic and socioeconomic factors. See Calvo (2006) and the citations therein for an up-to-date summary of the literature in this area.

5. Health alone may not be the sole determinant of whether someone is able to work. Nagi (1965, 1976, 1991) views disability as the interaction between the individual's disability and the demands presented by his or her social and physical environments. Consequently, as Jette and Badley (2000) lay out, varying levels of accommodation as well as an individual's own personality and characteristics can affect the likelihood of working with a disability. Burkhauser, Butler, and Gumus (2004) find that following the onset of a work-limiting condition, employer accommodation delays the time between onset and claiming Social Security Disability Insurance benefits.

6. The same pattern of differential mortality gains is even more evident in the probability of 55-year-olds' surviving to 65: very little change for men until 1965 and a surge thereafter and a much smaller increase for women, who in 1965 already had much better survival rates. The probability of surviving to age 65 increased for 55-year-old men from 80 percent in 1965 to 89 percent in 2005 and for 55-year-old women from 90 to 93 percent.

7. The reported life expectancies are averages for the country as a whole. One study divides the population into "eight Americas" and finds huge divergences (Murray and others, 2006). The gap in life expectancy at birth between the 3.4 million high-risk urban black males and the 5.5 million Asian females was 20.7 years in 2001. Within the sexes, the life expectancy gap between the best-off and worst-off groups was 15.4 years for males (Asians versus high-risk urban blacks) and 12.8 years for females (Asians versus low-income southern rural blacks). The disparities were caused primarily by chronic diseases and injuries. Between 1982 and 2001 the ordering and magnitude of the differences in life expectancies among the eight Americas remained largely unchanged.

8. Fuchs (1984). For a study of alternative measures of age, see Shoven (2007).

9. Cutler, Liebman, and Smyth (2006).

10. Fries (1983).

11. Manton (1982).

12. Gruenberg (1977).

13. The following discussion is based on the sequence presented in Cutler (2001).

14. Waidmann, Bound, and Schoenbaum (1995).

15. See Freedman and others (2004). The five surveys included the Health and Retirement Study (HRS), the Medicare Current Beneficiary Survey (MCBS), the National Health Interview Survey (NHIS), the National Long-Term Care Survey (NLTCS), and the Supplements on Aging (SOAs).

16. The sample consisted of 15,000 who were surveyed on previous surveys and 5,000 who passed age 65 since the previous survey (Manton and Gu 2001).

17. Manton, Gu, and Lamb (2006).

18. For an extensive discussion of this issue, see Fogel and Costa (1997).

19. Cutler (2001).

20. Fries and others (1996).

21. Cutler (2001).

22. Cutler (2001).

23. Cutler (2001) argues that the onset of conditions has not receded, while Fogel (2003) asserts that the average age of onset of chronic disease occurs more than a decade later.

24. For a review of the literature, see Cutler, Deaton, and Lleras-Muney (2006).

25. Costa (2005); Cutler (2001).

26. Cutler (2001).

27. Costa (2005).

28. Lakdawalla, Bhattacharya, and Goldman (2004).

29. Johnson (2004a); Steuerle, Spiro, and Johnson (1999).

30. Case and Deaton (2003).

31. Manton and Gu (2001).

32. The percentage of men and women ages 65 and older with a college degree increased from 9 percent in 1980 to 19 percent in 2006, and the share without a high school diploma dropped from 59 to 24 (U.S. Census Bureau and Bureau of Labor Statistics, Current Population Survey, 1980 and 2005).

33. Schoeni, Freedman, and Wallace (2001).

34. Smith (2004).

35. Goldman and Smith (2002) find that, in a randomized trial in which one group of diabetics was placed in a group with enforced treatment, the biggest beneficiaries of enforced treatment are those with the least education.

36. Insight from correspondence with Dora Costa.

37. Cutler and Meara (2001).

38. Costa (2005, p. 30).

39. Waidmann, Bound, and Schoenbaum (1995).

40. Waidmann, Bound, and Schoenbaum (1995). From the mid-1960s until the mid-1970s, Social Security Disability Insurance benefits rose, while eligibility requirements became less strict. Until the Social Security Administration and Congress started to tighten these requirements in 1976, the availability of disability insurance may have influenced workers' view of their health and ability to work.

41. Cutler, Liebman, and Smyth (2006) compare health status in the 1960s and 1970s with that of today and, as discussed below, find significant improvement. The study used two measures that are consistent over time: the share of people in the last two years of their life (a period when disability is high); and the share of people who report themselves in fair or poor health. The reported data, however, do not provide a clear indication of what happened during the 1970s.

42. The National Center for Health Statistics redesigned the NHIS questionnaire format in 1982 and again in 1997. The NHIS asks all adult respondents whether they are unable to perform their major activity because of health problems; are limited in their ability to perform their major activity; and are limited in any activity. Before 1982 men were asked these questions in regard to paid work, while women who identified their major activity as "keeping house" were asked about their ability to perform housework. Starting in 1982, the question asking respondents to identify their "major activity" changed to give men and women the same set of choices (working, keeping house, going to school, or something else). Additionally, regardless of what respondents identified as their major activity, all of those under age 70 were asked about their ability to work. Those who did not report their major activity as working were asked a set of follow-up questions from which a work limitation response could be constructed. In 1997 changes were made in the wording, structure, and context of questions, and the collection process changed from paper to laptop computers.

43. The NHIS also asks directly about certain impairments (such as deaf in both ears, blind in both eyes) of a subset of survey respondents. This design allows researchers to explore the people who have similar impairments but report no work limitations.

44. The incidence of health care problems as reported by the health care system, by contrast, increased over this period. This could be due to improvements in diagnosis as well as to a rise in health care problems. Even if the increase reflects an actual increase in underlying problems, the ability of the health care system to ameliorate, control, and eliminate such problems has improved. Trends in health status are thus better captured by changes in self-reported status (Cutler and Richardson 1997). Self-reported health status is also a more accurate predictor of labor supply decisions (Blau and Gilleskie 2001). We thank the anonymous reviewer for directing our attention to these publications.

45. See Burkhauser and others (2002) for an assessment of the limitations of the CPS for measuring the portion of the population with disabilities. In fact, both surveys may understate the percentage of the population with impairments, because having an impairment, even a serious one, does not necessarily mean the individual

will not work. For example, according to the 1996 NHIS, 31 percent of those blind in both eyes reported no work limitation, and 26 percent of those with cerebral palsy reported no work limitation. Therefore, both estimates exclude those sufficiently integrated into the workforce that they do not report a work limitation. For any given person, the likelihood of employment depends on the interaction of state of health, functional capacity, the nature of the work, and the possibilities for work accommodation (Chan, Tan, and Koh 2000).

46. Idler and Kasl (1991).

47. Following Cutler, Liebman, and Smyth (2006).

48. Banks and others (2006). The U.S. data came from the HRS and the U.K. data from the Longitudinal Study on Aging, which was designed to have directly comparable measures of health, income, and education. These surveys were supplemented by surveys that contain comparable biological disease markers for respondents, to determine whether any health differences could be attributed to differential propensities to report illness.

49. For example, among those aged 55–64, diabetes is twice as prevalent in the United States as in Great Britain; only one-fifth of this difference can be explained by risk factors.

50. Lakdawalla, Bhattacharya, and Goldman (2004).

51. People were classified as having a *disability* based on their answer to a question regarding personal care, which was asked of all respondents reporting an activity limitation. People were placed into one of the following three categories depending on their answers: unable to attend to personal care needs, limited in performing other routine tasks, and not limited in attending to personal care or performing routine tasks. The trends are the same regardless of the definition of disability adopted.

52. The authors acknowledge that the primary weakness of emphasizing obesity growth as the major source of the rising incidence of disability is its prevalence across all age groups, including the elderly, for whom disability rates have not increased.

53. Autor and Duggan (2006) argue that for low-wage workers Social Security Disability Insurance (SSDI) has become more attractive for two reasons. First, the benefits are indexed to the average wage index, which now exceeds real wage growth of low-wage workers. Second, administrative changes have made it easier to qualify for benefits when an individual has difficulty finding employment. Using data from the Survey of Income and Program Participation (SIPP), the study estimates that the rate of SSDI receipt among high school dropouts increased dramatically between 1984 and 2004.

Chapter 3

1. A 1570 census of the poor in Norwich, England, thus found three widows, ages 74, 79, and 82, "almost past work" but still earning a small income from spinning. Estates left by the elderly in colonial America often included tools used in less strenuous trades, such as tailoring, spinning, shoemaking, and weaving. Well into the nine-

teenth century about half of all 80-year-old men in America still worked (Thane 2000); (Sass 1997).

2. The census measured the gainful employment rate until 1940 and then the labor force participation rate, defined as the percentage of the population working or actively looking for work.

3. See Graebner (1980).

4. Costa (2000).

5. Life expectancy at age 20 for men in 1900 was forty-four years, compared to fifty-nine years in 2000 (U.S. Social Security Administration 2003). Also see Lee (2001) for the rapid rise in the expected length of retirement of workers entering the labor force between 1850 and 1990.

6. Costa (1998).

7. Costa (1998).

8. Moen (1987); Margo (1993); Sass (1997).

9. For a discussion of the rise of employer pensions and their role in the labor market, see Sass (1997); Gustman, Mitchell, and Steinmeier (1994).

10. Favorable tax provisions had a limited effect on coverage before the war, as less than 10 percent of the adult population typically paid tax. But the postwar growth of mass income taxation made pensions far less costly to employers and workers and encouraged their spread.

11. Stock and Wise (1990) demonstrate, using data from a large firm with a traditional defined benefit plan, that workers respond to the forward-looking "option value" of continued work. That is, they continue to work if the expected value of retirement wealth will be worth more if they retired tomorrow rather than if they retired today.

12. The change was made primarily to help younger widows and to allow wives, who were presumed to be two to three years younger than their husbands, to claim benefits at the same time as their husbands. Since it seemed unfair to require women workers to wait until a later age for benefits than women nonworkers, the EEA was introduced for all women (Congressional Budget Office 1999).

13. Gustman and Steinmeier (1986); Rust and Phelan (1997); Burtless and Quinn (2000); Coile and Gruber (2000). In addition, Blau (1998) concludes that the availability of Social Security benefits is very important to the retirement decision, while changes in Social Security benefits over time have been considerably less important. On the other hand, Gruber (2000) finds a sizable labor supply response to the level of disability benefits when comparing labor force participation in the Quebec system and in the rest of Canada, where benefits were increased. Butrica, Smith, and Steuerle (2006) point out that one effect of earlier retirements is a reduction in income tax revenues.

14. For example, suppose a person will live for twenty years and is entitled to a pension of $15,000 a year at age 65; lifetime benefits will equal $300,000 (20 x $15,000). To keep lifetime benefits constant, if that employee retired at 55 his annual benefit should be only $10,000 a year (30 x $10,000 = $300,000). But traditional

defined benefit plans typically provided far more because they used an actuarial reduction that was smaller than the full reduction. That is, they pay, say, $12,000 at age 55, which means that the worker in this example who retires at 55 would receive substantially more in lifetime pension benefits than if he were to retire at 65. The exercise is actually somewhat more complicated because the employee adds to his age-65 pension if he continues to work.

15. Often, working beyond the full retirement age results in negative pension accruals. The law requires that the wage increases of those who work beyond the full retirement age be reflected in higher retirement benefits. But it does not prevent firms from capping the years of service used to calculate benefits; nor does it require firms to provide actuarial adjustments for the fact that participants will receive benefits for fewer years (McGill and others 1996).

16. Hamermesh (2005) argues that early retirement may also result from the rigidities imposed by market work schedules. Using the American Time Use Survey, he finds that work is associated with fixed time costs that alter the mix of nonmarket activities, reducing leisure and increasing the time allocated to housework. Market work also raises the cost of switching among nonmarket activities and alters the time allocated to different nonmarket activities compared to that chosen in the absence of the market constraint. All these effects are more burdensome on low-income households, because high-income households can buy market substitutes.

17. For more details, see Purcell (2005).

18. Friedberg (2007); Burtless and Quinn (2002).

19. Under current law, individuals with less than $25,000 and married couples with less than $32,000 of combined income do not have to pay taxes on their Social Security benefits. (Combined income is adjusted gross income as reported on tax forms plus nontaxable interest income plus one-half of Social Security benefits.) Above those thresholds, recipients must pay taxes on either 50 percent or 85 percent of their benefits. Individuals must pay 50 percent if their combined income is between $25,000 and $34,000 and 85 percent if it is above $34,000. A couple must pay 50 percent if their combined income is between $32,000 and $44,000 and 85 percent if it is above $44,000 (U.S. House of Representatives, Committee on Ways and Means 2000).

20. Spouses are entitled to the greater of their own earned benefit or a benefit based on one-half of their spouse's primary insurance amount (the benefit payable at the full retirement age).

21. Munnell and Soto (2005).

22. Munnell, Sanzenbacher, and Soto (2007). Including the value of the survivor benefit, which is generally unchanged, Social Security's replacement of preretirement earnings would decline even more.

23. Benefits were cut about 1.1 percent a year until reaching a 6.7 percent reduction for the cohorts turning 62 between 2000 and 2005; the 1.1 percent annual cuts then resume with the cohort turning 62 in 2017 and reach the full 13.3 percent reduction for cohorts turning 62 in 2022 and after.

24. Before the introduction of early retirement, the earnings test was a tax in that benefits lost in one year did not produce a gain in benefits in later years. It also remained a tax for employment after the full retirement age, as the increase in benefits had not been actuarially fair. See Gustman and Steinmeier (1999, 2001) for the public's general ignorance of Social Security rules.

25. Friedberg (1998, 2000); Loughran and Haider (2005); Friedberg and Webb (2006); Gustman and Steinmeier (2007); Gruber and Orszag (2003).

26. Coile and Gruber (2000); Pingle (2006). Coile and Gruber (2000) note that in a context in which workers make their retirement decisions based on the full future stream of Social Security benefits, raising the delayed retirement credit could have a larger effect than raising the full retirement age. Changing the full retirement age has offsetting income and substitution (accrual) effects on labor supply, but a change in the delayed retirement credit has only positive incentives for work, at least until age 65. After age 65 the income effect of a higher delayed retirement credit discourages continued work, while the substitution effect rewards it. Before age 65 the study shows that raising the delayed retirement credit from 5 percent to 8 percent would increase labor force participation by age 65 by four percentage points.

27. Friedberg and Webb (2005); Munnell, Cahill, and Jivan (2003).

28. Another factor that could cause those with 401(k)s to work longer is exposure to market risk. In 2002, 21 percent of respondents in an AARP survey of 50- to 70-year-olds who had not yet retired reported that they had postponed their retirement as a result of stock market losses (AARP 2002a). Some researchers (Eschtruth and Gemus 2002; Cahill, Giandrea, and Quinn 2006) agree that those covered by defined contribution plans are sensitive to fluctuations in the stock market and that the collapse of the stock market might explain why the labor force participation rate for older workers (55–64) jumped two percentage points between early 2000 and 2002, an unprecedented increase during a recession, when labor force participation usually declines. This view is consistent with studies by Gustman and Steinmeier (2002b) and Coronado and Perozek (2003), who find that the unexpected positive shocks to wealth as a result of the stock market boom of the 1990s led to some additional retirement. Other researchers (Coile and Levine 2006) argue that few households had substantial stock holdings and that, if indeed workers were so sensitive to stock market fluctuations, participation should have dropped as the market recovered, which did not happen.

29. Clark and Schieber (2002).

30. In cash balance plans, as in traditional defined benefit plans, the employer makes the contributions, owns the assets, selects the investments, and bears the risk. The Pension Benefit Guaranty Corporation also insures the benefits. To the employee, however, cash balance plans look very much like defined contribution plans. The employer typically contributes 4–5 percent of the worker's pay to a "notional" account and provides an interest credit on the balances. Employees receive regular statements and generally withdraw the balance as a lump sum when they retire or terminate employment. Since these plans are not back loaded, employees

suffer no loss in benefits as they move from job to job, and therefore the plans would not be expected to affect mobility. Bank of America created the first cash balance plan in 1985, and by 2003 these plans accounted for 22 percent of employees and 26 percent of assets in defined benefit plans (Buessing and Soto 2006). Since 2003 extensive litigation has brought the expansion of cash balance plans to a virtual halt. The Pension Protection Act of 2006 clarified the legality of converting defined benefit plans to cash balance form and so might cause renewed interest in cash balance plans among employers.

31. Coronado and Copeland (2003) offer another perspective on the reasons for the shift to cash balance plans. They contend that these conversions occurred in competitive industries with tight labor markets and were done largely to improve compensation for a more mobile workforce.

32. Massachusetts Office of the Governor (2001).

33. The share of men ages 55–60 in a job that requires "lots of physical effort none or almost none of the time" increased from 31 percent to 39 percent between 1992 and 2002 (Johnson 2004a).

34. Blau (1998), using the Retirement History Survey, finds that 30–40 percent of husbands and wives leave the labor force within a year of each other. Hurd (1990), using the Social Security Administration's New Benefit Survey, estimates that a quarter of husbands and wives retire a year apart. Johnson and Favreault (2001), looking at married couples in the 1998 wave of the Health Retirement Study, calculates that 22–40 percent of spouses retire within two years of each other. These studies, which control for other factors that could influence such proximity in the timing of retirement, show that spouses tend to retire at the same time because they want to spend time together. Gustman and Steinmeier (2002a), using the HRS, find that a measure of how much each spouse values spending time in retirement with the other accounts for a good part of the decision to retire. Including this measure in simulations doubles the frequency of predicted joint retirements. See also Johnson (2004b). Sociologists appear to have identified the importance of joint decisionmaking early. Smith and Moen (2004) provide a summary of the literature and then explore how the process of decisionmaking affects outcomes in terms of satisfaction for each spouse separately and for the couple as a unit. Using data on 241 retired respondents from Cornell's Retirement and Well-Being Study, the authors find that if the husband perceives his wife as having influenced his retirement decision, both he and his wife are more likely to be satisfied with his retirement. In contrast, retired wives and husbands, both independently and jointly, are more likely to be satisfied when the wives perceive the husbands as *not* influential in their retirement decision.

35. Schirle (2007), using data from the U.S. March Current Population Survey, the Canadian Labour Force Survey, and the U.K. Labour Force Survey, finds that husbands treat the leisure time of their wives as complementary to their own leisure at older ages and that a large portion of the recent increases in older men's participation rates may be explained as a response to the recent increase in older women's participation rates.

36. Researchers find that the provision of both pre- and postretirement health care coverage by an employer significantly influences the retirement decision, with retiree coverage having a strong positive influence and preretirement coverage having a negative influence. Gustman and Steinmeier (1994); Karoly and Rogowski (1994); and Rust and Phelan (1997).

37. A study by Gustman and Steinmeier (2006) finds that Social Security changes increase the number of 65-year-old married men in the labor force by about two percentage points, with a somewhat smaller effect at older ages. Given the low labor force participation rates at these ages, the increases are not trivial.

38. Haider and Loughran (2001).

39. Indeed, Lahey, Kim, and Newman (2006) find that retirees who return to work are no less financially prepared than their counterparts who remain retired. Instead, the factors for returning to work are the availability of health insurance, whether the initial retirement was voluntary, and the degree of satisfaction with retirement. Maestas (2005), using the Health and Retirement Study, also concludes that financial pressures are not the reason for "unretirement."

40. Costa (1998) cautions researchers not to put too much emphasis on the recent uptick in labor force participation of older workers. As long as retirement remains an attractive option and incomes continue to rise, people will want to use at least some of their increased wealth for retirement. Even if income during people's working years continues to rise, however, the question is whether the prospective decline in retirement income provided by Social Security and employer plans will provide the impetus for continued work.

41. Mermin, Johnson, and Murphy (2006), using the Health and Retirement Study, report a significant increase between 1992 and 2004 in the expected probability among workers ages 51–56 of working full time past age 62 (47–51 percent) and past age 65 (27–33 percent). Controlling for other factors, self-employment, education, and earnings increase work expectations, while defined benefit pension coverage, employer-sponsored retiree health benefits, and household wealth reduce expectations.

42. Munnell and Sundén (2006). Data from the 2004 Survey of Consumer Finances show that the median value of combined 401(k) and IRA assets for all households is $35,000 (Bucks, Kennickell, and Moore, 2006).

43. Virtually every survey reports that baby boomers plan to work longer or work in retirement (AARP 1999, 2003; Towers Perrin 2003). But surveys also show that retirees were often forced to leave the workforce earlier than planned. Sun Life Financial's 2006 online survey on forced retirement reports that nearly a quarter of retirees are forced into retirement earlier than planned (Sun Life Financial 2006). Prudential Financial (2005) reports that 38 percent of current retirees claim they retired involuntarily. Flippen and Tienda (2000), using waves 1 and 2 from the Health and Retirement Study, find that older black, Hispanic, and female workers experience more involuntary job separation in the years before retirement, leading to extended periods of joblessness and eventual retirement.

44. The Current Population Survey has asked respondents about job tenure since 1973. Tenure supplements are available: 1973, 1978, 1981, 1983, 1987, 1991, 1996, 1998, 2000, 2002, and 2004. All data are from the Workplace Topics I (January–February) supplements, although the 1973 tenure data are from the displaced worker supplement. The question changed slightly over the period. In 1973, 1978, and 1981, the question refers to time working at the present job or business, while for 1983 and later the question refers to working "continuously" for the present employer. If respondents experience temporary separations, their responses would indicate less tenure in more recent surveys despite the same underlying behavior.

45. Neumark (2000); Gottschalk and Moffitt (1999).

46. Friedberg and Owyang (2004), using data from the Federal Reserve's Survey of Consumer Finances, also conclude that current and remaining job tenure fell over the period 1983–2001. They attribute some of the change to the movement from defined benefit to defined contribution plans. On the other hand, Stevens (2005) comes to the conclusion that nothing has changed. Using three data sets that follow people over an extended period of time, the author concludes that, despite some ups and downs, the average tenure of workers in the longest job in their careers remained virtually unchanged between 1969 and 2002 (21.9 and 21.4 years). Stevens, however, does not focus on older workers. That the average tenure in 1969 was 21.9 years could also be seen as indicating unusual stability, as 1969 is just twenty-four years after the end of the Second World War, which was disruptive of careers.

47. Allen, Clark, and McDermed (1988). Gustman and Steinmeier (1993) emphasize how small pension wealth is early in workers' careers and argue that the main impact of defined benefit pensions would be to deter mobility for long-tenured workers.

48. Specifically, for each survey it is possible to identify those working full time at ages 55, 60, and so on who are still with the same employer they worked for at age 50. Mechanically, this exercise involves simply asking, say, the 55-year-old full-time worker how long he has been with his current employer. If the response is five years or more, the worker is classified as working with his age-50 employer.

49. The table shows that the percentage not working in each educational group increased between 1983 and 2004, but also shows that the overall percentage not working remained unchanged at 36 percent. This is explained by the rapid increase in educational attainment, which resulted in a big decline in the proportion of older men with less than a high school diploma, who have very low rates of participation, and an increase in the proportion with a college diploma or more, who have high rates of participation.

50. Farber (2006) also notes an increase in churning among younger workers. That is, the proportion of workers in their 30s with less than one year of tenure has increased, suggesting a reduced tendency for younger cohorts to settle into career positions.

51. Abraham and Houseman (2007) claim that part of the problem is that many older workers do not know how to go about looking for a new job. They also used

waves 1–7 of the Health and Retirement Study to measure the extent to which people who planned to change their hours or jobs were able to follow through. After four years, 80 percent of those who said they planned to retire were out of the workforce. Those who said they planned to never stop working were working. But only half of those planning to reduce their hours and just a third of those planning to change their jobs had followed through. Those who failed to realize their plans were twice as likely to stop work altogether as to continue working. Individuals with low education had the most difficulty making the transitions. In addition, Chan and Stevens (2001), using the Health and Retirement Study, find that displacement had an extremely negative effect on the probability of older workers' getting another job.

52. The survey asks workers whether they lost their jobs for one of the following reasons: their plant or company closed down or moved, their company had insufficient work, their position or shift was abolished, a seasonal job was completed, a self-operated business failed, and other reason. These data do not include all layoffs because the survey collects and reports information only on layoffs where the job itself is eliminated and only records one job loss for each individual. Nevertheless, this survey can be used to determine whether older workers are becoming more or less vulnerable to displacement.

53. Farber (2005), using the Displaced Worker Surveys, shows that the probability of displacement declines with age when men and women are measured together. Boisjoly, Duncan, and Smeeding (1998), using the Panel Study of Income Dynamics, find that the likelihood of involuntary joblessness for men with the same level of education is higher among younger men than among those over 50. Rodriguez and Zavodny (2000, 2003), using 1984–98 Displaced Worker Surveys, show that the probability of displacement decreases with age.

54. Becker (1975).

55. Johnson and Kawachi (2007).

56. For detailed Bureau of Labor Statistics projections of labor force growth in the shorter run, see Toossi (2004).

57. Welch (1979). A study by Freeman (1979) reaches similar conclusions.

58. Triest, Sapozhnikov, and Sass (2006).

59. Health insurance, which is especially costly for older workers, has clearly become an important factor attaching such workers to the labor force until age 65, when they become eligible for Medicare. To the extent that the decline in career employment reduces access to employer-provided health insurance, it reduces a major inducement to remain in the labor force.

60. U.S. Government Accountability Office (2001).

61. Montgomery (1988).

62. Tilly (1991).

63. Hutchens (2001).

64. Gustman and Steinmeier (2007).

65. The average retirement age is defined as the age at which 50 percent of the cohort is out of the labor force.

66. The increase began with individuals born in 1938, for whom the full retirement age is 65 plus two months, and increases two months a year until it reaches age 66. After a twelve-year hiatus, the full retirement age again increases by two months a year for workers born in 1955 until it reaches age 67 for individuals born in 1960 or later.

67. More specifically, benefits are reduced by 5/9ths of 1 percent for each month they are received before the full retirement age, up to thirty-six months, and 5/12ths of 1 percent for each month thereafter. This is equivalent to a 6.67 percent reduction for the first three years before full retirement age and 5 percent thereafter. With a full retirement age of 65, a person who claimed benefits at age 62 received monthly benefits 20 percent lower than the full amount. Raising the full retirement age, however, will increase the actuarial reduction for claiming benefits at age 62 from 20 percent to 30 percent.

68. Studies showing the availability of benefits as the major effect on retirement include Blau (1998), Burtless and Moffitt (1984), Hurd (1990), and Gruber and Wise (1998). In a study of twelve countries, Gruber and Wise (2002) conclude that, averaging across countries, a three-year delay in benefit eligibility would likely reduce the retirement of men ages 56–65 by 23–36 percent (closer to 36 percent in the long run).

69. Munnell, Sass, and Aubry (2006).

70. Munnell, Sass, and Aubry (2006); Burtless (1986); Costa (1998); Diamond and Gruber (1997); Friedberg and Webb (2005); Krueger and Pischke (1992); Samwick (1998).

71. U.S. Census Bureau and Bureau of Labor Statistics, Current Population Survey (1962–2006); U.S. Bureau of Labor Statistics (2007b).

72. For projections of the labor force participation for older men that are lower than those produced by the Bureau of Labor Statistics, see Fallick and Pingle (2007) and U.S. Social Security Administration (2006b).

Chapter 4

1. Goldin (2006).

2. The Second World War is widely seen as a major turning point in the history of women's employment. However, Goldin (1991) finds the war to have had a much more modest effect. Using two retrospective surveys, she shows that the majority of female wartime entrants had exited the labor force by 1950. While the war had a significant effect on women's employment during the 1940s, its lasting effect appears much more limited.

3. One question is whether women's increased labor force participation is a response to the disappointing earnings growth of their husbands. Juhn and Murphy (1997), using the March Current Population Survey and the 1960 census, looked at earnings and employment changes for couples at different points in the earnings distribution and find that, while low-wage men suffered the greatest declines in earnings

and employment, the wives of middle- and high-wage men made the greatest employment and earnings gains. This finding is consistent with Cancian, Danziger, and Gottschalk (1993), who report that the rising correlation of wives' and husbands' earnings contributed significantly toward rising inequality in family incomes. Devereux (2004) also concludes that assortative mating led to increased inequality but argues that the increase would have been greater had not wives of low-wage workers responded to the slow growth in their husbands' earnings with an increase in their labor supply.

4. Goldin and Katz (2002) present both descriptive time-series and cross-state and cross-cohort econometric evidence that shows, for young unmarried women, the pill lowered the costs of long-duration professional education and raised the age at first marriage.

5. Blau and Kahn (2005), using March Current Population Survey data, examine married women's labor supply from 1980 to 2000 and find that the labor supply curve for married women shifted sharply to the right in the 1980s, with an additional small shift in the 1990s. A further additional factor affecting their labor supply was the decline in their husbands' real wages in the 1980s. Even more significant, over the 1980–2000 period women's own wage elasticity declined 50–56 percent, while the elasticity with respect to their husbands' wage fell 38–47 percent.

6. Goldin (1990) claims that this phenomenon reflects the increasing divorce rates and career orientation of women.

7. The poverty threshold for a single-person household is $10,839 a year in current 2007 dollars; the near-poverty threshold (150 percent of the poverty threshold) is $16,259 a year (U.S. Census Bureau 2007b).

8. Women and men in part-time jobs were paid roughly $14 an hour, while women working full time earned about $15 an hour and men more than $17 an hour (U.S. Census Bureau and Bureau of Labor Statistics, Current Population Survey, 2005). Part-time workers also receive less in pension and health benefits; while 73 percent of standard full-time workers have health insurance through their employer, only 17 percent of standard part-time workers do (U.S. Government Accountability Office 2000).

9. The reduction in the gender gap since 1980 occurred as women increasingly entered traditionally male occupations. Predominantly female occupations pay less than male occupations, even after controlling for the characteristics of the workers and the jobs. Over the same period, women also invested in education, increased their commitment to the labor force, and improved their job skills. Nevertheless, experts suggest that the pay gap is unlikely to vanish completely. Women continue to confront discrimination in the labor market. Similarly, they also retain primary responsibility for housework and child care, which reduces their labor force attachment. The narrowing of the gender gap has been primarily associated with new cohorts of young women, each doing better than the one before. But the high wage ratios of younger women tend to decline as they age, reflecting both the tendency of women to drop out of the labor market for family reasons and also possible barriers

to advancement in the workplace. For a more complete discussion of these issues, see Blau and Kahn (2000, 2004).

10. U.S. Social Security Administration (2004).

11. U.S. Social Security Administration (2007b).

12. These data are for cohort life expectancy as of 2006. Cohort life expectancy reflects mortality improvements expected in the future (U.S. Social Security Administration 2007a).

13. McGarry and Schoeni (2005)

14. Munnell and Soto (2007). Married women are entitled to three types of benefit: a benefit based on their own earnings record; a spouse's benefit equal to 50 percent of their husband's primary insurance amount (the benefit unreduced for early retirement) if that exceeds their own benefit, while their spouse is alive; and a survivor's benefit should their husband die, equal to 100 percent of their husband's actual benefit, if that exceeds their own benefit. In the case of a married woman who earned less than her husband, two factors are important for the claiming decision. First, the survivor benefit is solely determined by her husband's earnings history, and the actuarial reductions or increases reflect his early or delayed claiming. That is, from her perspective, the survivor's benefit is a fixed amount to be received after her husband's death. To maximize that fixed annual amount, a woman would like her husband to delay claiming. If the couple is trying to maximize the benefits it receives, delay by the husband is also usually the better choice. Ironically, in deciding when the husband should claim, it is the wife's life expectancy, rather than the husband's, that should be considered, as that determines how long the benefit is expected to be in force. Second, the decision over which the wife has control is when to claim the benefits she receives until the death of her husband. In deciding when the wife should claim, it is the husband's shorter life expectancy that should be considered, as that determines how long this benefit is expected to be in force (to be replaced upon the husband's death with the survivor benefit). Because the couple can expect to receive these benefits for a period shorter than the life expectancy of the average person, the wife has an incentive to claim as soon as possible.

15. U.S. Internal Revenue Service (2007).

16. Munnell and Zhivan (2006).

17. While the preceding discussion focuses on the personal income tax, McCarty (1990), using the Retirement History Survey, finds that a high net payroll tax is a labor supply disincentive for many married women, particularly those near retirement age. Most women have taxable earning below the maximum and therefore face the payroll tax rate at the margin. Also, the net rate is often high for women because, as discussed below, many receive benefits as spouses and widows rather than on the basis of their own earnings, so their payroll tax payment does not enhance their future benefits.

18. According to the 2006 Current Population Survey, just over 50 percent of full-time women and men ages 25–64 are covered by an employer-sponsored plan.

19. Munnell and Sass (2005); for a detailed analysis of annuity pricing by gender, see Campbell and Munnell (2002).

20. Under current law, calculating initial benefits involves four steps. First, a worker's previous earnings are restated in terms of today's wages by indexing past earnings to wage growth. Second, earnings for the highest thirty-five years are then averaged and divided by twelve to calculate average indexed monthly earnings. Third, the Social Security benefit formula is applied to the average indexed monthly earnings to yield the primary insurance amount, the benefit payable at the full retirement age. Finally, benefits are adjusted to produce permanently lower benefits for those who claim before the full retirement age and higher benefits for those who delay retirement.

21. U.S. Social Security Administration (2007b). The fact that a greater proportion of women than men claim benefits early might seem surprising, since women are expected to live longer than men. In fact, fewer single women than men do claim benefits early, so the seeming anomaly rests with married women. Ironically, in maximizing the value of her benefits, the relevant planning period for the wife is the time until her husband dies and she becomes eligible for a widow's benefit. That is, her life expectancy becomes irrelevant, and the relevant life expectancy is that of her husband. In this way, her choice mirrors that facing a single man. Because these benefits are expected to be received for a period shorter than the life expectancy of the average person, she has an incentive to claim as soon as possible. And this pattern is evident in the data (Munnell and Soto 2007).

22. Szinovacz, DeViney, and Davey (2001), using data from the first two waves of the National Survey of Families and Households, find that individuals who made financial contributions to children outside the household and white women with resident children are less likely to retire. Among African Americans, household effects are more complex.

23. Metropolitan Life Insurance Company (1999).

24. Blau (1998), using the Retirement History Survey, finds that for 30–40 percent of married couples, the spouses left the labor force within a year of each other. Hurd (1990), using the Social Security Administration's New Benefit Survey, estimates that, for a fourth of couples, husbands and wives retired within one year of each other. Johnson (2004b), using Health and Retirement Study data from 1992–2002, finds that 19 percent of married couples retired in the same year as each other. Johnson and Favreault (2001), looking at married couples in the 1998 wave of the Health and Retirement Study, calculate that 22–40 percent of husbands and wives retired within two years of each other.

25. Models estimated by Gustman and Steinmeier (2000) and Hurd (1990) support the hypothesis that husbands and wives view their own leisure and that of their spouse as complementary. Coile (2003), using the Health and Retirement Study, finds that people respond not only to the financial incentives of their own Social Security and employer-provided benefits but also to spillover effects from their spouse's incentives. Coile interprets these results as an indication that spouses are eager to coordinate their retirements.

26. Johnson and Favreault (2001).

27. National Center for Health Statistics, *Current Estimates* (1981, 2005).

28. Divorce after a ten-year marriage entitles the unmarried person to Social Security spouse benefits of a living insured worker who is age eligible and survivor benefits of a deceased insured worker.

29. Interestingly, Gray (1998) argues that the reassignment of property rights brought about by major changes in divorce laws led to an increase in labor supply by those who were favored by such changes and a decrease in labor supply by those who were disadvantaged. That is, the increase in property rights enhanced the wife's bargaining position within the marriage, and she chose to use some of this increased power to work more. This finding contradicts the more intuitive results by Peters (1986) and Parkman (1992), who conclude that residence in a unilateral divorce state has a positive effect on married women's labor force participation. Gray argues that states with high rates of female labor force participation may be the ones most likely to adopt unilateral divorce laws, so cross-sectional analysis might show a positive relationship even if behavior did not change after enactment of such laws. Gray uses two years of data, one before and one after enactment, to eliminate the possible bias.

30. The Health and Retirement Study is conducted by the Institute for Social Research at the University of Michigan and is made possible by funding from the National Institute on Aging. More information is available at the ISR website (http://hrsonline.isr.umich.edu/). See Juster and Suzman (1995) for a detailed overview of the survey.

31. In addition, the Health and Retirement Study includes data on children of the Depression (1923–30) and on those born before 1923.

32. The following analysis is based on Munnell, Cahill, and Jivan (2003). It differs primarily in the definition of pension coverage. In this study, pension coverage pertains to the individual rather than the household and to the current job only.

33. The results for demographic characteristics are consistent with expectations. Being in fair or poor health dramatically lowers the likelihood of employment for both nonmarried and married women. Similarly, for both nonmarried and married women, having been divorced raises the likelihood of working by 4–7 percent. Age has a slight negative effect, and being nonwhite has a slight positive effect on the probability of married women's being employed.

34. Although individuals with a stronger taste for work may accumulate more financial assets, we do not control for it. Despite that, in our analysis financial wealth has a negative effect on the probability of being employed and is statistically significant. Controlling for taste would make the effect of financial wealth more negative.

35. Total financial wealth is equal to the value of assets in stocks, bonds, checking accounts, certificates of deposit, IRAs, and any other account, minus household debt. All wealth variables are measured in $100,000 increments.

36. Having been divorced and faced with the responsibility of supporting oneself increases the likelihood of working for both single and married women.

37. Whenever possible, both respondents' retirement expectations and independent variables are defined as of 1992. For a few individuals, information on expected retirement age was taken from later waves, and some information on expected Social Security benefits was taken from later waves to avoid significantly reducing the sample size. Limiting the sample to those who are currently employed reduces the number of observations from 12,650 to 8,370. Missing information—primarily for benefits under defined benefit plans, defined contribution plans, Social Security, and expected retirement age—further reduces the sample to 4,955. Another 652 respondents were missing pension wealth information for their previous jobs. The equation was estimated both with and without these individuals, and the results are virtually identical. Since their inclusion did not change the results, we kept them in the sample.

38. The other demographic variables play the predicted role. Fair or poor health leads to earlier expected retirement ages. Being nonwhite also reduces the expected retirement age (by one or two years). For previously divorced married women, the divorce variable is insignificant.

39. A number of variables are included to measure women's attachment to the labor force: part-time work, hours worked, or having a physically demanding job. None of these variables affect women's expected retirement age. Even self-employment has no effect on expected retirement age for women, which is quite surprising because the flexibility associated with this form of employment increases the expected retirement age for men significantly.

40. Employee Benefit Research Institute (1992–2007).

41. Explanatory variables include those from the original 1992 regression of expected retirement age and new "shock" variables. The original variables are age, health, college, self-employment status, retiree health insurance, and indicators for defined benefit and defined contribution coverage. The shock variables— deterioration in health status, deterioration in spouse's health status, change in total financial wealth, retirement of spouse, switching jobs, and onset of caring for parents—are likely reasons that people might change their retirement plans.

42. The results show that, of the initial variables, only two are important: age and fair or poor health. The older the women the less likely they are to revise their retirement plans and retire early. That result seems reasonable in that the closer women are to actual retirement the more accurately they can plan. In contrast, women who initially say that their health is fair or poor have a greater likelihood of retiring earlier than they said they would. It seems likely that women with health problems underestimate the extent to which these problems will affect their ability to work. Having a college education, being self-employed, and having retiree health insurance do not have a statistically significant effect when it comes to retiring earlier than planned.

43. Deterioration reflects a decline in the respondent's assessment from excellent, very good, or good to fair or poor or from fair to poor.

Chapter 5

1. Shephard (2000, p. 535).
2. Shephard (1999, p. 331).
3. Munnell, Sass, and Soto (2006).
4. Of the employers that responded to the question, 22 percent said physical health and stamina had a negative impact on the productivity of older white-collar workers and 34 percent said it had a negative impact on the productivity of older rank-and-file workers; but no employer said the effect was "very negative" (as opposed to "somewhat negative") for white-collar workers, and only 2 percent said the effect was "very negative" for rank-and-file workers. Data were collected for the Munnell, Sass, and Soto (2006) survey and are available upon request from the authors.
5. Judge and others (1994).
6. Surveys that report positive employer evaluations of the emotional capabilities of older workers include Kreps (1977); Barth, McNaught, and Rizzi (1993); AARP (2000); Marshall (2001); McGregor and Gray (2002); Guest and Shacklock (2005); Henkens (2005); and Munnell, Sass, and Soto (2006).
7. Verhaegen and Salthouse (1997).
8. Earles and others (1997); Anstey and others (2005).
9. Avolio and Waldman (1994); Park, Nisbett, and Hedden (1999); Maitland and others (2000); Deary and others (2000).
10. Warr (1994); Wilson and others (2002); Anstey and others (2005).
11. Surveys that report negative employer evaluations of the flexibility or learning ability of older workers include Kreps (1977); Rosen and Jerdee (1977); Barth, McNaught, and Rizzi (1993); Taylor and Walker (1998); AARP (2000); Marshall (2001); McGregor and Gray (2002); Henkens (2005); and Munnell, Sass, and Soto (2006).
12. Schwartzman and others (1987); Blum, Jarvik, and Clark (1970).
13. Colonia-Willner (1998).
14. Rybash, Hoyer, and Roodin (1986).
15. AARP (2005); Munnell, Sass, and Soto (2006).
16. Ahituv and Zeira (2005); Beckmann (2005); and Reinhard Hujer and Dubravko Radić, "Age and Skill Biased Technological Change: A Multiple Treatment Approach Using a Linked Employer-Employee Dataset, 2005" (http://doku.iab.de/veranstaltungen/2006/cafe_2006_k1_radic.pdf). Beckmann (2005) and Hujer and Radić find that organizational change, as well as technical change, leads to earlier exits by older workers. Aubert, Caroli, and Roger (2004) also find that older workers have lower "experience" premiums in organizationally and technically dynamic firms. These patterns, however, might not reflect a decline in the ability to learn and adapt, which is more important in such industries and organizations. Firm-specific human capital and seniority protections, which benefit older workers and provide protection against layoffs and dismissals, are less important in such industries and organizations.

That the lack of such advantages, rather than the decline in mental alacrity as workers age, might explain these relatively early retirements and relatively low experience premiums is suggested by the finding that older workers are not more likely to be dismissed than younger workers in high-tech industries. Aaronson and Housinger (1999).

17. Bartel and Sicherman (1993); Allen and de Grip (2005).

18. Workers in high-tech industries tend to be well educated and work in an intellectually stimulating environment. So even if they retain sufficient flexibility and learning ability to absorb what is taught in on-the-job training, older workers in general might not. One employer survey, however, finds essentially no difference in evaluations of older white-collar and rank-and-file workers in terms of their flexibility and ability to learn. Munnell, Sass, and Soto (2006).

19. Abramovitz and David (2000).

20. Goldin (1998).

21. The educational attainment of workers entering the labor force was taken from 2006 Current Population Survey data for workers aged 25–34.

22. Triest, Sapozhnikov, and Sass (2006).

23. Neuman and Weiss (1995).

24. Triest, Sapozhnikov, and Sass (2006).

25. A study of occupations with a disproportionate share of older workers finds that many, such as farmers, tool and die makers, and clerical and rail workers, are employed in occupations projected to decline (Dohm 2000).

26. Rather than using wages as a measure of productivity, researchers primarily focus on measuring and explaining the extent to which wages deviate from productivity as workers age.

27. Boot (1995).

28. U.S. Bureau of Labor Statistics (1957); Mark (1957); Kutscher and Walker (1960); Walker (1964). Also see U.S. Bureau of Labor Statistics (1956, 1960).

29. Waldman and Avolio (1986); McEvoy and Cascio (1989).

30. Hægeland and Klette (1999); Haltiwanger, Lane, and Speltzer, (1999); Ilmakunnas, Maliranta, and Vainiomäke (1999); Andersson, Holmlund, and Lindh (2002); Crépon, Deniau, and Pérez-Duarte (2002). Hellerstein and Neumark (1995) and Hellerstein, Neumark, and Troske (1999) do not find a downturn in productivity as workers age. See Skirbekk (2003) for a discussion of these studies.

31. Kotlikoff and Gokhale (1992).

32. The study developed age-productivity profiles for five types of workers: male and female office workers, male and female sales people, and male managers (as managers were mainly men).

33. Frazis and others (1998).

34. Keese (2006).

35. A large literature explores the extent and rationale of sticky wages in the U.S. economy. Campbell and Kamlani (1997), Groshen and Schweitzer (1996), Kahn

(1997), Jacoby and Mitchell (1990), and Altonji and Devereaux (1999) provide useful introductions.

36. Figure 5-3 understates the growth of earnings for individual workers as tenure rises, since the workers with less tenure in the figure are also younger, and younger cohorts can be expected to earn higher wages than their elders at any given level of tenure. The earnings of workers with thirty-five years of tenure (not shown) actually decline. This could reflect higher-wage workers' either retiring relatively early or cutting back their hours. As most workers retire before reaching thirty-five years of tenure, the lower average wages for the relatively few workers with that amount of tenure cannot be interpreted as a downturn in the return to tenure. In most organizations, workers in younger cohorts will generally earn higher wages at any given combination of age and tenure. In the Towers Perrin (2005) sample of Fortune 1000 firms, earnings are actually greatest for workers age 55. Wage growth slows but generally does not turn down at the end of a worker's career. So workers who are 55 today will earn more when 60 and 65 but less than workers who are 55 when they are 60 and 65. Houthakker (1959).

37. Graebner (1980); Sass (1997); also see Lazear (1979).

38. Lazear (1979); Hutchens (1986); Kotlikoff and Gokhale (1992); and Hu (2003). Consistent with the career employment model, most employers adopted an actuarial costing method (entry age normal) that spread the cost of a defined benefit pension across the worker's entire career (Sass 1997).

39. Ippolito (1990).

40. Munnell and Sundén (2004). Employers with about 25 percent of total defined benefit participants have converted their plans to a cash balance format (Pension Benefit Guaranty Corporation 2004) in which the value of benefits is also unaffected by age. The annual benefit in a cash balance plan is an employer contribution of a fixed percentage of earnings to an individual account, with all workers included in the plan. For discussions of the factors underlying the shift to 401(k)s and cash balance plans, also see Aaronson and Coronado (2005), Coronado and Copeland (2003), Friedberg and Owyang (2004), Sass (1997), and Schieber (2007).

41. While not all low-wage workers are covered by an employer-provided health insurance plan, many are. Among full-time, full-year workers in their 40s, more than 40 percent of those who earn less than $25,000 a year and more than two-thirds of those who earn between $25,000 and $45,000 a year are covered by a plan. (Among full-time, full-year workers in their 40s, less than 10 percent earn less than $25,000 a year and 25 percent earn between $25,000 and $40,000 a year.) Authors' calculations from U.S. Census Bureau and Bureau of Labor Statistics, Current Population Survey (2006).

42. Scott, Berger, and Garen (1995) report the results of a 1991 survey of employers, finding that both the presence and generosity of employer-provided health insurance significantly reduce the likelihood that the employer will hire 55–64-year-old workers. The researchers corroborate these results using data from the Current Population Survey Employee Benefit Supplements. As health insurance costs increased

from 6.1 percent of worker compensation in 1991 to 7.7 percent in 2006, these costs likely represents an even greater impediment to the employment of older workers today. Also see Lahey (2007).

43. Hægeland and Klette (1999); Haltiwanger, Lane, and Speltzer (1999); Ilmakunnas, Maliranta, and Vainiomäki (1999); Kotlikoff and Gokhale (1992); Andersson, Holmlund, and Lindh (2002); Crépon, Deniau, and Pérez-Duarte (2002). Hellerstein and Neumark (1995) and Hellerstein, Neumark, and Troske (1999), who do not find productivity turning down as workers age, do not find compensation exceeding productivity as workers age.

44. Lee (2005).

45. Von Wachter (2007).

46. Munnell, Sass, and Soto (2006). These results are broadly consistent with other survey results, such as those cited in note 11.

47. Munnell and others (2006b). See U.S. Census Bureau and Bureau of Labor Statistics, Displaced Workers Survey.

48. Munnell, Sass, and Aubry (2006); Eschtruth, Sass, and Aubry (2007).

49. Aaronson and Sullivan (1998). See chapter 3 for a discussion of this issue.

50. Johnson and Kawachi (2007).

51. U.S. Department of Labor (1965).

52. Hutchens (1988, 1993).

53. Hirsch, Macpherson, and Hardy (2000).

54. Eran Yashiv, "Evaluating the Performance of the Search and Matching Model," 2004 (www.tau.ac.il/˜yashiv/yashiv_aug8pdf).

55. Towers Perrin (2005).

56. Munnell, Sass, and Soto (2006).

57. AARP (2002b).

58. Bendick, Jackson, and Romero (1996); Lahey (2005).

59. Marshall (2001); Metcalf and Meadows (2006).

60. Munnell, Sass, and Soto (2006); Rosen and Jerdee (1977); Lyon and Pollard (1997). Also see McGregor and Gray (2002); House of Lords (2003); Smith and Harrington (1994).

61. Triest, Sapozhnikov, and Sass (2006).

62. Murphy and Zábonjík (2007).

63. See Benitez-Silva (2002) for a discussion of search costs from the worker's perspective.

64. Chan and Stevens (2001).

65. The limited data available from the Current Population Survey do not indicate a significant difference by educational attainment in this 75 percent figure for the switchers' reemployment wage.

66. Johnson and Kawachi (2007).

67. Judy and D'Amico (1997); Committee for Economic Development (1999); Nyce and Schieber (2002); Robson (2001); U.S. Government Accountability Office (2001, 2004); Towers Perrin (2005); Ernst and Young (2006).

68. A labor shortage is a shortage at current wage rates. In a market economy such shortages tend to dissipate through an increase in wages or through the use of second-choice options, such as older workers.

69. Bosworth, Bryant, and Burtless (2004).

70. The discussion in the remainder of this section largely follows the analysis in Freeman (2006). Also see Cappelli (2003).

71. Dohm (2000).

72. Dohm (2000). Private sector industries facing labor shortages due to retirements include aerospace and defense, utilities, and oil and gas. Shortages are also projected in health care, especially for nurses, who already are in short supply. Rappaport and Stevenson (2004); Ernst and Young (2006).

73. On a scale from 1 to 10, employers with half of their workforce age 50 or over were only 0.3 points more likely to create such opportunities than employers with 10 percent of their workers age 50 or over. By contrast, employers expecting "significant" employment growth were 0.9 points more likely to create opportunities than employers expecting "not much change" in employment levels. Eschtruth, Sass, and Aubry (2007).

74. Employers characterizing the effect on the knowledge base as "highly positive" are 0.6 points more likely, on a scale from 1 to 10, to create opportunities for half of those who wanted to stay than employers characterizing the effect as "neutral." Eschtruth, Sass, and Aubry (2007).

Chapter 6

1. Mosisa and Hipple (2006).

2. Mosisa and Hipple (2006).

3. For projections of labor force participation rates, see Toossi (2005), U.S. Social Security Administration (2007b), Fallick and Pingle (2007), and Munnell and Sass (2007).

4. The discrepancies were greatest in the following areas: willingness to be flexible about doing varying tasks, willingness to participate in training and retraining programs, willingness to try new approaches to problems, willingness to learn and use new technology, and understanding of new technology (AARP 2005).

5. Johnson and Kawachi (2007).

6. Abraham and Houseman (2007).

7. A study based on pre- and postretirement interviews with nearly a hundred middle-income individuals finds that frustrations on the job are often the proximate cause of retirement, frustrations that elicit a different response when workers are middle-aged (Weiss 2005).

8. For example, see Employee Benefit Research Institute (1992–2007).

9. Munnell, Sass, and Aubry (2006).

10. While the study finds that employers are generally lukewarm about retaining older workers past their traditional retirement age, those that place a high value on

the contribution such workers could make to the organization's knowledge base and those that face staffing shortages (though due more to expected employment growth than to a surge of retirements) are more likely to create opportunities for such workers (Eschtruth, Sass, and Aubry 2007).

11. For introductions to the large literature on the management of educated workers, see Mintzberg (1998), Drucker (1999), and Davenport (2005).

12. Researchers reporting a low level of employer action in addressing the aging of the workforce include Robson (2001), U.S. Government Accountability Office (2001), Collison (2005), Morton and others (2005), and Ernst and Young (2006).

13. Ernst and Young (2006, p. 8).

14. Blinder (2006) makes the argument that the types of jobs likely to be outsourced to emerging economies are those that can easily be delivered or performed electronically. This shift may affect both low- and high-skilled workers, as more types of work can be performed in this manner.

15. Hutchens (1993); Blank (1998); Nollen, Eddy, and Martin (1977); Friedberg (2004).

16. Rappaport and Stevenson (2004).

17. Committee for Economic Development (1999).

18. An additional factor raising the cost of recruiting older workers is that older workers tend to be less aggressive in searching for a good match than someone younger, as they have less expected time in the labor market to recoup their investment of time and money (Benítez-Silva 2006).

19. Han and Moen (1999); Kohli and Rein (1991); Guillemard and van Gunsteren (1991).

20. AARP (2004).

21. Hutchens (2003).

22. Brown and Schieber (2003).

23. Rebick (1994); Casey (2004).

24. IBM, "Why Transition to Teaching?" 2007 (www-01.ibm.com/ibm/transitiontoteaching/why/index.html).

25. Pension Protection Act (PPA) of 2006 (section 905). Before the enactment of the PPA, defined benefit pension plans could not make in-service payments to covered employees before the plan's designated normal retirement age (Hutchens 2003).

26. Passing much of the cost of health insurance on to employees in a cafeteria arrangement with a pro rata employer contribution would seem to be the most promising approach. Addressing the problem by adjusting wages would likely be more difficult. As the correct adjustment would depend on the particular worker's age, wage, and reduction in hours, it appears difficult to develop a uniform policy for all.

27. One proposal would allow workers aged 65 and over to opt out of the program (Burkhauser and Quinn 1997); another would allow workers to opt out of the program once they reach the earliest age of eligibility for benefits, age 62 (Munnell 2006); another would declare workers paid up after forty years of contributions (Goda and others 2006).

28. Earnings before age 60 are indexed to the present by the growth of national average earnings to age 60 and by the consumer price index after age 62.

29. Continued employment will raise a worker's PIA only if his or her earnings are greater than the indexed earnings in some past year.

30. Laitner and Silverman (2006). Economists generally hold that the burden of paying the payroll tax falls primarily on workers by reducing their wages by the amount the employer pays. However, employment decisions, not just wage rates, could be influenced by the payroll tax that employers must or must not pay. Exempting employers from paying payroll tax would clearly make older workers more attractive. In some instances this would result in employers' bidding up their wages, passing along the payroll tax reduction. But in other instances it would result in employers' deciding to retain or hire older workers that they otherwise would not. They would pocket some or all of the payroll tax reduction to offset a decline in productivity or a rise in other compensation costs.

31. The Social Security Administration estimates that raising the averaging period from thirty-five to forty years would eliminate 24 percent of the program's seventy-five-year deficit (U.S. Social Security Administration 2005).

32. Goda and others (2006).

33. Gustman and Steinmeier (2005).

34. As shown in figure 6-5, workers with a full retirement age of 66 get a monthly benefit one-third greater if they claim at 66 rather than 62. These increases from the age 62 benefit are much the same at any full retirement age.

35. Keeping the EEA at 62, as life expectancies lengthen, effectively shifts Social Security benefits toward middle age (Steuerle and Spiro 1999).

36. Cahill and Munnell (2004).

37. At age 60 African American men have 2.7 years less life expectancy than white men (17.8 versus 20.5 years) and African American women have 1.8 years less life expectancy than white women (21.9 versus 23.7 years). National Center for Health Statistics, Life Tables 2003.

38. Various studies using the Health and Retirement Study find that early claimants on average are neither less healthy nor less wealthy than those who claim later. Burkhauser, Couch, and Phillips (1996); Congressional Budget Office (1999); Panis and others (2002).

39. Sass, Sun, and Webb (2007).

40. Cahill and Munnell (2004).

41. Zhivan and others (2008).

42. Estimates of the effects of an elastic EEA are for men and based on an EEA of 62 for men with less than half average lifetime earnings, rising to 64 for men with average lifetime earnings. Preliminary work suggests that a worker's EEA could be set at age 55 based on the worker's lifetime earnings up to that point, as lifetime earnings at 55 are highly correlated with lifetime earnings at age 62. Setting a worker's EEA at 55 would allow a reasonable amount of time for individuals to make their work and retirement plans. Zhivan and others (2008).

43. Gruber and Orszag (1999, 2003).

44. U.S. House of Representatives (2000).

45. Penner, Perun, and Steuerle (2002).

46. Note that the proposed expansion of the SCHIP program, which uses government funds to provide health care for children in households with incomes below a specified threshold, would lower the employer's cost of providing health insurance for young and middle-aged workers, increasing the cost differential between young and old workers.

47. Von Wachter (2002); Ashenfelter and Card (2002).

48. For example, OECD (2006).

49. Rix (2004).

50. See U.S. Government Accountability Office (2003a, 2003b, and 2005) for the uncertainty surrounding the effectiveness of U.S. public sector training programs; LaLonde (1995) for the consensus view that success has been limited; and Osterman (2005) for a somewhat more optimistic appraisal.

51. The U.S. Department of Labor has recognized the need to revamp the services the One-Stops provide to older job seekers. Its 2004 "Protocol for Serving Older Workers" (Employment and Training Administration 2004) emphasizes that these workers will remain in the labor force longer and have valuable skills that employers need. In addition to urging expanded training opportunities, it recommends help in using online job-matching services, such as Monster.com and CareerBuilder.com. It also promotes the use of labor market intermediaries that connect older workers and employers (as AARP has done with Home Depot) and programs that help older job seekers become self-employed, an important option for many older workers. The protocol also recommends training programs for One-Stop staff "on the unique aspects of serving mature workers."

52. AARP (2002b).

53. Workers, for example, cannot be dismissed because their compensation is rising. But can employers adjust their compensation package to control compensation creep—the tendency of compensation to rise with age? Or is this a discriminatory reduction in the compensation of older workers, who have earned their compensation by fulfilling the conditions set down by the employer? The difficulty the courts have in determining whether conversions of defined benefit pension plans to cash balance formats are discriminatory illustrates the ambiguity of what constitutes discrimination. We thank the publisher's anonymous reviewer for pointing out the ambiguous nature of the Age Discrimination in Employment Act of 1967 and the cash balance example.

54. Neumark (2001).

55. Lahey (2006).

Chapter 7

1. Kaiser Family Foundation (2006).

2. The term *phased retirement* is sometimes limited to full-time workers reducing their hours in their current job. For example, see Hutchens and Papps (2005) and Hutchens (2007). Our focus here is the broader concept of retirement in stages but not necessarily with the same employer.

3. U.S. Government Accountability Office (2001).

4. Discrete, routine, and self-contained tasks are most amenable to part-time employment; industries that must accommodate uneven demand across the work day—such as retailing, restaurants, and mass transit, which deliver services directly to people—can benefit by employing part-time workers. Blank (1998); Nollen, Eddy, and Martin (1977); Friedberg (1999); and Hutchens (2001).

5. Gustman and Steinmeier (2007).

6. For women, employment rates in 2005 were significantly higher at all ages because each successive cohort has higher labor force participation rates.

7. Autor and Duggan (2006).

References

Aaronson, Daniel, and Kenneth Housinger. 1999. "The Impact of Technology on Displacement and Reemployment." *Economic Perspectives* 23, no. 2: 14–30. Federal Reserve Bank of Chicago.

Aaronson, Daniel, and Daniel Sullivan. 1998. "The Decline of Job Security in the 1990s: Displacement, Anxiety, and Their Effect on Wage Growth." *Economic Perspectives* 22, no. 1: 17–43. Federal Reserve Bank of Chicago.

Aaronson, Stephanie, and Julia Coronado. 2005. "Are Firms or Workers behind the Shift away from DB Pension Plans?" Finance and Economic Decision Series 2005-17. U.S. Federal Reserve Board.

AARP. 1999. *Baby Boomers Envision Their Retirement: An AARP Segmentation Analysis.* Washington.

———. 2000. *American Business and Older Employees: A Summary of Findings.* Washington.

———. 2002a. *Impact of the Stock Market Decline on 50–70-Year-Old Investors.* Washington.

———. 2002b. *Staying Ahead of the Curve: The AARP Work and Career Study.* Washington.

———. 2003. *Staying Ahead of the Curve: The AARP Working in Retirement Study.* Washington.

———. 2004. *Staying Ahead of the Curve 2004: Employer Best Practices for Mature Workers.* Washington.

———. 2005. *American Business and Older Employees: A Focus on Midwest Employers.* Washington.

Abraham, Katherine G., and Susan N. Houseman. 2007. "Removing Barriers for Work for Older Americans." Paper prepared for conference, A Future of Good Jobs: America's Challenge in the Global Economy. Washington.

Abramovitz, Moses, and Paul David. 2000. "American Macroeconomic Growth in the Era of Knowledge-Based Progress: The Long-Run Perspective." In *The Cambridge Economic History of the United States*, vol. 3, edited by Stanley L. Engerman and Robert E. Gallman. Cambridge University Press.

Ahituv, Avner, and Joseph Zeira. 2005. "Technical Progress and Early Retirement." Discussion Paper 2614. London: Center for Economic Policy.

Allen, Jim, and Andries de Grip. 2005. "Skill Obsolescence, Lifelong Learning, and Labour Market Participation." Paper prepared for the EALE/SOLE World Conference. San Francisco, June 3–5.

Allen, Steven, Robert Clark, and Ann McDermed. 1988. "The Pension Cost of Changing Jobs." *Research on Aging* 10, no. 4: 459–71.

Altonji, Joseph G., and Paul J. Devereux. 1999. "The Extent and Consequences of Downward Nominal Wage Rigidity." Working Paper 7236. Cambridge, Mass.: National Bureau of Economic Research.

Ameriks, John, and others. 2007. "Six Paths to Retirement." Valley Forge, Pa.: Vanguard Center for Retirement Research.

Andersson, Frederik, Bertil Holmlund, and Thomas Lindh. 2002. "Labor Productivity, Age, and Education in Swedish Mining and Manufacturing, 1985–96." Uppsala University, Department of Economics.

Anstey, Kaarin J., and others. 2005. "Biomarkers, Health, Lifestyle, and Demographic Variables as Correlates of Reaction Time Performance in Early, Middle, and Late Adulthood." *Quarterly Journal of Experimental Psychology*, Section A58, no. 1: 5–21.

Arizona Mature Workforce Initiative. 2006. *The Arizona Mature Workforce Initiative Year One: Outcomes and Recommendations*. Phoenix: Governor's Council on Workforce Policy.

Ashenfelter, Orley, and David Card. 2002. "Did the Elimination of Mandatory Retirement Affect Faculty Retirement?" *American Economic Review* 92, no. 4: 957–80.

Aubert, Patrick, Eve Caroli, and Muriel Roger. 2004. "New Technologies, Workplace Organization, and the Age Structure of the Workforce: Firm-Level Evidence." Working Paper. Paris: National Institute for Statistics and Economic Studies.

Autor, David H., and Mark G. Duggan. 2006. "The Growth in the Social Security Disability Rolls: A Fiscal Crisis Unfolding." *Journal of Economic Perspective* 20, no. 3: 71–96.

Avolio, Bruce J., and David A. Waldman. 1994. "Variations in Cognitive, Perceptual, and Psychomotor Abilities across the Working Life Span: Examining the Effects of Race, Sex, Experience, Education, and Occupational Type." *Psychology and Aging* 9, no. 3: 430–42.

Banks, James, and others. 2006. "Disease and Disadvantage in the United States and in England." *Journal of the American Medical Association* 295, no. 17: 2037–45.

Bartel, Ann P., and Nachum Sicherman. 1993. "Technological Change and Retirement Decisions of Older Workers." *Journal of Labor Economics* 11, no. 1: 162–83.

Barth, Michael C., William McNaught, and Philip Rizzi. 1993. "Corporations and the Aging Work Force." In *Building the Competitive Workforce: Investing in Human Capital for Corporate Success*, edited by Philip H. Mirvis. New York: John Wiley and Sons.

Becker, Gary. 1975. *Human Capital*. Columbia University Press.

Beckmann, Michael. 2005. "Age-Biased Technological and Organizational Change: Firm-Level Evidence and Management Implications." Working Paper. University of Munich, School of Management.

Bendick, Marc, Jr., Charles W. Jackson, and J. Horacio Romero. 1996. "Employment Discrimination against Older Workers: An Experimental Study of Hiring Practices." *Journal of Aging and Social Policy* 8, no. 4: 25–46.

Benitez-Silva, Hugo. 2002. "Job Search Behavior at the End of the Life Cycle." Working Paper 2002-10. Chestnut Hill, Mass.: Center for Retirement Research.

———. 2006. "Job Search Behavior of Older Americans." Working Paper. SUNY at Stony Brook, Economics Department.

Blank, Rebecca M. 1998. "Contingent Work in a Changing Labor Market." In *Generating Jobs: How to Increase Demand for Less-Skilled Workers*, edited by Richard B. Freeman and Peter Gottschalk. New York: Russell Sage.

Blau, David M. 1998. "Labor Force Dynamics of Older Married Couples." *Journal of Labor Economics* 16, no. 3: 595–629.

Blau, David M., and Donna B. Gilleskie. 2001. "The Effect of Health on Employment Transitions of Older Men." In *Worker Well-Being in a Changing Labor Market*, edited by Solomon W. Polachek. Amsterdam: JAI.

Blau, Francine D., and Lawrence M. Kahn. 2000. "Gender Differences in Pay." *Journal of Economic Perspectives* 14, no. 4: 75–99.

———. 2004. "The US Gender Pay Gap in the 1990s: Slowing Convergence." Working Paper 10853. Cambridge, Mass.: National Bureau of Economic Research.

———. 2005. "Changes in the Labor Supply Behavior of Married Women: 1980–2000." Working Paper 11230. Cambridge, Mass.: National Bureau of Economic Research.

Blinder, Alan S. 2006. "Offshoring: The Next Industrial Revolution?" *Foreign Affairs* (March–April): 113–28.

Blum, J. E., L. F. Jarvik, and E. T. Clark. 1970. "Rate of Change on Selective Tests of Intelligence: A Twenty-Year Longitudinal Study of Aging." *Journal of Gerontology* 25, no. 3: 171–76.

Boisjoly, Johanne, Greg J. Duncan, and Timothy Smeeding. 1998. "The Shifting Incidence of Involuntary Job Losses from 1968 to 1992." *Industrial Relations* 37, no. 2: 207–31.

Boot, H. M. 1995. "How Skilled Were Lancashire Cotton Factory Workers in 1833?" *Economic History Review* 48, no. 2: 283–303.

Bosworth, Barry P., Ralph C. Bryant, and Gary Burtless. 2004. "The Impact of Aging on Financial Markets and the Economy: A Survey." Brookings.

Bowen, William, and T. Finnegan. 1969. *The Economics of Labor Force Participation.* Princeton University Press.

Brown, Kyle N., and Sylvester J. Schieber. 2003. "Structural Impediments to Phased Retirement." Technical and Policy Paper. Arlington, Va.: Watson-Wyatt.

Bucks, Brian, Arthur Kennickell, and Kevin Moore. 2006. "Recent Changes in U.S. Family Finances: Evidence from the 2001 and 2004 Survey of Consumer Finances." *Federal Reserve Bulletin* 92: A1–A38.

Buessing, Marric, and Mauricio Soto. 2006. "The State of Private Pensions: Current 5500 Data." Issue in Brief 42. Chestnut Hill, Mass.: Center for Retirement Research.

Burkhauser, Richard V., John S. Butler, and Gulcin Gumus. 2004. "Dynamic Programming Model Estimates of Social Security Disability Insurance Application Timing." *Journal of Applied Econometrics* 19: 671–85.

Burkhauser, Richard V., Kenneth A. Couch, and John W. Phillips. 1996. "Who Takes Early Social Security Benefits? The Economic and Health Characteristics of Early Beneficiaries." *Gerontologist* 36, no. 6: 789–99.

Burkhauser, Richard V., and Joseph F. Quinn. 1997. "Implementing Pro-Work Policies for Older Americans in the Twenty-First Century." Paper prepared for the Forum on Older Workers, U.S. Senate Subcommittee on Aging.

Burkhauser, Richard V., and others. 2002. "Self-Reported Work-Limitation Data: What They Can and Cannot Tell Us." *Demography* 39, no. 3: 541–55.

Burtless, Gary. 1986. "Social Security, Unanticipated Benefit Increases, and the Timing of Retirement." *Review of Economic Studies* 53, no. 5: 781–805.

Burtless, Gary, and Robert Moffitt. 1984. "The Effect of Social Security Benefits on Labor Supply of the Aged." In *Retirement and Economic Behavior*, edited by Henry Aaron and Gary Burtless. Brookings.

Burtless, Gary, and Joseph F. Quinn. 2000. "Retirement Trends and Policies to Encourage Work among Older Americans." Paper prepared for the Annual Conference of the National Academy of Social Insurance. Washington.

———. 2002. "Is Working Longer the Answer for an Aging Workforce?" Issue in Brief 11. Chestnut Hill, Mass.: Center for Retirement Research.

Butrica, Barbara A., Karen E. Smith, and C. Eugene Steuerle. 2006. "Working for a Good Retirement." Discussion Paper 06-03. Washington: Urban Institute.

Butrica, Barbara A., and others. 2006. "The Implicit Tax on Work at Older Ages." *National Tax Journal* 59, no. 2: 211–34.

Cahill, Kevin E., Michael Giandrea, and Joseph Quinn. 2006. "A Micro-Level Analysis of Recent Increases in Labor Force Participation among Older Men." Working Paper 400. U.S. Bureau of Labor Statistics.

Cahill, Kevin E., and Alicia H. Munnell. 2004. "What Would Be the Effect of Raising the Earliest Eligibility Age for Social Security?" New York: Russell Sage.

Calvo, Esteban. 2006. "Does Working Longer Make People Healthier and Happier?" Work Opportunities Brief 2. Chestnut Hill, Mass.: Center for Retirement Research.

Campbell, Carl M., and Kunal S. Kamlani. 1997. "The Reasons for Wage-Rigidity: Evidence from a Survey of Firms." *Quarterly Journal of Economics* 112, no. 3: 759–89.

Campbell, Sheila, and Alicia H. Munnell. 2002. "Sex and 401(k) Plans." Just the Facts 4. Chestnut Hill, Mass.: Center for Retirement Research.

Cancian, Maria, Sheldon Danziger and Peter Gottschalk. 1993. "Working Wives and Family Income Inequality among Married Couples." In *Uneven Tides: Rising Inequality in America*, edited by Sheldon Danziger and Peter Gottschalk. New York: Russell Sage.

Cappelli, Peter. 2003. "Will There Really Be a Labor Shortage?" *Organizational Dynamics* 44, no. 2: 221–33.

Case, Anne C., and Angus Deaton. 2003. "Broken Down by Work and Sex: How Our Health Declines." Working Paper 9821. Cambridge, Mass.: National Bureau of Economic Research.

Casey, Bernard. 2004. "Reforming the Japanese Retirement Income System: A Special Case?" Global Issue in Brief 4. Chestnut Hill, Mass.: Center for Retirement Research.

Centers for Medicare and Medicaid Services. Various years. *Annual Report of the Boards of Trustees of the Federal Hospital Insurance and Federal Supplementary Medical Insurance Trust Funds.* U.S. Department of Health and Human Services.

Chan, Gregory, V. Tan, and David Koh. 2000. "Aging and Fitness to Work." *Occupational Medicine* (Oxford) 50, no. 7: 483–91.

Chan, Sewin, and Ann Huff Stevens. 2001. "Job Loss and Employment Patterns of Older Workers." *Journal of Labor Economics* 19, no. 2: 484–521.

Clark, Robert L., and Sylvester J. Schieber. 2002. "Taking the Subsidy out of Early Retirement: The Story behind the Conversion to Hybrid Pensions." In *Innovations in Managing the Financial Risks of Retirement*, edited by Olivia Mitchell and others. University of Pennsylvania Press.

Coile, Courtney. 2003. "Retirement Incentives and Couples' Retirement Decisions." Working Paper 4. Chestnut Hill, Mass.: Center for Retirement Research

Coile, Courtney, and Jonathan Gruber. 2000. "Social Security and Retirement." Working Paper 7830. Cambridge, Mass.: National Bureau of Economic Research.

Coile, Courtney C., and Phillip B. Levine. 2006. "Bulls, Bears, and Retirement Behavior." *Industrial and Labor Relations Review* 59, no. 3: 408–29.

Collison, Jessica. 2005. *The Future of the U.S. Labor Pool.* Alexandria, Va.: Society for Human Resource Management.

Colonia-Willner, R. 1998. "Practical Intelligence at Work: Relationship between Aging and Cognitive Efficiency among Managers in a Bank Environment." *Psychology and Aging* 13, no. 1: 45–57.

Committee for Economic Development. 1999. "New Opportunities for Older Workers: A Statement on National Policy by the Research and Policy Committee of the Committee for Economic Development." New York.

Congressional Budget Office. 1999. "Raising the Earliest Eligibility Age for Social Security Benefits."

———. 2004. "Retirement Age and the Need for Saving."

Coronado, Julia Lynn, and Phillip C. Copeland. 2003. "Cash Balance Pension Plan Conversions and the New Economy." Finance and Economics Discussion Series 2003-63. U.S. Federal Reserve Board of Governors.

Coronado, Julia Lynn, and Maria Perozek. 2003. "Wealth Effects and the Consumption of Leisure: Retirement Decisions during the Stock Market Boom of the 1990s." Finance and Economics Discussion Series 2003-20. U.S. Federal Reserve Board of Governors.

Costa, Dora L. 1998. *The Evolution of Retirement: An American Economic History, 1880–1990.* University of Chicago Press.

———. 2000. "The Wage and the Length of the Work Day: From the 1890s to 1991." *Journal of Labor Economics* 18, no. 1: 156–81.

———. 2005. "Causes of Improving Health and Longevity at Older Ages: A Review of the Explanations." *Genus* 61, no. 1: 21–38.

Crépon, Bruno, Nicolas Deniau, and Sebastien Pérez-Duarte. 2002. "Wages, Productivity, and Worker Characteristics: A French Perspective." Working Paper. Paris: Institut National de la Statistique et des Etudes Economiques.

Currie, Janet, and Brigitte C. Madrian. 1999. "Health, Health Insurance, and the Labor Market." In *Handbook of Labor Economics,* edited by Orley C. Ashenfelter and David Card. Vol. 3C. Amsterdam: Elsevier Science.

Cutler, David. 2001. "Declining Disability among the Elderly." *Health Affairs* 20, no. 6: 11–27.

Cutler, David, Angus Deaton, and Adriana Lleras-Muney. 2006. "The Determinants of Mortality." Working Paper 11963. Cambridge, Mass.: National Bureau of Economic Research.

Cutler, David, Jeffrey B. Liebman, and Seamus Smyth. 2006. "How Fast Should the Social Security Eligibility Age Rise?" Working Paper NB04-05. Cambridge, Mass.: National Bureau of Economic Research.

Cutler, David, and Ellen Meara. 2001. "Changes in the Age Distribution of Mortality over the 20th Century." Working Paper 8556. Cambridge, Mass.: National Bureau of Economic Research.

Cutler, David M., and Elizabeth Richardson. 1997. "Measuring the Health of the U.S. Population." *Brookings Papers on Economic Activity: Microeconomics:* 217–82.

Davenport, Tom H. 2005. *Thinking for a Living: How to Get Better Performance and Results from Knowledge Workers*. Harvard Business School Press.

Deary, Ian J., and others. 2000. "The Stability of Individual Differences in Mental Ability from Childhood to Old Age: Follow-Up of the 1932 Scottish Mental Survey." *Intelligence* 28, no. 1: 49–55.

Delorme, Luke, Alicia H. Munnell, and Anthony Webb. 2006. "Empirical Regularity Suggests Retirement Risks." Issue in Brief 41. Chestnut Hill, Mass.: Center for Retirement Research.

Deschryvere, Matthias. 2005. "Health and Retirement Decisions: An Update of the Literature." Research Report 6. Brussels: European Network of Economic Policy Research Institutes.

Devereux, Paul J. 2004. "Changes in Relative Wages and Family Labor Supply." *Journal of Human Resources* 39, no. 3: 696–722.

Diamond, Peter, and Jonathan Gruber. 1997. "Social Security and the U.S." Working Paper 6097. Cambridge, Mass.: National Bureau of Economic Research.

Dohm, Arlene. 2000. "Gauging the Labor Force Effects of Retiring Baby Boomers." *Monthly Labor Review* 123, no. 7: 17–25.

Drucker, Peter. 1999. "Knowledge-Worker Productivity: The Biggest Challenge." *California Management Review* 41, no. 2: 79–94.

Earles, Julie K., and others. 1997. "Interrelations of Age, Self-Reported Health, Speed, and Memory." *Psychology and Aging* 12, no. 4: 675–83.

Employee Benefit Research Institute. Various years. *Retirement Confidence Survey.* Washington.

Employment and Training Administration. 2004. "Protocol for Serving Older Workers." U.S. Department of Labor.

Ernst and Young. 2006. "The Aging of the U.S. Workforce: Employer Challenges and Responses." Washington.

Eschtruth, Andrew, and Jonathan Gemus. 2002. "Are Older Workers Responding to the Bear Market?" Issue in Brief 5. Chestnut Hill, Mass.: Center for Retirement Research.

Eschtruth, Andrew D., Steven A. Sass, and Jean-Pierre Aubry. 2007. "Employers Lukewarm about Retaining Older Workers." Work Opportunities for Older Americans Series 10. Chestnut Hill, Mass.: Center for Retirement Research.

Fallick, Bruce, and Jonathan Pingle. 2007. "The Effect of Population Aging on Aggregate Labor Supply in the U.S." In *Labor Supply in the New Century,* edited by Katharine Bradbury, Christopher L. Foote, and Robert Triest. Conference Series 52. Federal Reserve Bank of Boston.

Farber, Henry S. 2005. "What Do We Know about Job Loss in the United States, 1984–2004?" Working Paper 498. Princeton University, Industrial Relations Section.

———. 2006. "Is the Company Man an Anachronism? Trends in Long-Term Employment in the U.S., 1973–2005." Working Paper 508. Princeton University, Industrial Relations Section.

Flippen, Chenoa, and Marta Tienda. 2000. "Pathways to Retirement: Patterns of Labor Force Participation and Labor Market Exit among the Preretirement Population, by Race, Hispanic Origin, and Sex." *Journal of Gerontology* Series B 55, no. 1: S14–S27.

Fogel, Robert. 2003. "Changes in the Process of Aging during the Twentieth Century: Findings and Procedures of the Early Indicators Project." Working Paper 9941. Cambridge, Mass.: National Bureau of Economic Research.

Fogel, Robert, and Dora L. Costa. 1997. "A Theory of Technophysio Evolution with Some Implications for Forecasting Population, Health Care, and Pension Costs." *Demography* 31, no. 1: 49–66.

Frazis, Harley, and others. 1998. "Results from the 1995 Survey of Employer-Provided Training." *Monthly Labor Review* 121, no. 6: 3–13.

Freedman, Vicki, and others. 2004. "Resolving Inconsistencies in Trends in Old-Age Disability: Report from a Technical Working Group." *Demography* 41, no. 3: 417–41.

Freeman, Richard B. 1979. "The Effect of Demographic Factors on Age-Earnings Profiles." *Journal of Human Resources* 14, no. 3: 289–318.

———. 2006. "Is a Great Labor Shortage Coming? Replacement Demand in the Global Economy." Working Paper 12541. Cambridge, Mass.: National Bureau of Economic Research.

Friedberg, Leora. 1998. "The Social Security Earnings Test and Labor Supply of Older Men." In *Tax Policy and the Economy*, edited by James Poterba. MIT Press.

———. 1999. "The Trend toward Part-Time Work among Older Workers." Paper prepared for the NBER Summer Institute. Cambridge, Mass., July 17.

———. 2000. "The Labor Supply Effects of the Social Security Earnings Test." *Review of Economics and Statistics* 82, no. 1: 46–63.

———. 2004. "The Trend toward Part-Time Work among Older Workers." University of Virginia, Department of Economics.

———. 2007. "The Recent Trend toward Later Retirement." Issues in Brief 9. Chestnut Hill, Mass.: Center for Retirement Research.

Friedberg, Leora, and Michael T. Owyang. 2004. "Explaining the Evolution of Pension Structure and Job Tenure." Working Paper 10714. Cambridge, Mass.: National Bureau of Economic Research.

Friedberg, Leora, and Anthony Webb. 2005. "Retirement and the Evolution of Pension Structure." *Journal of Human Resources* 40, no. 2: 281–308.

———. 2006. "Persistence in Labor Supply and the Response to the Social Security Earnings Test." Working Paper 2006-27. Chestnut Hill, Mass.: Center for Retirement Research.

Fries, James F. 1983. "The Compression of Morbidity." *Milbank Memorial Fund Quarterly* 61, no. 3: 397–419.

Fries, James F., and others. 1996. "Reduction in Long-Term Disability in Patients with Rheumatoid Arthritis by Disease-Modifying Antirheumatic Drug-Based Treatment Strategies." *Arthritis and Rheumatism* 39, no. 4: 616–22.

Fuchs, Victor R. 1984. "'Though Much Is Taken': Reflections on Aging, Health, and Medical Care." *Milbank Memorial Fund Quarterly* 62, no. 2: 143–66.

Goda, Gopi Shah, and others. 2006. "Removing the Disincentives in Social Security for Long Careers." Working Paper 13110. Cambridge, Mass.: National Bureau of Economic Research.

Goldin, Claudia. 1990. *Understanding the Gender Gap*. Oxford University Press.

———. 1991. "The Role of World War II in the Rise of Women's Employment." *American Economic Review* 81, no. 4: 741–56.

———. 1998. "America's Graduation from High School: The Evolution and Spread of Secondary Schooling in the Twentieth Century." *Journal of Economic History* 58, no. 2: 345–74.

———. 2006. "The Quiet Revolution That Transformed Women's Employment, Education, and Family." Working Paper 11953. Cambridge, Mass.: National Bureau of Economic Research.

Goldin, Claudia, and Lawrence F. Katz. 2002. "The Power of the Pill: Oral Contraceptives and Women's Career and Marriage Decisions." *Journal of Political Economy* 110, no. 4: 730–70

Goldman, Dana P., and James P. Smith. 2002. "Can Patient Self-Management Help Explain the SES Health Gradient?" *Proceedings of the National Academy of Sciences USA* 99, no. 16: 10929–34.

Goss, Stephen C., and Alice H. Wade. 2002. "Estimates of Financial Effects for Three Models Developed by the President's Commission to Strengthen Social Security." Social Security Administration, Office of the Chief Actuary.

Gottschalk, Peter, and Robert Moffitt. 1999. "Changes in Job Instability and Insecurity Using Monthly Survey Data." *Journal of Labor Economics* 17, no. 4: S91–S126.

Graebner, William. 1980. *A History of Retirement: The Meaning and Function of an American Institution, 1885–1978*. Yale University Press.

Gray, Jeffrey S. 1998. "Divorce-Law Changes, Household Bargaining, and Married Women's Labor Supply." *American Economic Review* 88, no. 3: 628–42.

Groshen, Erica L., and Mark E. Schweitzer. 1996. "Macro- and Microeconomic Consequences of Wage Rigidity." Working Paper 9607. Federal Reserve Bank of Cleveland.

Gruber, Jonathan. 2000. "Disability Insurance Benefits and Labor Supply." *Journal of Political Economy* 108, no. 6: 1162–83.

Gruber, Jonathan, and Peter Orszag. 1999. "What to Do about the Social Security Earnings Test?" Issue in Brief 1. Chestnut Hill, Mass.: Center for Retirement Research.

———. 2003. "Does the Social Security Earnings Test Affect Labor Supply and Benefits Receipt?" *National Tax Journal* 56, no. 4: 755–73.

Gruber, Jonathan, and David Wise. 1998. "Social Security and Retirement: An International Comparison." *American Economic Review* 88, no. 2: 158–63.

———. 2002. "Social Security Programs and Retirement around the World: Micro Estimation." Working Paper 9407. Cambridge, Mass.: National Bureau of Economic Research.

Gruenberg, E. M. 1977. "The Failure of Success." *Milbank Memorial Fund Quarterly* 55, no. 1: 3–24.

Guest, Ross, and Kate Shacklock. 2005. "The Impending Shift to an Older Mix of Workers: Perspectives from the Management and Economics Literatures." *International Journal of Organisational Behaviour* 10, no. 3: 713–28.

Guillemard, Anne Marie, and Herman van Gunsteren. 1991. "Pathways and Prospects: A Comparative Interpretation of the Meaning of Early Exit." In *Time for Retirement: Comparative Studies of Early Exit from the Labor Force*, edited by Martin Kohli and others. Cambridge University Press.

Gustman, Alan, Olivia S. Mitchell, and Thomas Steinmeier. 1994. "The Role of Pensions in the Labor Market: A Survey of the Literature." *Industrial and Labor Relations Review* 47, no. 3: 417–38.

Gustman, Alan, and Thomas Steinmeier. 1986. "A Structural Retirement Model." *Econometrica* 54, no. 3: 555–84.

———. 1993. "Pension Portability and Labor Mobility: Evidence from the Survey of Income and Program Participation." *Journal of Public Economics* 50, no. 3: 299–323.

———. 1994. "Employer-Provided Health Insurance and Retirement Behavior." *Industrial and Labor Relations Review* 48, no. 1: 124–40.

———. 1999. "What People Don't Know about Their Pensions and Social Security: An Analysis Using Linked Data from the Health and Retirement Study." Working Paper 7368. Cambridge, Mass.: National Bureau of Economic Research.

———. 2000. "Retirement in a Family Context: A Structural Model for Husbands and Wives." *Journal of Labor Economics* 18, no. 3: 503–45.

———. 2001. "Imperfect Knowledge, Retirement, and Saving." Working Paper 8406. Cambridge, Mass.: National Bureau of Economic Research.

———. 2002a. "Social Security, Pensions and Retirement Behavior within the Family." Working Paper 8772. Cambridge, Mass.: National Bureau of Economic Research.

———. 2002b. "Retirement and the Stock Market Bubble." Working Paper 9404. Cambridge, Mass.: National Bureau of Economic Research.

———. 2005. "The Social Security Early Entitlement Age in a Structural Model of Retirement and Wealth." *Journal of Public Economics* 89, nos. 2 and 3: 441–63.

———. 2006. "How Changes in Social Security Affect Retirement Trends." Working Paper 127. Retirement Research Center, University of Michigan.

———. 2007. "Projecting Behavioral Responses to the Next Generation of Retirement Policies." Working Paper 12958. Cambridge, Mass.: National Bureau of Economic Research.

Hægeland, Torbjorn, and Tor Jakob Klette. 1999. "Do Higher Wages Reflect Higher Productivity? Education, Gender, and Experience Premiums in Matched Plant Worker Data Set." In *The Creation and Analysis of Employer-Employee Matched Data*, edited by John C. Haltiwanger and others. Amsterdam: Elsevier.

Haider, Steven, and David Loughran. 2001. "Elderly Labor Supply: Work or Play?" Working Paper 4. Chestnut Hill, Mass.: Center for Retirement Research.

Haltiwanger, John C., Julia I. Lane, and James R. Speltzer. 1999. "Productivity Differences across Employers: The Roles of Employer Size, Age, and Human Capital." *American Economic Review* 89, no. 2: 94–98.

Hamermesh, Daniel S. 2005. "Why Not Retire? The Time and Timing Costs of Market Work." Working Paper 104. University of Michigan, Retirement Research Center.

Han, Shin-Kap, and Phyllis Moen. 1999. "Clocking Out: Temporal Patterning of Retirement." *American Journal of Sociology* 105, no. 1: 191–236.

Hellerstein, Judith K., and David Neumark. 1995. "Are Earnings Profiles Steeper than Productivity Profiles? Evidence from Israeli Firm-Level Data." *Journal of Human Resources* 30, no. 1: 89–112.

Hellerstein, Judith K., David Neumark, and Kenneth R. Troske. 1999. "Wages, Productivity, and Worker Characteristics: Evidence from Plant-Level Production Functions and Wage Equations." *Journal of Labor Economics* 17, no. 3: 409–46.

Henkens, Kene. 2005. "Stereotyping Older Workers and Retirement: The Managers' Point of View." *Canadian Journal of Aging* 24, no. 4: 353–66.

Hirsch, Barry T., David A. Macpherson, and Melissa A. Hardy. 2000. "Occupational Age Structure and Access for Older Workers." *Industrial and Labor Relations Review* 53, no. 3: 401–18.

House of Lords, Select Committee on Economic Affairs. 2003. "Aspects of the Economics of an Ageing Population." Session 2002–03, Fourth Report. London.

Houthakker, H. S. 1959. "Education and Income." *Review of Economic Statistics* 41, no. 1: 24–28.

Hu, Luojia. 2003. "The Hiring Decisions and Compensation Structures of Large Firms." *Industrial and Labor Relations Review* 56, no. 4: 663–81.

Hurd, Michael D. 1990. "The Joint Retirement Decision of Husbands and Wives." In *Issues in the Economics of Aging*, edited by David A. Wise. University of Chicago Press.

Hutchens, Robert. 1986. "Delayed Payment Contracts and a Firm's Propensity to Hire Older Workers." *Journal of Labor Economics* 4, no. 4: 439–57.

———. 1988. "Do Job Opportunities Decline with Age?" *Industrial and Labor Relations Review* 42, no. 1: 89–99.

———. 1993. "Restricted Job Opportunities and the Older Worker." In *As the Workforce Ages: Costs, Benefits and Policy Challenges*, edited by Olivia Mitchell. Ithaca: ILR Press.

———. 2001. "Employer Surveys, Employer Policies, and Future Demand for Older Workers." Retirement Research Consortium, Demand for Older Workers. Brookings.

———. 2003. "The Cornell Study of Employer Phased Retirement Policies: A Report on Key Findings." Cornell University, School of Industrial and Labor Relations.

———. 2007. "Worker Characteristics, Job Characteristics, and Opportunities for Phased Retirement." Discussion Paper 2564. Bonn: Institute for the Study of Labor.

Hutchens, Robert, and Kerry Papps. 2005. "Developments in Phased Retirement." In *Reinventing the Retirement Paradigm*, edited by Robert Clark and Olivia Mitchell. Oxford University Press.

Idler, Ellen, and Stanislav Kasl. 1991. "Health Perceptions and Survival: Do Global Evaluations of Health Status Really Predict Mortality?" *Journal of Gerontology* 46: S55–S65.

Ilmakunnas, P., M. Maliranta, and J. Vainiomäki. 1999. "The Role of Employer and Employee Characteristics for Plant Productivity." Working Paper 223. Helsinki School of Economics and Business Administration.

Ippolito, Richard A. 1990. "Toward Explaining Earlier Retirement after 1970." *Industrial and Labor Relations Review* 43, no. 5: 556–69.

Jacoby, Sanford M., and Daniel J. B. Mitchell. 1990. "Sticky Stories: Economic Explanations of Employment and Wage Rigidity." *American Economic Review* 80, no. 2: 33–37.

Jette, Alan M., and Elizabeth Badley. 2000. "Conceptual Issues in the Measurement of Work Disability." In *Survey Measurement of Work Disability: Summary of a Workshop,* edited by Nancy Mathiowetz and Gooloo S. Wunderlich. Washington: National Academy Press.

Johnson, Richard. 2004a. "Trends in Job Demands among Older Workers, 1992–2002." *Monthly Labor Review* 127, no. 7: 48–56.

———. 2004b. "Do Spouses Coordinate Their Retirement Decisions?" Issue in Brief 19. Chestnut Hill, Mass.: Center for Retirement Research.

Johnson, Richard W., and Melissa M. Favreault. 2001. "Retiring Together or Working Alone: The Impact of Spousal Employment and Disability on Retirement Decisions." Working Paper 1. Chestnut Hill, Mass.: Center for Retirement Research.

Johnson, Richard W., and Janette Kawachi. 2007. "Job Changes at Older Ages: Effects on Wages, Benefits, and Other Job Attributes." Working Paper 4. Chestnut Hill, Mass.: Center for Retirement Research.

Judge, Timothy A., and others. 1994. "1994 Employee Age as a Moderator of the Relationship between Ambition and Work Role Affect." Working Paper 20. Center for Advanced Human Resource Studies, Cornell University.

Judy, Richard W., and Carol D'Amico. 1997. *Workforce 2020: Work and Workers in the 21st Century*. Indianapolis: Hudson Institute.

Juhn, Chinhui, and Kevin M. Murphy. 1997. "Wage Inequality and Family Labor Supply." *Journal of Labor Economics* 15, no. 1: 72–97

Juster, F. Thomas, and Richard Suzman. 1995. "An Overview of the Health and Retirement Study." *Journal of Human Resources* 30, no. 5: S7–S56.

Kahn, Shulamit. 1997. "Evidence of Nominal Wage Stickiness from Microdata." *American Economic Review* 87, no. 5: 993–1008.

Kaiser Family Foundation. 2006. *Kaiser/HRET Survey of Employer-Sponsored Health Benefits.* Washington.

Karamcheva, Nadia, and Alicia H. Munnell. 2007. "Why Are Widows So Poor?" Issue in Brief 9. Chestnut Hill, Mass.: Center for Retirement Research.

Karoly, L. A., and J. A. Rogowski. 1994. "The Effect of Access to Postretirement Health Insurance on the Decision to Retire Early." *Industrial and Labor Relations Review* 48, no. 1: 103–23.

Keese, Mark. 2006. "Live Longer, Work Longer: A Synthesis Report of the Ageing and Employment Policies Project." Paris: OECD.

Kohli, Martin, and Martin Rein. 1991. "The Changing Balance of Work and Retirement." In *Time for Retirement: Comparative Studies of Early Exit from the Labor Force*, edited by Martin Kohli and others. Cambridge University Press.

Kotlikoff, Laurence J., and Jagadeesh Gokhale. 1992. "Estimating a Firm's Age-Productivity Profile Using the Present Value of Workers' Earnings." *Quarterly Journal of Economics* 107, no. 4: 1215–42.

Kreps, Juanita. 1977. "Age, Work, and Income." *Southern Journal of Economics* 43, no. 4: 1423–37.

Krueger, Alan B., and Jörn-Steffen Pischke. 1992. "The Effect of Social Security on Labor Supply: A Cohort Analysis of the Notch Generation." *Journal of Labor Economics* 10, no. 4: 412–37.

Kutscher, Ronald E., and James F. Walker. 1960. "Comparative Job Performance of Office Workers by Age." *Monthly Labor Review* 83, no. 1: 39–43.

Lahey, Joanna. 2005. "Do Older Workers Face Discrimination?" Issue in Brief 33. Chestnut Hill, Mass.: Center for Retirement Research.

———. 2006. "How Do Age Discrimination Laws Affect Older Workers?" Work Opportunities for Older Americans Series 5. Chestnut Hill, Mass.: Center for Retirement Research.

———. 2007. "Does Health Insurance Affect the Employment of Older Workers?" Issue Brief 8. Chestnut Hill, Mass.: Center for Aging and Work/Workplace Flexibility.

Lahey, Karen E., Doseong Kim, and Melinda L. Newman. 2006. "Full Retirement? An Examination of Factors That Influence the Decision to Return to Work." *Financial Services Review* 15, no. 1: 1–19.

Laitner, John, and Dan Silverman. 2006. "Social Security Reform: Changing Incentives for When to Retire." Paper prepared for annual meeting of the American Economic Association. Boston.

Lakdawalla, Darius, Jayanta Bhattacharya, and Dana Goldman. 2004. "Are the Young Becoming More Disabled?" *Health Affairs* 23, no. 1: 168–76.

LaLonde, Robert J. 1995. "The Promise of Public Sector-Sponsored Training Programs." *Journal of Economic Perspectives* 9, no. 2: 149–68

Lazear, Edward D. 1979. "Why Is There Mandatory Retirement?" *Journal of Political Economy* 87, no. 6: 1261–84.

Lee, Chulhee. 2001. "The Expected Length of Male Retirement in the United States, 1850–1990." *Journal of Population Estimates* 14, no. 4: 641–50.

———. 2005. "Labor Market Status of Older Males in the United States, 1880–1940." *Social Science History* 29, no. 1: 77–105.

Loughran, David S., and Steven Haider. 2005. "Do Elderly Men Respond to Taxes on Earnings?" Working Paper WR-223-1. Santa Monica, Calif.: Rand.

Lyon, Phil, and David Pollard. 1997. "Perceptions of the Older Employee: Is Anything Really Changing?" *Personnel Review* 26, no. 4: 245–57.

Maestas, Nicole. 2005. "Back to Work: Expectations and Realizations of Work after Retirement." Working Paper WR-196-1. Santa Monica, Calif.: Rand.

Maitland, Scott B., and others. 2000. "Gender Differences and Changes in Cognitive Abilities across the Adult Life Span." *Aging, Neuropsychology, and Cognition* 7, no. 1: 32–53.

Manton, Kenneth. 1982. "Changing Concepts of Morbidity and Mortality in the Elderly Population." *Milbank Memorial Fund Quarterly* 60: 183–244.

Manton, Kenneth, and XiLiang Gu. 2001. "Changes in the Prevalence of Chronic Disability in the United States Black and Non-Black Population above Age 65, from 1982 to 1999." *Proceedings of the National Academy of Sciences USA* 98 no. 1: 6354–59.

Manton, Kenneth, XiLiang Gu, and Vicki Lamb. 2006. "Change in Chronic Disability from 1982 to 2004/2005 as Measured by Long-Term Changes in Function and Health in the U.S. Elderly Population." *Proceedings of the National Academy of Sciences USA* 103, no. 48: 18374–79.

Margo, Robert A. 1993. "The Labor Force Participation of Older Americans in 1900: Further Results." *Explorations in Economic History* 30, no. 3: 409–23.

Mark, J. A. 1957. "Comparative Job Performance by Age." *Monthly Labor Review* 80: 1467–71.

Marshall, Victor W. 2001. "Canadian Research on Older Workers." Paper prepared for conference, International Association on Gerontology. Vancouver.

Massachusetts Office of the Governor. 2001. "Massachusetts, Toward a New Prosperity: Building Regional Competitiveness across the Commonwealth." Boston.

Mayfield, Demmie, Gail McLeod, and Patricia Hall. 1974. "The CAGE Questionnaire: Validation of a New Alcoholism Screening Instrument." *American Journal of Psychiatry* 131, no. 10: 1121–23.

McCarty, Therese. 1990. "The Effect of Social Security on Married Women's Labor Force Participation." *National Tax Journal* 43, no. 1: 95–110.

McEvoy, Glenn M., and Wayne F. Cascio. 1989. "Cumulative Evidence of the Relationship between Employee Age and Job Performance." *Journal of Applied Psychology* 74, no. 1: 11–17.

McGarry, Kathleen, and Robert F. Schoeni. 2005. "Widow(er) Poverty and Out-of-Pocket Medical Expenditures Near the End of Life." *Journal of Gerontology* Series B 60, no. 3: S160–S168.

McGill, Dan M., and others. 1996. *Fundamentals of Private Pensions*. Philadelphia: University of Pennsylvania Press.

McGregor, Judy, and Lance Gray. 2002. "Stereotypes and Older Workers: The New Zealand Experience." *Social Policy Journal of New Zealand* 19: 163–77.

Mermin, Gordon B. T., Richard W. Johnson, and Dan Murphy. 2006. "Why Do Boomers Plan to Work So Long?" Retirement Project Discussion Paper 06-04. Washington: Urban Institute.

Metcalf, Hilary, and Pamela Meadows. 2006. "Survey of Employers' Policies, Practices, and Preferences Relating to Age." Research Report 325. DTI Employment Relations Research Series 49. U.K. Department for Work and Pensions.

Metropolitan Life Insurance Company. 1999. "The MetLife Juggling Act Study: Balancing Caregiving with Work and the Costs Involved." New York.

Mintzberg, Henry. 1998. "Covert Leadership: Notes on Managing Professionals— Knowledge Workers Respond to Inspiration, Not Supervision." *Harvard Business Review* 76, no. 6: 140–47.

Moen, Jon R. 1987. "Essays on the Labor Force and Labor Force Participation Rates: The United States from 1860 through 1950." Ph.D. dissertation, University of Chicago.

Montgomery, Mark. 1988. "On the Determinants of Employer Demand for Part-Time Workers." *Review of Economics and Statistics* 70, no. 1: 112–17.

Morton, Lynn, and others. 2005. *Managing the Mature Workforce*. New York: Conference Board.

Mosisa, Abraham, and Steven Hipple. 2006. "Trends in Labor Force Participation in the United States." *Monthly Labor Review* 129, no. 10: 35–57.

Munnell, Alicia H. 2003. "The Declining Role of Social Security." Just the Facts 6. Chestnut Hill, Mass.: Center for Retirement Research.

———. 2006. "Policies to Promote Labor Force Participation of Older People." Working Paper 2. Chestnut Hill, Mass.: Center for Retirement Research.

Munnell, Alicia H., Kevin E. Cahill, and Natalia Jivan. 2003. "How Has the Shift to 401(k)s Affected the Retirement Age?" Issue in Brief 13. Chestnut Hill, Mass.: Center for Retirement Research.

Munnell, Alicia H., Francesca Golub-Sass, and Andrew Varani. 2005. "How Much Are Workers Saving?" Issue in Brief 34. Chestnut Hill, Mass.: Center for Retirement Research.

Munnell, Alicia H., Geoffrey Sanzenbacher, and Mauricio Soto. 2007. "Working Wives Reduce Social Security Replacement Rates." Issue in Brief 15. Chestnut Hill, Mass.: Center for Retirement Research.

Munnell, Alicia H., and Steven Sass. 2005. "401(k) Plans and Women: A 'Good News/Bad News' Story." Just the Facts 13. Chestnut Hill, Mass.: Center for Retirement Research.

———. 2007. "The Labor Supply of Older Americans." In *Labor Supply in the New Century*, edited by Katharine Bradbury, Christopher L. Foote, and Robert Triest. Federal Reserve Bank of Boston.

Munnell, Alicia H., Steven A. Sass, and Jean-Pierre Aubry. 2006. "Employer Survey: 1 of 4 Boomers Won't Retire Because They Can't." Work Opportunities Brief 6. Chestnut Hill, Mass.: Center for Retirement Research.

Munnell, Alicia H., Steven A. Sass, and Mauricio Soto. 2006. "Employer Attitudes toward Older Workers: Survey Results." Work Opportunities for Older Americans Series 6. Chestnut Hill, Mass.: Center for Retirement Research.

Munnell, Alicia H., and Mauricio Soto. 2005 "What Replacement Rates Do Households Actually Experience in Retirement?" Working Paper 10. Chestnut Hill, Mass.: Center for Retirement Research.

————. 2007. "When Should Women Claim Social Security Benefits?" *Journal of Financial Planning* 20, no. 6: 58–65.

Munnell, Alicia H., and Annika Sundén. 2004. *Coming Up Short: The Challenge of 401(k) Plans.* Brookings.

————. 2006. "401(k) Plans Are Still Coming up Short." Issue in Brief 43. Chestnut Hill, Mass.: Center for Retirement Research.

Munnell, Alicia H., Anthony Webb, and Francesca Golub-Sass. 2007. "Is There Really a Retirement Savings Crisis? An NRRI Analysis." Issue in Brief 11. Chestnut Hill, Mass.: Center for Retirement Research.

Munnell, Alicia H., and Natalia Zhivan. 2006. "Earnings and Women's Retirement Security." Working Paper 12. Chestnut Hill, Mass.: Center for Retirement Research.

Munnell, Alicia H., and others. 2006a. "Will We Have to Work Forever?" Issues in Brief 4. Chestnut Hill, Mass.: Center for Retirement Research.

Munnell, Alicia H., and others. 2006b. "Has the Displacement of Older Workers Increased?" Working Paper 17. Chestnut Hill, Mass.: Center for Retirement Research.

Murphy, Kevin J., and Ján Zábonjík. 2007. "Managerial Capital and the Market for CEOs." Working paper. Kingston, Ontario, Canada: Queens' University.

Murray, Christopher J. L., and others. 2006. "Eight Americas: Investigating Mortality Disparities across Races, Counties, and Race-Counties in the United States." *PLoS Medicine* 3, no. 9: 1513–24.

Nagi, Saad. 1965. "Some Conceptual Issues in Disability and Rehabilitation." In *Sociology and Rehabilitation,* edited by Marvin Sussman. Washington: American Sociological Association.

————. 1976. "An Epidemiology of Disability among Adults in the United States." *Milbank Memorial Fund Quarterly* 54: 439–67.

————. 1991. "Disability Concepts Revisited: Implications for Prevention." In *Disability in America: Toward a National Agenda for Prevention,* edited by Institute of Medicine. Washington: National Academy Press.

National Center for Education Statistics. 2007. *Digest of Education Statistics 2006.* U.S. Department of Education.

National Center for Health Statistics. Various years. Life Tables. Centers for Disease Control and Prevention.

————. Various years. Current Estimates from the National Health Interview Survey.

————. 1995a. *Advance Report of Final Divorce Statistics, 1989 and 1990.*

————. 1995b. *Advance Report of Final Marriage Statistics, 1989 and 1990.*

————. 1999–2006. Births, Marriages, Divorces, and Deaths.

————. 2002. "Mean Age of Mother, 1970–2000." *National Vital Statistics Reports* 51, no. 1.

————. 2005. *Summary Health Statistics for the U.S. Population: National Health Interview Survey, 2003.* Vital and Health Statistics, series 10, no. 224.

————. 2006. "Trends in Health and Aging" (www.cdc.gov/nchs/agingact.htm).

Neuman, Shoshana, and Avi Weiss. 1995. "On the Effects of Schooling Vintage on Experience-Earnings Profiles: Theory and Evidence." *European Economic Review* 39, no. 5: 943–55.

Neumark, David. 2000. "Changes in Job Stability and Job Security: A Collective Effect to Untangle, Reconcile, and Interpret the Evidence." In *On the Job: Is Long-Term Employment a Thing of the Past?* edited by David Neumark. New York: Russell Sage.

————. 2001. "Age Discrimination Legislation in the United States." Working Paper 8152. Cambridge, Mass.: National Bureau of Economic Research.

Nollen, Stanley D., Brenda B. Eddy, and Virginia H. Martin. 1977. "Permanent Part Time Employment: The Manager's Perspective." Employment and Training Administration, Office of Research and Development PB-268-390. Georgetown University, School of Business Administration.

Nyce, Steven A., and Sylvester J. Shieber. 2002. "The Decade of the Employee: The Workforce Environment in the Coming Decade." *Benefits Quarterly* 18, no. 1: 60–79.

OECD. 2006. "Live Longer, Work Longer." Paris.

Osterman, Paul. 2005. "Employment and Training Policies: New Directions for Less Skilled Adults." Paper prepared for Urban Institute Conference, Workforce Policies for the Next Decade and Beyond. Washington, November 11.

Panis, Constantijn, and others. 2002. *The Effects of Changing Social Security Administration's Early Entitlement Age and the Normal Retirement Age.* Santa Monica, Calif.: Rand.

Park, D. C., R. Nisbett, and T. Hedden. 1999. "Aging, Culture, and Cognition." *Journal of Gerontology* Series B 54, no. 2: 75–84.

Parkman, Allen M. 1992. "Unilateral Divorce and the Labor-Force Participation of Married Women, Revisited." *American Economic Review* 82, no. 3: 671–78.

Penner, Rudolph G., and Richard W. Johnson. 2006. "Health Care Costs, Taxes, and the Retirement Decision: Conceptual Issues and Illustrative Simulations." Working Paper 20. Chestnut Hill, Mass.: Center for Retirement Research.

Penner, Rudolph G., Pamela Perun, and Eugene Steuerle. 2002. "Legal and Institutional Impediments to Partial Retirement and Part-Time Work by Older Workers." Washington: Urban Institute.

Pension Benefit Guaranty Corporation. 2004. *Pension Insurance Data Book 2004.* Washington.

Peters, H. Elizabeth. 1986. "Marriage and Divorce: Informational Constraints and Private Contracting." *American Economic Review* 76, no. 3: 437–54.

Pingle, Jonathan F. 2006. "Social Security's Delayed Retirement Credit and the Labor Supply of Older Men." Finance and Economics Discussion Series 2006-37. U.S. Federal Reserve Board.

Prudential Financial. 2005. "Roadblocks to Retirement: A Report on What Happens When Living Life Today Gets in the Way of Financial Security Tomorrow." Newark.

Purcell, Patrick J. 2005. "Older Workers: Employment and Retirement Trends." Congressional Research Service.

Rappaport, Anna, and Matt Stevenson. 2004. "Staying Ahead of the Curve 2004: Employer Best Practices for Mature Workers." Washington: AARP.

Rebick, Marcus. 1994. "Rewards in the Afterlife: Late Career Job Placements as Incentives in Japanese Firms." *Journal of Japanese and International Economies* 9, no. 1: 1–25.

Rix, Sara E. 2004. "Aging and Work—A View from the United States." 2004-02. Washington, DC: AARP.

Robson, William B. P. 2001. "Aging Populations and the Workforce: Challenges for Employers." Winnipeg: British–North American Committee.

Rodriguez, Daniel, and Madeline Zavodny. 2000. "Are Displaced Workers Now Finished at Age Forty?" *Economic Review* 85, no. 2: 33–47.

———. 2003. "Changes in the Age and Education Profile of Displaced Workers." *Industrial and Labor Relations Review* 56, no. 3: 498–510.

Rosen, Benson, and Thomas H. Jerdee. 1977. "Too Old or Not Too Old." *Harvard Business Review* 55, no. 6: 97–106.

Ruggles, Steven, and Matthew Sobek. 2004. *Integrated Public Use Microdata Series, Version 3.0.* Minneapolis: Minnesota Population Center.

Rust, John, and Christopher Phelan. 1997. "How Social Security and Medicare Affect Retirement Behavior in a World of Incomplete Markets." *Econometrica* 65, no. 4: 781–831.

Rybash, John M., William J. Hoyer, and Paul A. Roodin. 1986. *Adult Cognition and Aging: Developmental Changes in Processing, Knowing, and Thinking.* New York: Pergamon.

Samwick, Andrew A. 1998. "New Evidence on Pensions, Social Security, and the Timing of Retirement." *Journal of Public Economics* 70, no. 2: 207–36.

Sass, Steven A. 1997. *The Promise of Private Pensions: The First Hundred Years.* Harvard University Press.

Sass, Steven A., Wei Sun, and Anthony Webb. 2007. "Why Do Married Men Claim Social Security Benefits So Early? Ignorance or Caddishness?" Working Paper 2007-17. Chestnut Hill, Mass.: Center for Retirement Research.

————. 2008. "Why Do Married Men Claim Social Security Benefits So Early? Ignorance, Caddishness, or Something Else?" Issue in Brief 3. Chestnut Hill, Mass.: Center for Retirement Research.

Schieber, Sylvester J. 2007. "Pension Aspirations and Realizations: A Perspective on Yesterday, Today, and Tomorrow." Arlington, Va.: Watson-Wyatt.

Schirle, Tammy. 2007."Why Have the Labour Force Participation Rates of Older Men Increased since the Mid-1990s?" Working Paper. Wilfrid Laurier University, Department of Economics.

Schoeni, Robert F., Vicki A. Freedman, and Robert B. Wallace. 2001. "Persistent, Consistent, Widespread, and Robust? Another Look at the Trends in Old-Age Disability." *Journal of Gerontology* Series B 56, no. 4: S206–S218.

Scholz, John Karl, Ananth Seshadri, and Surachai Khitatrakun. 2006. "Are Americans Saving Optimally for Retirement?" *Journal of Political Economy* 114, no. 4: 607–43.

Schwartzman, A. E., and others. 1987. "Stability of Intelligence. A 40-Year Follow-Up." *Canadian Journal of Psychology* 41, no. 2: 244–56.

Scott, Frank A., Mark G. Berger, and John E. Garen. 1995. "Do Health Insurance and Pension Costs Reduce the Job Opportunities of Older Workers?" *Industrial and Labor Relations Review* 48, no. 4: 775–91.

Shephard, Roy J. 1999. "Age and Physical Work Capacity." *Experimental Aging Research* 25, no. 4: 331–43.

————. 2000. "Aging and Productivity: Some Psychological Issues." *International Journal of Industrial Ergonomics* 25, no. 5: 535–45.

Shoven, John B. 2007. "New Age Thinking: Alternative Ways of Measuring Age, Their Relationship to Labor Force Participation, Government Policies, and GDP." Working Paper 13476. Cambridge, Mass.: National Bureau of Economic Research.

Skirbekk, Vegard. 2003. "Age and Individual Productivity: A Literature Survey." Working Paper 28. Rostock, Germany: Max Planck Institute for Demographic Research.

Skolnik, Alfred. 1976. "Private Pension Plans, 1950–1974." *Social Security Bulletin* 39, no. 6: 3–17.

Smith, Deborah B., and Phyllis Moen. 2004. "Retirement Satisfaction for Retirees and Their Spouses: Do Gender and the Retirement Decision-Making Process Matter?" *Journal of Family Issues* 25, no. 2: 262–85.

Smith, James P. 2004. "Unraveling the SES Health Connection." *Aging, Health, and Public Policy: Demographic and Economic Perspectives,* special issue, *Population and Development Review* 30: 108–32.

Smith W. J., and K. V. Harrington. 1994. "Younger Supervisor–Older Subordinate Dyads: A Relationship of Cooperation or Resistance?" *Psychological Reports* 74, no. 3: 803–12.

Soldo, Beth, and others. 2006. "Cross-Cohort Differences in Health on the Verge of Retirement." Working Paper 12762. Cambridge, Mass.: National Bureau of Economic Research.

Sorokina, Olga, Anthony Webb, and Dan Muldoon. 2008. "Pension Wealth and Income: 1992, 1998, and 2004." Issue in Brief 1. Chestnut Hill, Mass.: Center for Retirement Research.

Steuerle, Eugene, and Christopher Spiro. 1999. "Adjusting for Life Expectancy in Measures of Labor Force Participation." Straight Talk on Social Security and Retirement Policy 10. Washington: Urban Institute.

Steuerle, Eugene, Christopher Spiro, and Richard W. Johnson. 1999. "Can Americans Work Longer?" Straight Talk on Social Security and Retirement Policy 5. Washington: Urban Institute.

Stevens, Ann Huff. 2005. "The More Things Change, the More They Stay the Same: Trends in Long-Term Employment in the United States, 1969–2002." Working Paper 11878. Cambridge, Mass.: National Bureau of Economic Research.

Stock, James H., and David A. Wise. 1990. "Pensions, the Option Value of Work, and Retirement." *Econometrica* 58, no. 5: 1151–80.

Sun Life Financial. 2006. "Forced Retirement Survey" (prepared by Harris Interactive). Wellesley Hills, Mass.

Szinovacz, Maximiliane, Stanley DeViney, and Adam Davey. 2001. "Influences of Family Obligations and Relationships on Retirement: Variations by Gender, Race, and Marital Status." *Journal of Gerontology* Series B 56, no. 1: S20–S27.

Taylor, Philip, and Alan Walker. 1998. "Employers and Older Workers: Attitudes and Employment Practices." *Ageing and Society* 18: 641–58.

Thane, Pat. 2000. *Old Age in English History: Past Experiences, Present Issues.* Oxford University Press.

Tilly, Chris. 1991. "Reasons for the Continuing Growth of Part-Time Employment." *Monthly Labor Review* 114, no. 3: 10–18.

Toossi, Mitra. 2004. "Labor Force Projections to 2012: The Graying of the U.S. Workforce." *Monthly Labor Review* 128, no. 2: 37–57.

———. 2005. "Labor Force Projections to 2014: Retiring Boomers." *Monthly Labor Review* 128, no. 11: 25–44.

Towers Perrin. 2003. "Back to the Future: Redefining Retirement in the 21st Century." Washington: AARP.

———. 2005. "The Business Case for Workers Age 50+." Washington: AARP.

Triest, Robert K., Margarita Sapozhnikov, and Steven A. Sass. 2006. "Population Aging and the Structure of Wages." Working Paper 5. Chestnut Hill, Mass.: Center for Retirement Research.

United Nations Economic Commission for Europe. 2003. *Trends in Europe and North America: The Statistical Yearbook of the Economic Commission for Europe, 2003.*

University of Michigan. Various years. Health and Retirement Study.

U.S. Bureau of Labor Statistics. 1956. "Job Performance and Age: A Study in Measurement." Bulletin 1203.

———. 1957. "Comparative Job Performance by Age: Large Plants in Men's Footwear and Household Furniture Industries." Bulletin 1223.

———. 1960. "Comparative Job Performance by Age: Office Workers." Bulletin 1273.

———. 2007a. Labor Force Statistics from the Current Population Survey.

———. 2007b. Projected Labor Force Data.

U.S. Census Bureau. 2007a. "Historical Income Tables–People."

———. 2007b. "Poverty Thresholds."

———. 2007c. "Median Income for 4-Person Families, by State".

U.S. Census Bureau and Bureau of Labor Statistics. Various years. Current Population Survey.

———. Various years. Displaced Workers Survey.

U.S. Department of Labor. 1965. *The Older American Worker.*

———. 1999. *Private Pension Plan Bulletin: Abstract of 1995 Form 5500 Annual Reports.*

———. 2006. *Annual Return/Report Form 5500 Series for Plan Year 2004.*

———. 2007. *Labor Force Statistics from the Current Population Survey: Employment and Unemployment.*

U.S. Federal Reserve Board. Various years. Survey of Consumer Finances.

U.S. Government Accountability Office. 2000. *Contingent Workers: Incomes and Benefits Lag behind Those of Rest of Workforce.* GAO/HEHS-00-76.

———. 2001. *Older Workers: Demographic Trends Pose Challenges for Employers and Workers.* GAO 02-85.

———. 2003a. *Workforce Investment Act: One-Stop Centers Implemented Strategies to Strengthen Services and Partnerships, but More Research and Information Sharing Is Needed.* GAO-3-725.

———. 2003b. *Multiple Employment and Training Programs: Funding and Performance Measures for Major Programs.* GAO-03-589.

———. 2004. *Workforce Challenges and Opportunities for the 21st Century: Changing Labor Force Dynamics and the Role of Government Policies.* GAO-04-845SP.

———. 2005. *Workforce Investment Act: Substantial Funds Are Used for Training, but Little Is Known Nationally about Training Outcomes.* GAO-05-650.

U.S. House of Representatives, Committee on Ways and Means. 2000. *Green Book.*

U.S. Internal Revenue Service. 2008. *2008 Federal Tax Rate Schedules.*

U.S. Social Security Administration. 2003. *Life Table Functions for Males and Females Born 1850–2000 Based on the Alternative II Mortality Probabilities from the 2003 Trustees Report.*

———. 2004. *Performance and Accountability Report for Fiscal Year 2004.*

———. 2005. *Social Security: Why Action Should Be Taken Soon.*

———. 2006a. *Income of the Aged Chartbook.*

———. 2006b. *The 2006 Annual Report of the Board of Trustees of the Old-Age, Survivors, and Disability Insurance Trust Funds.*

————. 2007a. *The 2007 Annual Report of the Board of Trustees of the Old-Age, Survivors, and Disability Insurance Trust Funds.*

————. 2007b. *The 2006 Annual Statistical Supplement.*

————. Various years. *Annual Report of the Board of Trustees of Trustees of the Old Age and Survivors and Disability Insurance Trust Funds.*

Verhaegen, Paul, and Timothy A. Salthouse. 1997. "Meta-Analyses of Age-Cognition Relations in Adulthood: Estimates of Linear and Non-Linear Age Effects and Structural Models." *Psychological Bulletin* 122, no. 3: 231–49.

Von Wachter, Till. 2002. "The End of Mandatory Retirement in the US: Effects on Retirement and Implicit Contracts." Working Paper 49. University of California, Berkeley, Center for Labor Economics.

————. 2007. "The Effect of Changes in Labor Demand on Retirement Outcomes of Older Workers." Paper prepared for the Retirement Research Conference. Washington, August 9–10.

Waidmann, Timothy A., John Bound, and Michael Schoenbaum. 1995. "The Illusion of Failure: Trends in the Self-Reported Health of the U.S. Elderly." *Milbank Quarterly* 73, no. 2: 253–87.

Waldman, David A., and Bruce J. Avolio. 1986. "A Meta-Analysis of Age Differences in Job Performance." *Journal of Applied Psychology* 71, no. 1: 33–38.

Walker, James F. 1964. "The Job Performance of Federal Mail Sorters by Age." *Monthly Labor Review* 87, no. 3: 296–301.

Warr, Peter. 1994. "Age and Job Performance." In *Work and Aging: A European Perspective*, edited by Jan Snel and Roel Cremer. London: Taylor and Francis.

Weiss, Robert S. 2005. *The Experience of Retirement.* Ithaca: ILR Press.

Welch, Finis. 1979. "Effects of Cohort Size on Earnings: The Baby Boom Babies' Financial Bust." *Journal of Political Economy* 87, no. 5: S65–S98.

Wilson, Robert S., and others. 2002. "Individual Differences in Rates of Change in Cognitive Abilities of Older Persons." *Psychology and Aging* 17, no. 2: 179–93.

Zhivan, Natalia, and others. 2008. "The Elastic EEA: A New Approach to Raising Social Security's Earliest Eligibility Age." Issue in Brief 2. Chestnut Hill, Mass.: Center for Retirement Research.

Index